Eliphas Lévi and the French Occult Revival

SUNY series in Western Esoteric Traditions

David Appelbaum, editor

Eliphas Lévi
and the
French Occult Revival

CHRISTOPHER McINTOSH

SUNY PRESS

First published 1972
Second impression, 1975
© Christopher McIntosh 1972, 2011

Published by State University of New York Press, Albany

All rights reserved

Printed in the United States of America

No part of this book may be used or reproducted in any manner whatsoever without written permission. No part of this book may be stored in a retrieval system or transmitted in any form or by any means including electronic, electrostatic, magnetic tape, mechanical, photocopying, recording or otherwise without the prior permission in writing of the publisher.

For information, contact State University of New York Press, Albany, NY
www.sunypress.edu

Production by Eileen Meehan
Marketing by Michael Campochiaro

Library of Congress Cataloging-in-Publication Data

McIntosh, Christopher, 1943–
    Eliphas Lévi and the French occult revival / Christopher McIntosh.
       p. cm. — (SUNY series in Western esoteric traditions)
    Originally published: London : Rider, 1972.
    Includes bibliographical references (p. 228–232) and index.
    ISBN 978-1-4384-3557-2 (hardcover : alk. paper)
    ISBN 978-1-4384-3556-5 (pbk. : alk. paper)
    1. Lévi, Éliphas, 1810–1875. 2. Occultism—France. I. Title.

BF1598.C6M3 2011
130.92—dc22
                                                                                    2010031936

10 9 8 7 6 5 4 3 2 1

Contents

	List of Illustrations	6
	Preface	7
	Introduction	11

PART ONE
The Age of Unreason

1.	The Rebirth of Magic	17
2.	The Occult and the Revolution	34
3.	Revolutionary Cults	44
4.	The Beginnings of Popular Occultism	49
5.	Magnetisers and Mediums	55
6.	The Holy King	61

PART TWO
Eliphas Lévi

7.	The Early Years	73
8.	The Radical	83
9.	Enter Eliphas Lévi	96
10.	The Magician	105
11.	The Pundit	124
12.	The Last Years	136
13.	Eliphas Lévi: An Assessment	141

PART THREE
Towards the Kingdom of the Paraclete

14.	The Heirs of Eliphas Lévi	157
15.	The War of the Roses	171
16.	The Magical Quest of J.-K. Huysmans	177
17.	Writers and the Occult	195
18.	Satanists and Anti-Satanists	206
19.	The Indian Summer of Occultism	219

	Appendix A	225
	Appendix B	226
	Select Bibliography	228
	Index	233

List of Illustrations

		facing page
FRONTISPIECE	Lévi's celebrated drawing of Baphomet or the Goat of Mendès	6
1	Tarot figures from Court de Gébelin	32
2	Tarot figures from Court de Gébelin	33
3	The Devil, from Oswald Wirth's Tarot	49
4	Hoene Wronski	80
5	Saint-Yves d'Alveydre	81
6	Eugène Vintras	96
7	Joseph-Antoine Boullan	97
8	Alphonse-Louis Constant in 1836	128
9	Constant in 1852	129
10	Constant as Eliphas Lévi in 1862	144
11	Frontispiece to Lévi's *Clés majeures et clavicules de Salomon*	145
12	Figures from Lévi's *Clés majeures*	176
13	Joseph Péladan	177
14a	Cartoons of Péladan	192
14b	The symbol of the Cabalistic Order of the Rosy Cross	192
15	Stanislas de Guaita	193

Lévi's celebrated drawing of *Baphomet* or the *Goat of Mendès*. Often misunderstood as satanic, it is in fact a combination of images representing Lévi's doctrine of polarities.

Preface to the New Edition

Bringing this book out again some four decades after it was first published has revived memories of the experience of writing it in the late 1960s and early 1970s. After publishing my first book, *The Astrologers and Their Creed* (London: Hutchinson, 1969), I was looking for another subject within the study of western esotericism—a field that was then in its early infancy and still largely outside the academic pale. Within the recent history of esotericism Eliphas Lévi (alias Alphonse-Louis Constant) was an important name. A few decades after his death he was enough of a legend to get a lengthy mention in Somerset Maugham's novel *The Magician* (1908) and a briefer one in H.P. Lovecraft's novella *The Case of Charles Dexter Ward* (written in 1927, first published in 1941), where he is referred to as "that cryptic soul who crept through a crack in the hidden door and glimpsed the frightful vistas of the void beyond" (op. cit., Part III, Ch. 6). Yet very little had been published in English about Lévi's life and work. It seemed to me that the time had come to fill the gap with a proper study of Lévi. The natural publisher was Rider, then part of the Hutchinson group, especially as Lévi's own works had appeared in English under that imprint. My friend and editor at Hutchinson, Dr. Daniel Brostoff, who was then in charge of Rider, was receptive to the idea but suggested that I extend the scope somewhat to include the wider occult revival in France, of which Lévi was part. I followed his suggestion accordingly, and when I began my research for the book I soon realized what an immensely rich subject I was dealing with.

Various countries have had their esoteric heydays, but the one that took place in France between approximately the late 18th century and the early 20th was one of the most fruitful. At its beginning stood a remarkable constellation of esoteric Freemasons, illuminati, mystics, alchemists, and ritual magicians, from whose milieu came movements such as Martinism. Their successors in the 19th century, apart from Lévi himself, included the occultist Papus (alias Dr. Gérard Encausse), whose influence stretched as far as the court of St. Petersburg, the counter-Pope Eugène Vintras, and the colourful Rosicrucian magus Joséphin Péladan, organizer of a cultural movement including art exhibitions that were closely connected with the Symbolist school of painting.

Any of these figures would deserve a biography to himself, but I chose to give pride of place to Lévi because of his particularly seminal influence both within France and internationally. Many of his ideas were admired by Madame Blavatsky and passed into Theosophy. The magicians of the Hermetic Order of the Golden Dawn were strongly influenced by him, as were writers such as Huysmans, Baudelaire and W.B. Yeats. And Aleister Crowley believed himself to be Lévi's reincarnation. As an artist he also has his place in esoteric history, if only because of his famous drawing of *Baphomet* or the *Goat of Mendès*, which has been reproduced innumerable times in books and magazines dealing with magic and the occult. This drawing was not included in the first edition of this book, but I have now made good the omission, and the picture is shown in Fig. 1. In the iconography of esotericism it has become one of those instantly recognized images like—in a wider context—Leonardo's *Vitruvian Man*, Salvador Dali's melting watches or Munch's *The Scream*. I even saw a plaster version of it in bright red, placed in the middle of a sort of Voodoo altar that had been set up as a museum exhibit. It is often—quite mistakenly—interpreted as a satanic image, and here I would like to correct this misconception.

The image symbolizes the process of working with the "Astral Light," a key concept for Lévi. The Astral Light is another name for the notion of an invisible, all-pervading fluid or medium on which thoughts can be imprinted and through which phenomena can be influenced. For Lévi it is the basis of all magical workings. In order to work with the Astral Light the magician has to be balanced between the forces and polarities that surround him, and it is this balance that is conveyed in the *Baphomet* image. The goat represents dense, earth-bound nature, but has angel's wings representing heavenly nature. It has female breasts but a male phallus. The four elements are shown by the hooves resting on the globe (earth), the fish scales on the belly (water), the wings (air) and the torch rising from the head (fire). Darkness and light are present in the black and white crescent moons and in the black and white serpents curled around the caduceus-like phallus.

The right arm points up, the left down, and the words written on the arms, "SOLVE" and "COAGULA" refer to the two key operations necessary to working successfully with the Astral Light. First the light must be fixed and concentrated (*coagula*) and then projected as a flow of energy (*solve*). In the centre of the goat's forehead is a pentagram, which for Lévi represents the dominion of will over the Astral Light. To see how quickly Lévi's drawing was misinterpreted one only needs to look at the 15th trump card, *Le Diable*, in the Tarot pack designed by Oswald Wirth and published in 1889 (Fig. 3). Here a grotesque caricature of Lévi's *Baphomet* appears as the Devil. It now has bat's wings instead of angel's wings, and the arms are pointing in the wrong directions—*coagula* should of course point to the earth and *solve* to heaven, as in Lévi's drawing. Wirth's picture was the forerunner of many subsequent distortions of Lévi's image.

It may seem surprising that—at least to my knowledge—no movement or school has emerged to perpetuate Lévi's ideas. This may be because it is rather difficult to extract a coherent message from his works. Lévi's writings poured from his pen in an inspired but often careless flow, and he hardly ever re-read or corrected drafts and printed proofs. Consequently his books are often rambling, verbose, badly structured and marred by mistakes. Nevertheless, if one perseveres with them one finds that they contain some fascinating ideas, which must have appeared new and exciting to his contemporaries and which continue to speak to many readers of today.

The appearance of this edition gives me the opportunity to add an important bibliographical reference. At the time this book first appeared it contained the only biography of Lévi in English, but in 1975 the University of Alabama Press published *Eliphas Lévi: Master of Occultism* by Thomas A. Williams, an excellent and most engaging study of Lévi and his ideas. In his preface, Williams, an American professor of romance languages, wrote: "Occult and esoteric thought has become an inescapable part of our contemporary intellectual climate. It is time for all of us to find out something—something reliable—about it ... but even as we set out to educate ourselves in this dark domain we confront a basic question: where do we begin? The path is dim and the forest obscure."

Today the path is a good deal less dim and the forest is progressively being charted, as esotericism becomes increasingly accepted within the academy as a legitimate area of study, as the re-appearance of this book in the SUNY Press Series in Western Esotericism shows. In a sense, the book has now come into its own, having gained an academic context that was lacking when it first appeared. It is a pleasure to know that it is now once again available to scholars who wish to explore the era of Lévi and the esoteric avatars who preceded and followed him.

Acknowledgments

First of all, a special thank-you to my former wife, Robina, who helped me with the research for this book, and whose advice and encouragement were invaluable. I am also most grateful to Gerald Yorke for lending me an important Lévi document and for reading the manuscript of the book and making valuable comments and suggestions. I am indebted, further, to Geoffrey Watkins who generously lent me some rare Lévi manuscripts and to Ellic Howe who supplied me with material and gave me much useful advice. My thanks are also due to the staffs of the Warburg Institute, the British Museum, the Bibliothèque Nationale and the Bibliothèque de l'Arsenal for their kind cooperation.

I should like to thank the following publishers for their permission to quote from books published by them: Cassell and Co., Honoré Champion, Corti, Dorbon, Hamish Hamilton, Jarrolds, Thomas Nelson and Sons, Oxford University Press, Plon, Presses Universitaires de France and Rider and Co. I am obliged to the British Museum for the use of plates 1, 2, and 15a, and to Robert Shackleton, literary excutor of the late Enid Starkie, for permission to quote from her biography of Rimbaud.

Introduction

Occult movements and secret cults have always played a significant part in society. Like a subterranean current they have moved beneath the ground of history, occasionally bursting forth to flow for a spell in the light of day, revealing some strange and exotic fish in the process. This book deals with one such bursting forth and with some of the interesting fish that it threw up.

One of the most colourful of these creatures was an ex-candidate for the priesthood called Alphonse Louis Constant, who came to public attention in the 1850s as Eliphas Lévi and under that name poured out a series of writings on magic which met with extraordinary success and were to have a widespread influence. It is strange that until now no detailed biography of Lévi has appeared in English. The only full study of his life is *Eliphas Lévi, rénovateur de l'occultisme en France*, by Paul Chacornac, which appeared in 1926. Naturally I have leaned very heavily on this book in my section on Lévi, but I have had access to certain documents which Chacornac does not mention and I have attempted something that is missing from his book, namely an assessment of Lévi's work. The only other detailed assessment that I know of is to be found in A. E. Waite's various introductions to his translations of Lévi's writings, which are rather scornful in tone and in my opinion do not do Lévi justice. Aleister Crowley was a more lively exegetist, but he went to the opposite extreme and looked upon Lévi as an occult genius of the highest order. I feel that the time has come for a more balanced judgement.

In view of all this it may be asked why I have not confined this book to Eliphas Lévi. The reason is that, while I feel a study of Lévi was necessary, I also felt that he needed to be set in his context and that both tasks could be accomplished in one volume. My readers will judge whether or not I have succeeded in this attempt. Lévi, as I say, needed to be set in his context, for he was part of an occult revival whose antecedents can be traced back to the years preceding the French Revolution and whose subsequent development can be followed forward to the First World War. There is, of course, something artificial about dividing the continuum of history up into sections in this way, but this is the only way that the historian can proceed, and I believe that the term 'occult revival' can meaningfully be used in relation to the period under discussion.

Parts of the ground covered in this book have been ably charted already, but the territory has never been mapped out in its entirety. This is surprising, as the French occultists were extremely influential both in their own country and abroad, and traces of their influence can be found in art, politics and literature. They also made certain very significant contributions to the occult tradition which are now taken for granted by modern occultists. The Tarot, for example, as a magical system, is an entirely French invention. It was Court de Gébelin, writing in the late eighteenth century, who first presented it as an occult device to the public, and it was Eliphas Lévi who connected it with the Cabala. The book on the Tarot written by Lévi's successor Papus is still a standard work on the subject today.

The French occult revival is also interesting from an historical point of view. Why, we may ask, did such a revival begin in the sceptical climate of eighteenth-century France? Was it partly perhaps because the sceptic is more vulnerable to persuasion than the religious man? A person who has a strong faith rooted in an accepted religious tradition will, in a sense, be inoculated against outlandish beliefs. The sceptic, on the other hand, weakens his defences by denying a fundamental part of his nature, namely the need for religious belief; thus he is an easy prey for the self-appointed prophet or messiah with some colourful new cult to offer.

This, however, is only part of the explanation. One must also take into account the social and political crisis that was brewing up in France at the time of the beginning of the occult revival—and indeed continued to come to the boil at intervals throughout the nineteenth century. The occult revival began when the old order was crumbling. Revolution was in the air. It was a time of disillusion and uncertainty. The same conditions prevailed in Rome during the period of political turbulence that preceded the coming to power of Julius Caesar; and again later on when the Roman Empire was crumbling. All of these periods gave birth to a variety of extravagant cults.

This study may bring accusations that I have paddled for too long in too narrow a backwater—though I think that I am in less danger of facing this charge than I would have been ten years ago. At the time of writing the subject of occult movements is beginning to be taken more seriously by social historians, and recently quite a number of books have appeared which have brought the light of objective historical analysis to bear on various sections of the history of occultism. I hope that this book will add some more light to the subject. The story I have told is an extraordinary and colourful one; it is also, I believe, an important one.

PART ONE

The Age of Unreason

I The Rebirth of Magic

A French Countess tells in her memoirs[1] of a bizarre character who arrived in Paris in the 1720s and soon had the court and the salons buzzing with stories of his remarkable deeds. He was reported to be fluent in every European language, as well as Chinese, Arabic and Sanskrit. He was a skilful pianist and also painted expertly in oils, achieving startling effects of colour, whose secret he refused to divulge. His appearance was striking, for he dressed very plainly, except for a large number of diamonds which he wore on his fingers, shoe-buckles, snuff-boxes and watches.

His origin was mysterious, but the commonest theory was that he was the youngest son of a dispossessed Transylvanian prince. He went by a number of names, among them the Marquis de Montferrat, Comte Bellamarre, Chevalier Schoening, Comte Soltikoff, Graf Tzarogy. But the name by which he was most widely known was Comte de Saint-Germain.

One incident related in the Countess's memoirs is enough to give an idea of the legend surrounding his person. At a gathering in Paris Saint-Germain was introduced to the Countess von Georgy, who, fifty years earlier, had been to Venice where her husband had been posted as ambassador. Recognising the name of Saint-Germain, she asked if by any chance his father had been in Venice at that time. Saint-Germain's reply was surprising: no, but he himself had been in Venice fifty years ago and, what was more, had paid court to the Countess.

' "Forgive me," said the Countess, but that is impossible; the Comte Saint-Germain I knew in those days was at least forty-five years old, and you, at the outside, are that at present."

' "Madame," replied the Count, smiling, "I am very old."

' "But then you must be nearly a hundred years old."

' "That is not impossible," the Count replied, and recounted some details which convinced the Countess, who exclaimed:
' "I am already convinced. You are a most extraordinary man, a devil."
' "For pity's sake!" exclaimed Saint-Germain in a thundering voice. "No such names!"
'He appeared to be seized with a cramp-like trembling in every limb, and left the room immediately.'

Similar stories about the strange Count crop up all over Europe. Evidently he was in England during the Jacobite Rebellion of 1745, and was arrested and held for a time as a spy. Horace Walpole confirms this in a letter to Sir Horace Mann, dated 9th December 1745:

'The other day they seized an odd man who goes by the name of Count Saint-Germain. He has been here these two years, and will not tell who he is or whence, but professes that he does not go by his right name. He sings and plays on the violin wonderfully, is mad and not very sensible.'

The Comte de Saint-Germain represents a recognisable type of semi-legendary figure who appears frequently in history. He has his counterpart in Appollonius of Tyana, the Greek sage, healer and wonder-worker of the first century A.D.; and in Christian Rosencreutz, the shadowy medieval figure, supposedly the founder of the Rosicrucian movement. Like both of these men, and like many another miraculous figure, Saint-Germain was credited with a journey to the East and a series of initiations into oriental mysteries. For example, at the court of the Shah of Persia he is supposed to have gathered his prodigious knowledge of precious stones, and in India his knowledge of alchemy.

It is impossible to say how many of the stories about Saint-Germain are true, but the very existence of the legend at this period of history is significant. It may seem surprising that the rational eighteenth century, and particularly the ultra-rational France, should encourage such a legend. But the fact is that the human mind abhors the absence of irrational belief, just as nature abhors a vacuum. Thus, the intellectuals who had initiated the revolt against the Christian Church were, by the middle of the eighteenth century, already becoming tired of their own scepticism and were looking around for a new faith to replace the one they had abandoned.

One manifestation of this search was the growth of freemasonry; and it is significant that Saint-Germain is credited with having been a leading light in the masonic movement. According to one account, for example, he was one of the French representatives at the great masonic convention that took place in Paris in 1785. He is also said to have initiated the Italian occultist Cagliostro, using a Templar ritual.

Although claiming to be of the greatest antiquity, the freemasonic movement in its present form dates from 1717 when the Grand Lodge of London was established. From England it spread quickly throughout Europe and also reached North America. The first French lodge, that of Brotherhood and Friendship, is believed to have been started at Dunkirk in 1721. But it was not until over twenty years later that a lodge officially recognised by the English Grand Lodge was set up in Paris. This probably took place in about 1743. In 1756 The Grand Lodge of France was founded. This later split up into factions, but was reassembled in 1771 by the Grand Duke of Luxembourg. A year later it was reconstituted as the Grand Orient of France.

By the time the Revolution broke out in 1789 there were between six and seven hundred lodges in France, totalling about 30,000 members.[2] One of the leaders of the movement was the Duke of Chartres, the future Philippe Egalité, who sided with the revolutionaries, but was eventually executed in 1793. In 1773 he was made Grand Master, and his sister, the Duchesse of Bourbon, was Grand Mistress of the women's lodges. In the provincial cities, and especially in Lyons, freemasonry had a strong following.

Because of the close-knit, federal structure of the masonic movement it had the appearance of a counter-Church, and to begin with was opposed by the authorities, though it fairly rapidly came to be tolerated. A bull against freemasonry was issued in 1738 by Pope Clement XII, but it was not recorded by the French parliament and had little effect. In 1789 twenty-six lodges were presided over by priests, and there were even lodges within certain religious houses.[3] It was not until the nineteenth century that freemasonry was to come into serious conflict with the Church.

The main appeal of freemasonry lay in the fact that it claimed to be the sole recipient and guardian of an ancient and powerful secret handed down from antiquity. The precise nature and provenance of this secret was naturally a matter of some dispute, and when the movement began to split into factions it was inevitable that each new order that appeared should lay claim to being the only 'true' masonry.

The idea of 'ancient wisdom' was not new. It had been propagated during the Renaissance by the scholars who revived the Hermetic teachings and espoused the Jewish Cabala. What was new about masonry was the fact that it constituted a widespread esoteric movement which, in spite of its warring factions, had a strong element of cohesion and central direction.

Most of the leading occultists of the eighteenth century were members of masonic or quasi-masonic fraternities. Those who were not masons were inevitably influenced indirectly by the movement. It was out of the masonic barrel, therefore, that there came most of the odd fish of eighteenth-century occultism.

Of these, one of the oddest was Martines de Pasqually, founder and self-appointed Grand Sovereign of a masonic rite called the Order of the Elect Cohens, the name being derived from the Hebrew word for priest.

Pasqually's origins, like those of Saint-Germain, are veiled in mystery. Some had it that he was a Spanish Jew. It is certain, however, that he was a Catholic, as there is a record of the baptism of his son. There is evidence that he was born in the parish of Notre-Dame de Grenoble, and that his father was a schoolmaster of Latin in the town. Pasqually's follower, J.-B. Willermoz, denies that he had any Jewish blood.

Of his childhood and youth almost nothing is known, but once again there is the well-worn legend of a journey to the Orient, and the acquisition of hidden wisdom in Egypt, Arabia, Palestine and China. The first solid fact known about him is that in 1754 at Montpelier he founded a society called the Scottish Judges—presumably the title referred to the Scottish rite of freemasonry. This society failed to get off the ground, and about six years later at Bordeaux he established his Order of the Elect Cohens, which soon gathered a substantial following.

The order practised a form of ceremonial magic, which Pasqually had derived partly from the Catholic mass and partly from Renaissance occult writers such as Cornelius Agrippa. Pasqually believed that he was in communication with unearthly beings, who endowed him with special powers. He claimed, for example, that he had been able to cure his wife of an illness by magical means.

One of his disciples was the Abbé Fournier, a cleric of Lyons, who told of his experiences with Pasqually in a book with the rather ponderous title *Ce que nous avons été, ce que nous sommes, et ce que nous deviendrons*. His first meeting with the master took place at a time when he was passing through an agony of religious doubt during which 'God accorded me the grace to meet a man who said to me in a friendly way: "You ought to come and see us, we are good men; you will open a book, you will glance at the first page, then at the middle of the book, and then at the end, reading only a few words, and you will know all that it contains;"' The strange man then pointed to the passers-by in the street. ' "Those people," he said "do not know why they are walking, but you . . ." he pointed to the Abbé, "you will know why you are walking."' Fournier was understandably taken aback by this curious man and at first imagined him to be a sorcerer, if not the devil himself. But evidently the lure of Pasqually's extravagant promises got the better of him, and he sought admission to the order. What Fournier's first reactions to the ceremonies were we do not know, but we do know, from letters exchanged between Pasqually and his closest disciples, roughly what form these ceremonies took.

Before the ritual the participants would have fasted for eleven hours. The fast was a well-established custom in magical rituals and, according to Pasqually, helped to free the soul and enable it to communicate with the 'centre of truth'.

The time at which the ceremony took place was usually regulated by celestial considerations, for Pasqually believed in an idiosyncratic type of astrology. 'The bodies of the universe,' he declared, 'are all vital organs of eternal life.'[4] Particularly influential were the moon, because of its proximity, and the sun, because life on earth was dependent on its light. Pasqually therefore chose the equinoxes for his most important rituals, and also regarded the crescent moon as propitious. These conditions encouraged the good spirits whose support was necessary for magical operations. One must, at all costs, avoid the demonic influences and evil intelligences that populate the astral domain.

René le Forestier, in his *La Franc-maçonnerie occultiste au XVIIIe siècle et l'ordre des Elus Coëns*, has pieced together a fascinating picture of the rituals practised by Pasqually's sect.

The simplest of these was the 'daily invocation' for which the adept had to trace a circle on the floor, at the centre of which he placed a candle and wrote the letter W. He then stood in the circle, holding a light to read his invocation which began: 'O Kadoz, O Kadoz, who will enable me to become as I was originally when a spark of divine creation? Who will enable me to return in virtue and eternal spiritual power . . . ?'

The more important rituals, however, took the form of a series of invocations which were performed over three consecutive days which had to fall between the new moon and the end of the first quarter. The details of the ritual, such as the tracing on the floor within which the adept operated, changed periodically as Pasqually was constantly revising the procedures and introducing new ones. A fairly constant feature, however, was the method used to produce a pungent aroma during the ceremony. The adept carried a small earthenware dish containing hot coals on which he periodically scattered a mixture containing the following ingredients: saffron, incense, sulphur, white and black poppy seeds, cloves, white cinnamon, mastic, sandarac, nutmeg and spore of agaric.[5]

The costume worn by the operator was probably also constant. Jacket, breeches and stockings were black. Over these he wore a long white robe with red borders, and over this were hung a blue ribbon, a black ribbon, a red sash and a green sash.[6]

As an example of the procedure carried out by the adept over three days, the following is an outline of the method proscribed by Pasqually in 1768. Every morning the adept began his day by reading the office of the Holy Spirit and when evening came he entered the privacy of his room at about ten o'clock. There he read some psalms and litanies from a missal and, having done this, was ready to draw the ceremonial tracing on the floor with a chalk. At the eastern side of the room he traced an approximate quarter segment with the point facing west, and then drew a line across the segment forming an isosceles triangle with the two radii. In the triangle he drew a small circle divided by a cross. Then he drew at the western side of the room a larger circle known as the 'circle of retreat' which was separated by two feet from the point of the segment. In this circle he drew the capital letters IAB and along the western branch of the cross in the small circle he put the letters RAP. This completed the tracing (see diagram opposite).

The operator then placed eight candles in the tracing: three at the point of the triangle, one beside the letters RAP, two at each end of the arc of the segment, one at the centre of the base of the triangle and one at the centre of the circle of retreat. He also wrote certain other mystical names.

The adept was then ready for the operation which had to begin at midnight precisely. When the twelve strokes began to sound he took off his shoes, removed the candle from the circle of retreat, lit it and placed it outside the circle on his right. He then lay down in the circle, face downwards, his forehead resting on his two fists. Having remained for six minutes in this position, he stood up and lit the candles in the segment. These he rearranged so that the one beside the letters RAP and the one at the base of the triangle were placed outside and opposite the centre of the arc. Then he knelt down in the segment, right knee on the ground and hands flat on the floor so that the tips of the forefingers came together at a right angle. Remaining in this position he repeated each of the names inscribed in the tracing, inserting them into the following formula which he recited three times for each name: *'In quali die . . . invocavero te, velociter exaudi me.'*[7] He then asked God to accord him the grace which he desired of 'a sincere heart, truly contrite and humble'.[8]

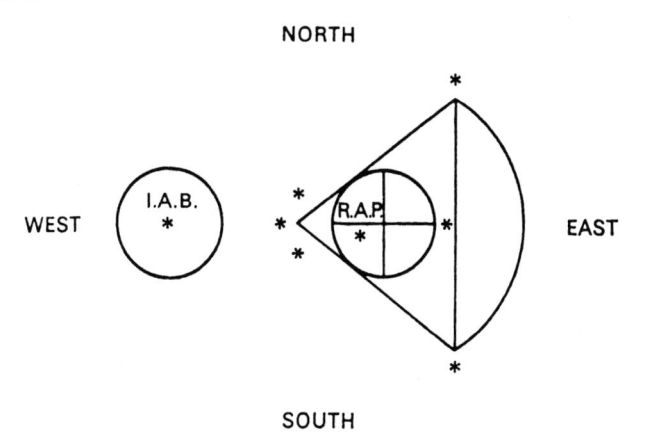

Floor tracing used in one of the rituals practised by Martines de Pasqually's Order of the Elect Cohens (the asterisks mark the points where candles were placed)

Taking the dish containing the glowing coals, he threw on to it a large pinch of the aromatic mixture and walked around the segment. Finally he sat down with the dish in the circle of retreat and settled down to a period of meditation.

On the first night the adept was only supposed to leave the circle between 1.30 and 2.00 in the morning. When he was finished he rubbed out all the figures traced on the floor, repeating as he did so invocations for the signs representing the good spirits and banishing formulae for those representing the bad. When all traces had been effaced he retired to bed.

The banishing of evil spirits and the invocation of good ones was an important part of Pasqually's rituals. Another ceremony, called the 'Work of the Equinox', included the following address to the evil demons:

'I conjure you, Satan, Beelzebub, Baran, Leviathan: all of you formidable beings, beings of iniquity, confusion and abomination, hearken and tremble at my voice and commandment; all of you great and powerful demons of the four universal regions and all of you demoniacal legions, subtle spirits of confusion, horror and persecution, hear my voice and tremble when it sounds among you and during your cursed operations; I command you by the one who has pronounced eternal death on all of you.' There then followed an address to each of the four main demons already mentioned beginning with Satan. 'On you, Satan, I impose excommunication, I tie and restrict you to your formidable region in the name of the Most High, God, the Eternal Avenger and Rewarder . . .' Then came an invocation of the good spirits. All this was carried out within a tracing similar to the one used for the ceremony already described.[9]

None of these rituals, however, was done primarily for the purpose of calling up particular spirits. The main aim was of a higher order, namely communication with what Pasqually called the 'Active and Intelligent Cause'. 'By this fact,' says A. E. Waite, 'the school of Martines de Pasqually is placed wholly outside the narrow limits and sordid motives of ceremonial magic.'[10]

Competence in these ceremonies was not the only thing required of the Elect Cohen. He was also required to follow certain rules of behaviour. For example, he was forbidden ever to consume the blood, fat or kidneys of any animal or to eat the flesh of domestic pigeons. He was not allowed, except with moderation, to indulge the senses, and had to eschew fornication.

The choice of the name 'Elect Cohens' reveals the Jewish inspiration of much of Pasqually's doctrine. Pasqually believed that the Jewish tradition had been perverted by its orthodox practitioners, but that certain 'true Jews' had preserved it in its purity. Clearly he believed that his order was in some sense helping to restore the true Judaism, by which he may have meant the Cabala as his theory of spirits corresponds closely to cabalistic doctrine. In the Cabala the number ten is given great significance —there are, for example, ten sephiroth, or spheres, on the Tree of Life. Pasqually believed in ten classes of spirit and held that ten was the divine number *par excellence*.

Pasqually continued to lead his group until the year 1772 when he sailed for Santo Domingo in the Caribbean, on a mission connected with some property he had there, leaving the Elect Cohens in the hands of his chief disciples, Bacon and Willermoz. He never returned and died at Port-au-Prince in 1774. His order died soon afterwards. Bacon joined another masonic order, the Grand Orient. Willermoz, after continuing the Elect Cohens for a time at Lyons, later went over to the Rite of Strict Observance, founded in 1754 by the German, Baron Hund.

While Pasqually had been operating at Bordeaux one of his followers had been a young army officer stationed in the town who devoted his ample leisure to the study of religion and philosophy. His name was Louis Claude de Saint-Martin, later to become famous for his writings under the name of 'Le Philosophe Inconnu'.

Saint-Martin recognised in Pasqually the master he was looking for, and in due course he was initiated into the Elect Cohens, the initiation taking place between 3rd August and 2nd October 1768. In 1771 he abandoned the military profession to devote himself entirely to contemplation and study.

At the time of Pasqually's death, Saint-Martin was living in Paris and writing his first treatise, *Of Errors and Truth*, in which he set out to teach the hidden principles behind all knowledge. It was the beginning of a long campaign of preaching his own highly individual brand of mysticism all over Europe. The greatest influence on his ideas was Jacob Boehme, the seventeenth-century German mystic whom he regarded as 'the greatest light that has appeared on earth since One who is the light itself'.[11] Saint-Martin believed in an ideal society based on a 'natural and spiritual theocracy' governed by men who would be chosen by God and who would regard themselves as 'divine commissioners' to guide the people. He died in 1803, having remained a strict Catholic all his life, in spite of the fact that his first treatise was placed on the Index. He left behind him a large volume of writing which continued to influence mystics and occultists right through the nineteenth century.

While Saint-Martin was writing *Of Errors and Truth*, and Bacon and Willermoz were going their separate ways, the faithful Abbé Fournier was busy trying to contact his departed master, Pasqually. He tried for a long time in vain, then one day success came. He described the event in *Ce que nous avons été*:

'At length, on a certain day, towards ten o'clock in the evening, I, being prostrated in my chamber, calling on God to assist me, heard suddenly the voice of M. de Pasqually, my director, who had died in the body more than two years previously. I heard him speaking distinctly outside my chamber, the door being closed, and the windows in like manner, the shutters also being secured. I turned in the direction of the voice, being that of the long garden belonging to the house, and thereupon I beheld M. de Pasqually with my eyes, who began speaking, and with him were my father and my mother, both also dead in the body. God knows the terrible night which I passed!'

Fournier relates that these visions of his parents and Pasqually continued for many years.

Another interesting group that flourished at this period was Antoine-Joseph Pernety's Illuminés d'Avignon. Pernety was a colourful character whose life is rather better documented than Pasqually's. He was born on 13th February 1716 at Roanne-en-Forez into a rather poor lower-middle-class family. He received his first education from his cousin, the Abbé Jacques Pernetti of Lyons, and early in life displayed unusual intellectual ability. Like many promising young men from the lower ranks of society he was oriented towards the Church and in 1732 he became a Benedictine, entering the abbey of Saint-Allire de Clermont. Later he was sent to the abbey of Saint-Germain in Paris to collaborate in the writing of a religious book.

At that time alchemy and the hermetic tradition were much in vogue, and in 1742 appeared *L'Histoire de la philosophie her-*

métique by the Abbé Langlet-Dufresnoy, which enjoyed great popularity. Pernety came across the book in the library at Saint-Germain and read it avidly. The fascination of alchemical symbolism took hold of him, and he immersed himself in the study of it. He conceived the theory that all ancient myths were hermetic allegories, which he expounded in a book published in 1758 entitled *Les Fables égyptiennes et grecques dévoilées et réduites au même principe avec une explication des hiéroglyphes de la guerre de Troie*. Both this and his later *Dictionnaire mytho-hermétique* came to be widely read.

Finding the life of a Benedictine monk too constricting, Pernety abandoned his religious habit and left the cloisters in 1765, though he continued to be referred to as Dom Pernety. He went first to Avignon which had developed into one of the main centres of freemasonry, partly under the influence of the many Jacobite *émigrés* who lived there. The first Avignon lodge was that of Saint-Jean d'Avignon, which was composed entirely of nobles. In 1749 a separate lodge was formed for the bourgeoisie, and later the two were fused as the lodge of Saint-Jean de Jerusalem. Subsequently a schismatic lodge was formed called the Sectateurs de la Vertu.

It was natural that shortly after arriving in Avignon, Pernety should become a freemason. In masonry he found ample scope for his hermetic interests, and he was soon propagating a rite of his own devising known as the *rite hermétique* or *rite de Pernety* which was adopted by the Sectateurs de la Vertu. The initiation consisted of six degrees:

1. *Vrai Maçon*
2. *Vrai Maçon de la Voie Droite*
3. *Chevalier de la Clef d'Or*
4. *Chevalier de l'Iris*
5. *Chevalier des Argonautes*
6. *Chevalier de la Toison d'Or*.

Pernety's rite was based entirely on alchemy, and initiates to the grade of *vrai maçon* were given an alchemical explanation of the masonic symbols. For example, the three symbols of the flaming star, the moon and the sun, with their corresponding inscriptions, were explained as follows: the word 'Force' inscribed on the flaming star, signified 'black matter' or putrefaction, the first stage in the alchemical process; the word 'Wisdom', inscribed on the moon, signified 'white matter' or purification, the second stage; the word 'Beauty', written on the sun, symbolised the final stage which produced 'red matter', the source of all good. In the other grades the candidate was taken through rituals based on Pernety's interpretations of ancient mythology. He later added another grade, *Chevalier du Soleil*, whose ritual, he claimed, contained a complete course of hermetism and gnosis.

Avignon at that time was still on papal territory, and the anti-masonic bull issued by Pope Clement XII in 1738 was enforceable there. Masons were therefore in constant danger of persecution. Finding that his situation was becoming perilous, Pernety left Avignon and made his way to Berlin where Frederick the Great, who was a francophile and a lover of philosophy, was extending a warm welcome to *émigré* French intellectuals. Frederick made Pernety a member of the Royal Academy of Berlin and gave him the post of curator of the royal library.

Pernety quickly made contact with occultists in Berlin and in due course became head of a small group of distinguished people who gathered together to discuss hermetic matters and to search for the philosopher's stone. He believed himself to be guided in his researches by an angel called Assadai who was prevented from returning to the higher regions until Pernety had discovered the secret of the Great Work. The group were also in touch with an entity called the Holy Word who informed Pernety that he was destined for the Great Work and that he would become a 'child of Sabaoth'. The entity also told him that a society would be formed as the nucleus for the new people of God, and that he and his friends had been chosen to be the centre of this society. New initiates were to be admitted by a ceremony known as consecration which was to take place on a hill near Berlin and was to continue every morning for nine days. The candidates were required to set up an altar of turf and to burn incense and swear to consecrate themselves to the service of God. Various members of the group went through this ceremony.

Pernety left Berlin in November 1783 and, after further travels, was instructed by the Holy Word to return to Avignon. On his return he became friendly with the Marquis de Vaucroze, who installed Pernety in a little house on his estate at Bédarrides, a few miles from Avignon. This territory was in one of the three fiefs of the archbishopric of Avignon which, although part of papal territory, were, by a strange anomaly, not under papal jurisdiction. Pernety was therefore able to carry on his activities without fear of persecution. The house, which he called Thabor, was the birthplace of the group that had been predicted in Berlin by the Holy Word. The new fraternity, which was called the Illuminés d'Avignon, was soon flourishing with a hundred members, all of whom were freemasons. They included Dr. Bouge, grand master of the lodge of Saint-Jean d'Ecosse à la vertu persecutée, the Marquis de Thomé, who later founded a Swedenborgian rite, and Esprit Calvert, professor of physiology and anatomy at the faculty of medicine of Avignon. Unlike Pernety's earlier rite, the Illuminés consisted of only two grades, *novice* and *illuminé moyen*, the leader of the group being known as *mage*. The house was equipped with a temple where the Great Work was pursued. The sort of alchemical activities that went on there can be deduced from a manuscript signed by Dr. Bouge setting out the procedure for making the elixir of the philosophers. This manuscript, which is still extant, is quoted by Joanny Bricaud in his fascinating study of Pernety, *Les Illuminés d'Avignon*. Part of it reads as follows:

'Take ten parts of philosophical mercury, place it in a matrass [glass vessel with a round or oval body and a long neck] or a philosopher's egg, together with one part of gold beaten into leaves; the gold will dissolve on the spot. Seal the vessel hermetically and expose it to the first degree of heat, and in forty days it will take on a black colour, blacker than the black of the blessed Raymond Lully, which is the raven's head that the philosophers talk of. But after this blackness has lasted forty days the matrass begins, little by little, to take on the colour of the cinders which the sages tell us on no account to despise because they are the beginning of our riches, and so, day by day, the substance begins to turn perfectly white, which is why we are told: whiten the mauve; but to do that it is necessary to raise the heat by one degree. After the blackness has lasted forty days the second degree of heat should be continued for about three months, as was the first degree, which makes six months in all for the first two degrees. The substance does not remain only white, but receives more colours of all kinds, and it is for this reason that the philosophers talk of watching the peacock's tail pass, after which begins the application of the third degree of heat. This lasts for about a month and a half, and then the substance takes on the colour of lemon, from which comes the saying of our masters that we must yellow a peacock by the third degree of heat; finally the fourth and last degree of heat must be given and continued for forty days so as to cause the substance to turn red, making nine months in all for the perfection of this work.'

Pernety's group carried on unmolested until the Revolution when there began a persecution of illuminist sects. Pernety was arrested in 1793. He was later released and went to live in Avignon where he died in 1796, guided to the last by the Holy Word. After his death the Illuminés d'Avignon declined, and by 1800 the membership had dwindled to fifteen. Soon after that it presumably died a natural death. One relic of Pernety's influence did, however, remain in freemasonry. The highest grade of his original rite which he had operated before going to Berlin, namely the grade of *Chevalier du Soleil*, was divided into two degrees and made the twenty-seventh and twenty-eighth grade of the Ancient and Accepted Scottish Rite. Pernety's writings also continued to be read long after his death.

Pernety's group was only one of an enormous proliferation of masonic and occult orders which grew up all over France in the latter half of the eighteenth century. There was, for example, the Rite of the Philalèthes, founded by Savalette de Langes, keeper of the royal treasury, in 1775. This combined the doctrines of Pasqually with those of Swedenborg. It was also, like Pernety's rite, tinged with alchemical doctrines. The rite had twelve degrees, of which the ninth was that of the Unknown Philosopher; this did not refer to Saint-Martin, but was the name of a spirit familiar to the celebrants of Pasqually's rituals. It is possible that this was the original inspiration for Saint-Martin's *nom de plume*.

Then there was the so-called Egyptian masonry of the Sicilian Cagliostro, whose strange life has been the subject of more than one biography. He claimed to have received, at the pyramids of Egypt, a full initiation into the 'mysteries of the veritable Grand Orient' and to be able to make gold and silver, renew youth, give physical beauty and evoke the spirits of the dead. He also proclaimed that he had lived for 2000 years. Cagliostro found France an ideal environment for his posturings and enjoyed enormous success in the salons.

Cagliostro's Egyptian rite, having been rejected in England, was received enthusiastically in France, and soon he had installed himself as High Priest of a Temple of Isis in the Rue de la Sondière in Paris. In 1785 he declared, apparently on Egyptian precedent, that women might be admitted to the mysteries of the pyramids, and in due course Madame de Lamballe and other ladies from the upper ranks of French society were admitted at the vernal equinox amid the oriental luxury of the temple of Isis. Cagliostro later moved to Rome, where he was arrested by the Inquisition and died in prison.

A visionary of a rather different kind, who also had an influence on French occultism, was the Swede Emanuel Swedenborg, who poured out his strange doctrines in *Arcana Coelestis, The Apocalypse Revealed, Four Preliminary Doctrines,* and *The True Christian Religion.* He held that since man is, in essence, a spirit, he is able to communicate with the instructed by spirits and angels, provided that God grants him the necessary receptivity. Swedenborg claimed that he himself enjoyed this privilege. Not only had he conversed with many types of spirit, but had been conducted by them to other planets, of whose inhabitants he gave detailed descriptions. At the same time as Pasqually was recruiting his first adepts, Swedenborg's writings were having a wide influence in France.

Another foreigner who influenced French occultism was the Austrian Franz Anton Mesmer (1734–1815), the pioneer of hypnotism. Mesmer had taken a medical degree at Vienna University, and for his doctorate had written a thesis entitled *de Planetarum Influxu in Corpore Humano* (*Of the Influence of the Planets on the Human Body*), in which he postulated the existence of a subtle fluid pervading all bodies and manifesting itself in the motions of the planets, and in tidal and atmospheric changes. When the ebb and flow of this fluid within the human body was out of harmony with the universal rhythm nervous or mental disorders resulted.

Soon after qualifying Mesmer began to apply this theory to the treatment of his patients, attempting to control the flow within the sick person by applying magnets to the body and by directing the fluid with a wand. He soon achieved some startling cures, the most famous being that of a young girl who had become blind through a nervous disorder. In spite of his fame and success the medical faculty at Vienna University refused to recognise his work, though he was given a warmer welcome in Bavaria and was admitted to the Munich Academy of Sciences. In 1778 he decided he needed a change of scene and departed for Paris, armed with a letter of recommendation from the Austrian Chancellor Kaunitz to the country's ambassador in Paris, Count Merci-Argentau. The Count introduced him to high French society and soon he was as famous in Paris as he had been in Vienna. It was not long before his sumptuous house in the Place Vendôme was full of people seeking treatment through what he called 'animal magnetism'.

Later he took a house at Creteil, a few miles from Paris, and continued his treatments there. One piece of apparatus was an oak barrel pierced with a number of holes through which protruded movable rods of iron. The patients sat round the barrel in a dimmed room, their hands joined and their knees and feet touching to ensure the circulation of the magnetic fluid. At the same time each patient would touch the afflicted part of his body with one of the iron rods. Appropriate music was provided sometimes by Mesmer himself who was an expert performer on the glass harmonica, a curious instrument consisting basically of a series of glass bowls, varying in size to provide a scale. From time to time Mesmer would walk round the circle, gazing penetratingly at each patient, speaking in a low voice, and waving his wand over their bodies. He wore a robe of lilac silk, trimmed with lace. A feature of his treatment was the inducing of a 'crisis' in the patient, after which the disorder supposedly disappeared.

Through his French disciple, Charles d'Eslon, he was introduced to the chief medical men of France, in the hope that he would gain in Paris the recognition that had eluded him in Vienna. In justification of his theories he wrote a *Mémoire sur la découverte du magnétisme animal*. But the Paris medical faculty, like the Vienna one, turned down his theories. A long struggle ensued, during which d'Eslon found himself outlawed because of his support for Mesmer. Finally, mainly through the influence of Marie Antoinette, a Royal Commission was appointed from the French Academy of Sciences consisting of a number of distinguished scientists including Lavoisier, Benjamin Franklin and the infamous Dr. Guillotin. Later a second commission, from the Royal Medical Society, also investigated Mesmer's case. Both judged animal magnetism to be spurious. Soon after-

1 Tarot card figures from Vol. 8 of Court de Gébelin's *Monde primitif* (published in 1781): top left, the Juggler; top right, the Fool; bottom left, the Emperor; bottom right, the Empress

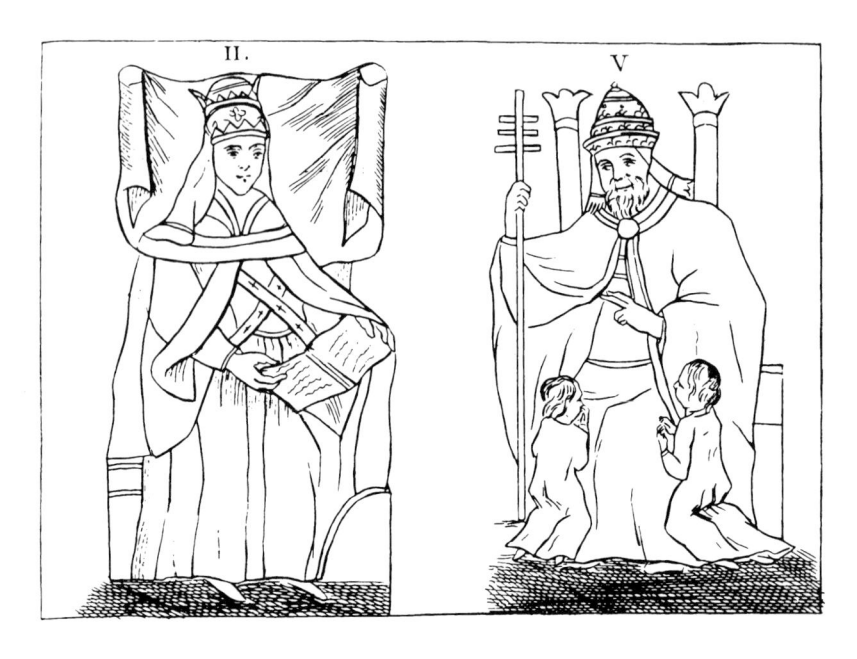

2 Court de Gébelin's Tarot (continued): top left, the High Priestess; top right, the High Priest; bottom left, the Chariot; bottom right, the Lovers

wards Mesmer left Paris; after further wanderings he ended up in Switzerland where he continued to propagate his theories until his death.

An extract from his *Mémoire* reads as follows:

'Animal magnetism is a fluid universally diffused; it is the medium of a mutual influence between the heavenly bodies, the earth, and animated bodies; it is everywhere continuous, so as to leave no void; its subtlety admits of no comparison; it is capable of receiving, propagating, communicating all the impressions of motion; it is susceptible of flux and reflux. The animal body experiences the effects of this agent; by insinuating itself into the substance of the nerves it affects them immediately . . . The action and the virtues of animal magnetism may be communicated from one body to another, animate and inanimate . . . It perfects the action of medicines; it excites and directs salutary crises in such a manner that the physician may render himself master of them . . . In animal magnetism, nature presents a universal method of healing and preserving mankind.'

This was indeed stuff to stir the imagination of occultists; and later on we find writers like Eliphas Lévi referring enthusiastically to animal magnetism.

1. Countess de B . . . *Chroniques de l'œil de bœuf.*
2. Adrien Dansette, *Religious History of Modern France.*
3. Ibid.
4. Auguste Viatte, *Les Sources occul'es du romantisme,* Ch. 2.
5. Op. cit., pp. 75–6.
6. Op. cit., p. 78.
7. 'At whatever time I shall invoke thee, hear me quickly.'
8. Op. cit. p. 79.
9. Op. cit., p. 81.
10. A. E. Waite, *The Life of Louis Claude de Saint-Martin.*
11. *Correspondence.* See A. E. Waite, *Life of Saint-Martin.*

C

2 The Occult and the Revolution

The members of Pasqually's Order of the Elect Cohens may have included one Jacques Cazotte, poet and author of a fanciful romance called *Le Diable amoureux*. Cazotte was evidently also a clairvoyant of remarkable power. In 1788 he was present at a dinner party in Paris given by the Duchesse de Gramont at which he made a prophecy concerning the Revolution.[1] This was recorded almost verbatim by another guest, Jean de la Harpe, a fanatical atheist and sceptic who intended to produce his record later and show the prediction to be false. As it turned out, La Harpe's notes were used for quite the opposite purpose.

Towards the end of dinner one of the many distinguished guests, Guillaume de Malesherbes, a minister and confidant of Louis XVI, proposed a toast 'to the day when reason will be triumphant in the affairs of men—a day which I shall never live to see'.

Cazotte did not respond to the toast; instead he rose and declared: 'Sir, you are wrong. You will live to see that day. It will come within six years.' He went on to say that the Revolution was not far ahead and that the lives of everyone in the room would be affected by it.

The guests clamoured to know what their fates were to be, and Cazotte turned first to the Marquis de Condorcet, who, he said, would die on the stone floor of a prison cell, having taken poison to cheat the executioner. Condorcet objected that such a prophecy could have little to do with the reign of reason, to which Cazotte replied that nevertheless this would take place under the so-called reign of reason; at that time, he added, the only temples in France would be dedicated to reason.

Another guest, Chamfort, a favourite of the King, remarked that Cazotte would not qualify as one of the priests of those temples, Cazotte answered him: 'You will be one . . . you will cut your veins twenty-two times with a razor, but still you will not die—until some months later.'

An equally grisly fate awaited another guest, Dr. Vicq d'Azyr, who was told: 'You will not open your veins yourself. At your own request someone will open them for you, six times in one day, and you will expire during the night.'

Turning to Jean Bailly, a distinguished astronomer, Cazotte informed him that in spite of his good deeds and great learning he would die on the scaffold at the hands of the mob. A similar fate awaited MM. Nicolai, Roucher and Malesherbes. Cazotte then sorrowfully told the Duchesse de Gramont that she too would be executed, along with many other great ladies. Furthermore the only victim allowed a confessor before he died would be the King himself.

When La Harpe sarcastically asked what lay in store for him, Cazotte replied that he would not die like the others, but would become a Christian. As for Cazotte himself, he would give no direct prediction as to his fate, but merely repeated the story of the man who, during the siege of Jerusalem, walked round the ramparts for seven successive days crying out: 'Woe to Jerusalem! Woe to Jerusalem!' At the last moment of his last round a huge stone from a Roman catapult hit and killed him.

Within six years all of Cazotte's predictions had been fulfilled to the letter. The Marquis de Condorcet poisoned himself in a prison cell. Chamfort, threatened with arrest, tried to kill himself by opening his veins, but he did not die until later as a result of bad medical treatment of his cuts. Dr. Vicq d'Azyr died in the manner predicted. Bailly, Roucher, Malesherbes and Nicolai were guillotined, as were the Duchesse de Gramont and the other ladies at the party. Jean de la Harpe became an ardent Catholic and entered a monastery. Cazotte himself was arrested and guillotined in 1792 on a charge of having tried to help the King escape. His prediction about the temples of reason was also correct, as I shall show in the next chapter.

La Harpe survived until 1803, and after his death the record of the prophecy was found among his papers. He had already given details of the prophecy to many of his friends, and the Baroness d'Oberkirch mentions in her memoirs having heard about it in 1789. There is therefore no possibility of the record having been forged.

Eliphas Lévi, in his *Doctrine et rituel de la haute magie*, says of the prophetic dinner party: 'Everyone present, La Harpe excepted, was an initiate who had divulged or at least profaned the mysteries. Cazotte, the most exalted of all in the scale of initiation, pronounced the sentence of death in the name of illuminism, and this sentence was executed variously but rigorously.'

Cazotte was also present at another remarkable prophecy concerning the Revolution when Cagliostro, at a masonic gathering in Paris, demonstrated his technique of prediction by numerology. After studying the numerical value of Louis XVI's name and various titles, Cagliostro warned the King to beware of death on the scaffold towards the thirty-ninth year of his life. A similar study of Marie Antoinette's name revealed that she too would die on the scaffold. Cagliostro went on to predict that the Princesse de Lamballe would escape the guillotine but be murdered by ruffians in the Rue des Ballets —a remarkably detailed prognostication which was fulfilled like the others. Cazotte stood up and asked Cagliostro what the name of the Bourbon's successor would be, to which Cagliostro replied that the question was in itself a prophecy; the numerical total of its letters revealed that the successor's name would be Napoleon Bonaparte and that he would end 'pacing the circle of a melancholy island'.[2]

One would not assume, from these accounts, that masonic initiates such as Cagliostro and Cazotte (for the latter certainly belonged to some masonic order) looked forward to the Revolution with any pleasure. But secret societies tend to get blamed for the ills of the world, and those who later looked for somewhere to lay the blame for the Revolution found in the masonic lodges and other secret groups an ideal target for their accusations.

An expatriate priest by the name of the Abbé Barruel, who had taken refuge in England from the ravages of the French Revolution, was the first proponent of the theory that the Revolution was the result of a secret conspiracy on the part of a number of sinister occult groups. He argued his case in a weighty, four-volume work entitled *Memoirs Illustrating the History of Jacobinism*. These were published in English translation in 1797 and found sympathetic readers among English opponents of the Revolution. The Abbé begins his treatise thus:

'At an early period of the French Revolution there appeared a

The Occult and the Revolution 37

sect calling itself Jacobin, and teaching that *all men were equal and free*! In the name of their equality and disorganising liberty, they trampled under foot the altar and the throne; they stimulated all nations to rebellion, and aimed at plunging them ultimately into the horrors of anarchy . . .

'Whence originated these men, who seem to arise from the bowels of the earth, who start into existence with their plans and their projects, their tenets and their thunders, their means and ferocious resolves; whence, I say, this devouring sect? Whence this swarm of adepts, these systems, this frantic rage against the altar and the throne, against every institution, whether civil or religious, so much respected by our ancestors?'

In the long and painstaking argument that follows Barruel depicts a conspiracy which, he claimed, began with the subtle anti-Christian propaganda of Voltaire and the compilers of the *Encyclopaedia*, which he calls an 'impious digest', and culminated in the execution of the King and the suppression of the Church.

So vivid is the Abbé's style, so persuasive his tone, and so painstaking in detail his treatise, that the reader is almost persuaded of the truth of his assertions, in spite of the fact that his almost fanatical hatred of the revolutionaries obviously stimulated his imagination to a high level of fantasy. Nevertheless, there is, as we shall see, a grain of truth in what he says. Furthermore his book gives some interesting information about freemasonry in general during the period leading up to the Revolution.

'During the last twenty years', he writes, 'it was difficult, especially in Paris, to meet persons who did not belong to the society of masonry.' He relates how he himself was invited to become a mason, but always refused. His friends, however, persisted, and one evening things came to a head:

'I was invited to a dinner at a friend's house and was the only prophane in the midst of a large party of Masons. Dinner over and the servants ordered to withdraw, it was proposed to form themselves into a lodge, and to initiate me. I persisted in my refusal, and particularly refused to take the oath of keeping a secret, the very object of which was unknown to me. They dispensed with the oath, but I still refused. They became more pressing, telling me that Masonry was perfectly innocent and that its morality was unobjectionable: In reply I asked whether it was better than that of the Gospel. They only answered by forming themselves into a lodge, when began all those grimaces and childish ceremonies which are described in books of masonry, such as Jachin and Boaz.[3] I attempted to make my escape, but in vain.'

Finding that there was no alternative, the Abbé decided to submit, but only on condition that he was not required to do anything that was against honour or conscience.

'At length the Venerable with the utmost gravity put the following question: "Brother, are you disposed to execute all the orders of the Grand Master, though you were to receive contrary orders from a King, an Emperor, or any other Sovereign whatever?" My answer was "No."—"What No," replies the Venerable with surprise! "Are you only entered among us to betray our secrets! Would you hesitate between the interests of Masonry and those of the prophane?—You are not aware then that there is not one of our swords but is ready to pierce the throat of a traitor." '

The Abbé persisted in his refusal. The Venerable grew angry. At length the Abbé threw off the bandage with which he had been blindfolded and shouted 'No' with great vehemence.

'Immediately the whole lodge clap their hands in sign of applause, and the Venerable compliments me on my constancy. "Such are the men for us, men of resolution and courage!"— "What" said I, "men of resolution! and who do you find who resist your threats! You, yourselves, gentlemen, have not all said YES to this question: and if you have said it, how is it possible that you can persuade me that your mysteries contain nothing against honour or conscience?

'The tone I assumed had thrown the Lodge into confusion. The brethren surrounded me, telling me that I had taken things too much in earnest, and in too literal a sense: that they had never pretended to engage in any thing contrary to the duties of every true Frenchman, and that in spite of all my resistance I should nevertheless be admitted. The Venerable soon restored order with a few strokes of his mallet. He then informed me that I was passed to the degree of *Master*, adding, that if the secret was not given to me, it was only because a more regular lodge, and held with the ordinary ceremonies, was necessary on such an occasion. In the mean while he gave me the signs and pass words for the third degree, as he had done for the other two.

This was sufficient for me to be admitted into a regular Lodge, and now we were all brethren. As for me, I had been metamorphosed into *apprentice, fellow-craft,* and *master* in one evening, without having ever dreamt of it in the morning.'

As an afterthought to this anecdote, the Abbé adds: 'In justice I am bound to declare, that, excepting the Venerable, who turned out a violent Jacobin, they all showed themselves loyal subjects at the Revolution.'

Barruel claimed that the fundamental purpose of French masonry was to subvert the basis of established society—a purpose which was made explicit in their innermost secret. He describes a meeting at which this secret was vouchsafed to an apprentice. After the apprentice had taken the oath 'the Master said the following words to him, which the reader may easily conceive have not escaped my memory, as I had expected them with so much impatience, "My dear brother, the secret of Masonry consists in these words EQUALITY AND LIBERTY; all men are equal and free; all men are brethren."' In another passage he explains that: 'In the higher degrees the twofold principle of liberty and equality is unequivocally explained *by war against Christ and his Altars, war against Kings and their Thrones!!!*' Barruel does, however, allow that the Jacobin interpretation of the principle is unknown to English masons, whom he is careful to exonerate from his charges.

In spite of Barruel's fantasies and exaggerations he does point out some interesting facts. In his first volume, for example, he discusses what he calls the 'Secret Academy', a group presided over by Voltaire and having among its members such subversive characters as d'Alembert, Diderot and Helvetius. This, according to Barruel, was a dangerous group, dedicated to the spreading of propaganda against religion, morals and government. He quotes a letter from Voltaire to Helvetius, dated 20th April 1761, in which occurs the passage: 'Let the Philosophers unite in *a brotherhood like the Free-Masons,* let them assemble and support each other; let them be faithful to the association.' This is an interesting remark, for it shows that the freemasons did set a kind of example to those who wished to band together for the reform of society.

In order to discover how much truth there is in Barruel's assertions it is necessary to examine the whole position of freemasonry in the years leading up to the Revolution. When we look closely at the movement we see that it occupied a unique position in the social structure; for in freemasonry the ideals of democracy and autocracy met.

As I have mentioned, the Grand Orient of France was finally established in 1772; and an examination of its constitution is important to an understanding of the nature of masonry. The constitution provided that each lodge would elect a venerable to lead it. The lodges would be represented at the Grand Orient by the venerables or by deputies chosen by the members. These representatives formed a kind of central legislative council, which in turn vested day-to-day executive power in a smaller group headed by the Grand Master and composed mainly of senior officers.

A circular issued by the Grand Orient on 18th March 1775 expressed the ideals of the constitution when it stated: 'The Grand Orient is nothing more than a body formed by the union of the free representatives of all the lodges: it is the lodges themselves and all the masons belonging to them who, via their representatives, give laws which they enforce with one hand and obey with the other. No one obeys a law that is not self-imposed. It is the most just, the most natural, and consequently the most perfect of governments.'

In spite of this claim there was a strong monarchical element in the constitution of the Grand Orient. The Grand Master was immovable, as was his second-in-command, the Administrator General. Gaston Martin, in his masterly study of freemasonry and the Revolution,[4] says 'The assembly was more like the council of a monarch than a Chamber of Deputies. The similarity went further: corresponding to the four traditional councils surrounding the sovereign were four chambers: the lodge of council; the chamber of Paris; the chamber of the provinces; and the chamber of administration.'

Nevertheless the masonic lodges provided an environment where members of different social strata could mix on more or less equal terms—a remarkable innovation considering the fossilised rigidity of social divisions in France at that time. Although the earliest lodges were confined to the nobility this situation did not last, and the bourgeoisie were admitted in full force. But the working class remained excluded for the following reason: the doctrine was held that the freemason was a free man and that those who depended on others for their living were not free. Many lodges were dominated by a single profession. For example, at Rennes, the Parfaite Union was composed largely of members of the legal profession, while the Parfaite Amitié was made up primarily of merchants.

The outstanding characteristic of the movement at this time was the high intellectual level of the members and their receptiveness to new ideas. As Martin says, 'Freemasonry incontestably represented the intellectual and moral élite of the nation.' A certain prestige came to be attached to belonging to the fraternity, and members of the bourgeoisie eager to display their intellectual superiority rushed to join. It was not surprising, therefore, that before long the movement had developed a vast and influential network reaching into every section of French society. There were lodges in the army and, as I mentioned before, even a number in religious houses. Many important names are to be found in the list of members of the Grand Orient. Among them were Voltaire, Bailly, Danton and Helvetius.

In 1779, a year after its formation, the Grand Orient had 104 lodges: 23 in Paris, 71 in the provinces, and 10 in the army. By 1789 its strength had grown to a total of 629 lodges. This rapid growth was explained partly by the infiltration of members of other organisations who wished to manœuvre the Grand Orient and turn its powerful influence to their own ends. The aims of the infiltrators divided themselves into three categories: quasi-mystical, religious, and political.

The quasi-mystical influence originated from the ideas of such men as Cagliostro, Mesmer, Swedenborg and Saint-Martin, whose teachings I discussed in the last chapter. The religious infiltration came mainly from the Jesuits, whose plan was a subtle one. Since the movement embraced both Catholic and Protestant, the Jesuits hoped to attract large numbers of Protestants into masonry and then gradually orient the movement back towards Catholicism, thus drawing the erring Protestants back into the fold. The political influences came to a large extent from German revolutionaries such as Weishaupt and Bode, who wanted to turn the whole masonic movement into an instrument for political reform.

Things came to a head at the great masonic congress at Wilhelmsbad in 1782. Here the rationalist revolutionaries, headed by Bode, were finally defeated by the moderates, causing a split in the movement in which the Bode faction allied themselves with the Bavarian Illuminati of Weishaupt. But the defeat of the political faction did not mean that the central body of masonry ceased to have any political importance. The fact that orthodox masonry in France, as represented by the Grand Orient, had renounced any extreme revolutionary aims probably enabled it in the end to have a greater effect politically.

The influence of freemasonry on the Revolution was not through any secret conspiracy of the kind envisaged by the Abbé Barruel. Nevertheless masonry did play an important part in paving the way for revolution. One of its most important functions was to act as a kind of proving ground for the ideals of the philosophers. In the masonic movement these were transformed from abstract speculation into practical action. This is how Martin sums it up:

'In this transformation of philosophical principles into political rules the rôle of freemasonry was of primary importance. This importance can be illustrated by the following comparison: with regard to the doctrines of liberty and equality freemasonry played the same role as a parliamentary commission does with regard to a proposed law. Having received a set of abstract theories, freemasonry extracted their practical possibilities and paved the way for their realisation.'

In 1789 the King decided to summon the States General, a decision in which the masons may have played a part, considering the number who were members of the King's entourage. During the elections to the States General the freemasons used the opportunity to put forward their schemes for reform. They did this, not directly, but through the *cahiers de doléances*, lists of grievances that were drawn up in each election district for transmission to the assembly. The speed with which these *cahiers* appeared and the cogency with which they were written indicated that the freemasons had long been prepared for such an opportunity to propagate their ideas of liberty and equality.

The masonic influence continued when the States General assembled. A large number of masons were elected, and in the Third Estate they were in a majority. As the revolution gathered momentum, however, forces began to build up that even the masons were powerless to check. The dreadful terror that reached its peak in the execution of the King was abhorrent to the civilised creed of the majority of masons.

The Occult and the Revolution 43

The scepticism that originally gave birth to masonry now began to take more extreme forms. The Catholic Church was systematically suppressed and many strange creeds now began to flourish in the open. It is to these that we shall now turn our attention.

---

1. My account of this affair is taken from *The Story of Fulfilled Prophecy*, by Justine Glass.
2. Justine Glass, *The Story of Fulfilled Prophecy*.
3. The twin symbolic pillars of the Temple of Solomon.
4. Gaston Martin, *La Franc-Maçonnerie française et la préparation de la révolution, 1926*.

3 Revolutionary Cults

A new social order demanded a new faith to go with it. But a faith, like a language, is not an easy thing to construct artificially, and it is not surprising that several different cults superseded one another in rapid succession during the early post-Revolution years. One of the first attempts was the revolutionary faith founded by Marie Joseph Chénier in which Christ was replaced by the Constitution as the source of goodness and the object of adoration. Incense was burned in honour of human society on the altar of the Fatherland. The liturgy was a hotch-potch of scraps borrowed from other religions.

At first the worship took the form of an awkward and rather preposterous mingling of Catholic observances with those of the constitutional cult. For example, on 14th July, the day chosen for the 'Feast of the Federation', a strange ceremony took place at the Champ-de-Mars where Talleyrand, Bishop of Autun, celebrated Mass at the Altar of the Fatherland. The 400 priests who surrounded him wore tricolour sashes over their robes. Lafayette, commander of the National Guard, provided the high point of the ceremony when he pronounced an oath of loyalty to the nation, the law and the King.[1]

In 1792 the Legislative Assembly decreed that an altar of the Fatherland be set up in every commune. Engraved on each altar was to be the Declaration of the Rights of Man, together with the inscription: 'The citizen is born, lives and dies for the Fatherland'[2] After the monarchy was removed in 1792 the ceremonies of the new faith became increasingly numerous and serious.

A number of other cults appeared in its wake. There was, for example, the worship of Reason which sprang up in the autumn of 1793, and which Cazotte had predicted in 1788 at the prophetic dinner. An example of the ceremonies of this cult is described in Adrien Dansette's *Religious History of Modern France*: 'A rock was placed in the choir of Notre Dame and on it a circular temple was erected, dedicated to "philosophy". On the morning of the 10th November, in the presence of members of the Commune, a procession of girls marched up and down the sides of the rock, saluting as they passed the Flame of Truth which burned half way up. An actress from the Opéra, dressed in white and wearing an azure cloak and red bonnet, came out of the temple and seated herself on a grass-covered throne. She was Reason and the girls chanted a hymn to her. Then, with the goddess borne on the shoulders of four citizens, the participants and spectators set off for the Convention . . . Similar ceremonies took place . . . all over the country where many churches had been converted into temples of Reason.'

These extraordinary antics illustrate an interesting and significant phenomenon. In all human behaviour there is a rational and an irrational element, neither of which can ever be entirely suppressed. In some societies these elements coexist in greater harmony than in others. In eighteenth-century France they seemed to conflict like partners in a forced marriage—inseparable but incompatible. So deeply rooted were religious attitudes in the French character that the designers of the new order found themselves unable to express their approval of any concept in terms of religious forms. Hence the paradox of Reason being dolled up in red, white and blue and worshipped as a goddess. There is a peculiarly French flavour about the performance.

In March 1794 Anaxagoras Chaumette, the main propagator of the worship of Reason, was executed, and his cult soon disappeared. It was followed by an attempt to return to some form of deistic religion, in which Robespierre was the main influence. He advocated a system based on highly general religious and moral principles, which soon took shape as the Cult of the Supreme Being. The sign 'Temple of Reason' which had hung on churches was replaced by one which proclaimed: 'The French people recognise the cult of the Supreme Being and the immortality of the soul.'

This new religion, like those which had preceded it, had to have its feasts: the first of these was held on 8th June 1794. Robespierre and the members of the Convention began the celebrations in an amphitheatre behind the palace of the Tuileries.

Robespierre made a speech in which he praised the great being who had 'placed remorse and fear in the heart of the triumphant oppressor and pride in the hearts of the innocent victims of oppression'. After a hymn had been sung by members of the Opéra, Robespierre descended from the steps of the rostrum and, carrying a torch in his hand, set fire to a group of monsters representing Atheism, Selfishness and Nothingness. When these had been consumed by the flames a statue of Wisdom rose in their place, somewhat blackened by smoke.

After this performance the members of the Convention proceeded to the Champ-de-Mars where another impressive display awaited them. Standing on a column, on top of a symbolic mountain, was a man with a silver trumpet; by signalling with blasts on the trumpet he directed a choir of men and women who sang a series of hymns appropriate to the occasion. Cannons thundered to the accompaniment of cries of 'Long live the Republic!' from the crowds.[3]

But this new religion did not last long. Robespierre was executed on 27th July 1794, a victim of the terror he had helped to create. The cult of the Supreme Being passed away, though vestiges of it remained—and still remain today—in the form of the revolutionary feasts.

After its demise there followed five years during which religious anarchy reigned. One of the cults that appeared during this period was that of the Théophilantropes. It began in 1796 when a bookseller called J. B. Chemin-Dupontés published a work written by himself and entitled *Manuel des Théoanthropophiles* (the name was later altered to the more euphonious *théophilantropes*) in which he outlined yet another religion to replace Catholicism which he regarded as inimical to free government. Chemin attempted to arrive at certain basic religious tenets which could be agreed on by everyone. Care was taken to avoid the appearance of a secret or exclusive cult. There were to be no rites, no priests, nothing that could cause offence to any sect. One of the publications of the Théophilantropes states that their dogmas are: 'those on which all sects are agreed ... their morality is that on which there has never been the slightest disagreement ... Even the name that they have given to their society expresses the double aim of all sects, that of encouraging men to worship God and to love their fellows.'[4]

A number of hymns were specially composed for the sect.

Revolutionary Cults 47

These presented 'an extract of all moralities, ancient and modern, stripped of any maxims too extreme in permissiveness or severity, or opposed to the principles of the Théophilantropes'.[5] The following is the first verse of one of these hymns:

> O, Dieu, dont l'Univers publie
> Et les bontés et la grandeur;
> Toi, qui nous accordas la vie,
> Reçois l'encens de notre cœur.
> Laisse à tes pieds dormir la foudre
> Dont tes bras peut réduire en poudre
> L'ingrat qui brise ton autel.
> De nos chants les Cieux retentissent;
> Sur des Enfans qui te benissent,
> Abaisse un regard paternel,
> Abaisse un regard paternel.[6]

In Chemin-Dupontés' *Code religieux et moral des Théophilantropes*, the fundamental precepts of the cult are set out. Chemin affirms that: 'The Théophilantropes believe in the existence of God and the immortality of the soul.' In another passage he exhorts his followers to 'love God, cherish your brothers, make yourself useful to your country.' The *Code Religieux* also reproduces a series of extracts from the works of a variety of writers of different religious persuasions. Here, for example, is a passage quoted from Confucius: 'It is pernicious to put one's joy in pride and vanity, in an idle and licentious life, in feasting and pleasures.'

There are also quotations relating to social and familial duties, taken from the book of an unnamed 'ancient sage of India'. The passage on social duties begins: 'Your food, your clothing, your domestic possessions, your security, your consolations, your pleasures, you owe to the existence of others, and you cannot enjoy them except in society.'

Trite and naive though the pronouncements of the Théophilantropes may seem, the cult is extremely significant historically. Here we have at attempt to find common ground between all religions and sects, an attempt which enlists the support of mysterious oriental sages—in short, exactly the sort of religious eclecticism that one associates with Theosophy and similar late-nineteenth-century phenomena. When the Theosophical Society was formed in 1875 it was not setting a precedent, but merely following one that had been established seventy-nine years earlier by the Théophilantropes.

The difference of three-quarters of a century, however, between the two movements is all-important. Whereas by 1875 Europe and America were ripe for a new religious syncretism, in 1796 only a small handful of people were free of the crude extremes of religious dogmatism and revolutionary atheism. Moreover, material and political problems were for the majority of greater concern that spiritual ones. The religious dilettante who was to become the mainstay of Theosophy was still a comparatively rare bird in the 1790s. Nevertheless there were enough of his kind to gain the Théophilantropes a considerable following for a time. The first service was held in 1797, and many prominent intellectuals and politicians joined the movement; soon Chemin's followers were sufficiently confident to establish a journal, *l'Echo des Théophilantropes*. But their success was short-lived. An extreme left-wing element began to dominate the religion, and the government withdrew its support. By then the novelty had worn off; the public became indifferent, and the cult of the Théophilantropes soon went the way of its predecessors.

In 1799 Napoleon Bonaparte seized power and initiated the re-establishment of orthodox Catholicism. The period of religious anarchy was at an end. Behind the scenes, however, the growth of occult movements continued.

1. Adrien Dansette, *Religious History of Modern France*.
2. Ibid.
3. Ibid.
4. *Recueil des cantiques, odes et hymnes, pour les fêtes publiques, religieuses et morales des Théophilantropes* (Paris, 1797).
5. Ibid.
6. Ibid.

3 The Devil, from the Tarot pack designed by Oswald Wirth in the late 19th century

4   The Beginnings of Popular Occultism

One of the celebrities who received a miraculous cure from Mesmer was an eccentric Protestant theologian from the Languedoc by the name of Court de Gébelin, who had been reduced to a bad physical condition by forty years of sleepless nights and overwork. When he presented himself at Mesmer's consulting rooms he had a badly swollen leg and a face 'as yellow as a quince'. He recorded his cure in a letter to the Secretary of the Academy of Dijon, dated 28th May 1783. Two or three days after his session with the magnetiser, he 'no longer had any pains or thirst. Soon my feet, which had been icy cold for twenty-five years, were moist and warm; all the callouses and corns had disappeared. The skin had become rejuvenated; I had feet like a fifteen-year-old . . . Such were the effects of animal magnetism in my case; and I am extremely grateful to him.'

But Court de Gébelin's feet are of less importance to this study than the influence which he exerted through his writing on certain trends in occultism. In 1772 he had issued a prospectus for a monumental work which he proposed to write, entitled *Le Monde primitif*—an undertaking which moved the encyclopaedist d'Alembert to remark that a work of such scope would require at least forty men to finish it. Nevertheless the first volume appeared in 1773, and the remaining volumes quickly followed. The book enjoyed an enormous success and was presented to the King. Court de Gébelin himself became famous.

Subsequent scholars have poured scorn on the superficial erudition of *Le Monde primitif*, and it would probably have passed completely into oblivion were it not for certain passages in it relating to the Tarot cards. In Volume 8 the author writes of the pack as follows:

'If one announced that there had existed for the last 3,757 years, and still existed, a work of the ancient Egyptians, one of the books saved from the flames that destroyed their superb libraries, and which contains their purest doctrine concerning certain interesting objects, everyone would no doubt be anxious to know such a precious and extraordinary book. If one added that this book is spread throughout a large part of Europe; that for many centuries it has been accessible to everyone, then the surprise would be even greater. But would it not reach its height if one declared that no one had ever suspected it of being Egyptian; that it was possessed as if it were of no value, and that no one had ever sought to decipher a single page; that the fruit of an exquisite learning is regarded as a mass of extravagant figures which are of no significance in themselves? This fact is nevertheless true, this Egyptian book . . . exists today.'

It is small wonder that these extravagant claims attracted attention, especially as Court de Gébelin included interpretations of the cards. This author's subsequent career is interesting, for in about 1776 he became a freemason and later president of a Paris lodge.

There was one person for whom Court de Gébelin's ideas on the Tarot were to have important consequences. This was a man named Alliette, who was destined to become another major propagandist of the Tarot pack. This Alliette is a somewhat mysterious figure. He appears to have started his career in humble circumstances living in Paris and giving lessons in mathematics. Evidently this was not a lucrative enough occupation, and he decided to seek a better source of income by telling fortunes with cards. In doing so he adopted the anagram of his name and called himself Etteilla.

Realising that his education was not sufficient for a would-be occultist he set about teaching himself, and by dint of wide reading succeeded in acquiring a sufficiently impressive appearance of learning. He advertised himself as a philosophical cabalist practising astrology, alchemy, cheiromancy and cartonomancy. The last word was his own invention, incorporating the word onomancy which means divination by names. He used it in preference to 'cartomancy' to describe his own system of telling fortunes with cards.

In 1753 he published *l'Abrégé de la cartonomancie*. This must have met with a lasting success, for it was reissued twenty

The Beginnings of Popular Occultism

years later. He also published a number of other works on various forms of fortune-telling, mainly connected with cards.

The appearance of *Le Monde primitif* and the interest it aroused in the Tarot presented an opportunity which Etteilla was quick to seize. He applauded Court de Gébelin's discoveries and added some claims of his own about the Tarot which went even further. He declared that the Tarot had been composed 171 years after the flood, that seventeen magi had collaborated for four years to produce it, and that Hermes Trismegistos himself had conceived the plan of the book, which was therefore called *The Book of Thoth*. It had been written, he said, on leaves of gold in a temple three leagues from Memphis.

Etteilla claimed to have known about the origin of the Tarot before Court de Gébelin, but it is likely that his ideas on the subject were based entirely on *Le Monde primitif*. This is suggested by an examination of his writings before and after the appearance of Court de Gébelin's book. *Etteilla ou Manière de se recréer*, published at Amsterdam in 1770, is a simple manual of fortune-telling with ordinary playing cards and contains no mention of the Tarot. His works on the Tarot, such as the *Dictionnaire synonimique du livre de Thot* were written after the appearance of *Le Monde primitif*.

In manner, Etteilla is described as being dignified and reserved. He was a man of few words and gave the impression of fearing to reveal too much to his listeners.[1] This must have had the desired effect of impressing his clients, for his fame spread rapidly, and he was kept busy casting horoscopes and making talismans to order. His customers were no doubt eager to employ the services of one who carried the mantle of the Comte de Saint-Germain, for Etteilla claimed to have been a pupil of that illustrious magus. In one of his books, *Les sept nuances de l'œuvre philosophique-hermétique*, he wrote that he had been 'a true disciple for about 20 years of M. de St.-Germain, the true cabalist'. He also claimed that he had been entrusted with the education of Saint-Germain's niece. When the newspapers announced the death of the Count, Etteilla stated publicly that the news was false and that his master would be seen again in Paris in 1787 or '88.

Etteilla's list of charges gives an idea of the range of services he offered and the profit he must have derived from his activities. The following are some extracts from his tariff.

For answering a question on the higher sciences	3 livres
For lessons in practical magic	3 livres
Casting a horoscope	50 livres
Reading of cards	24 livres
To resolve certain questions without previous work	6 livres
To be told the name of your genie, his nature, his qualities, his power in relation to human life, his element, his domain of protection etc.	12 livres
Interpreting a dream	6 livres
For making a talisman 8-10 louis, depending on the properties required and the difficulty of making the talisman	
For acting as a person's 'spiritual doctor' and 'perpetual soothsayer'	30 livres a month

Etteilla also derived income from a public course in 'cartonomancy' which consisted of six lessons costing three livres each. In 1788 he formed the Société littéraire des associés libres des interprètes du livre de Thot, which was carried on after his death on 12th December 1791.

Etteila's importance lies in the fact that he was the first French occultist to popularise a form of cabalism. Hitherto cabalistic ideas had been the preserve of scholars and esoteric orders. Now Etteilla had made certain cabalistic theories as accessible to the occult-minded public as were his simple forms of fortune-telling and cartonomancy. For example, he used the cabalistic doctrine known as the Schemhamphorasch, according to which there are seventy-two angels who guard over the world, corresponding to the seventy-two names of God.

Etteilla had a number of disciples, one of whom, a man named Hugand, published a work on cartonomancy in 1791 under the name of Jélalel. In an obituary pamphlet issued after Etteilla's death he wrote: 'Among the great men who have illuminated this eighteenth century was our master ... he is no longer, my brothers ... Etteilla is no longer! ... Posterity! You will judge whether or not Etteilla merits the honours of the French pantheon.'

But it is likely that more people remembered Etteilla in the terms of a satirical song composed about him while he was alive, entitled *Etteilla ou le Devin du Siècle*, which contained the lines:

Mais pour s'instruire, on va
On va
Chez le fameux Etteilla

While the disciples of Etteilla were carrying popular cabalism into the nineteenth century another form of Hebraic occultism was being propagated on a more scholarly level by Fabre d'Olivet (1767-1825). He came to Paris in 1780 and, following the wishes of his parents, went into the silk trade, but he was soon fired with a wish to pursue less mundane activities and began to devote himself to writing and composing music. He dreamed of undertaking a colossal work that would synthesise all facts accumulated by humanity. In pursuit of this objective he studied alone for twenty years, while earning his living as a minor employee in one of the ministries. He devoured ancient Greek and Latin authors and then turned his mind to Egyptology. In 1811 he claimed to have cured a deaf mute by a process discovered in deciphering a text from Pharaoh's temple.

The first fruits of his researches were published in *Les vers dorés de Pythagore expliqués*, which appeared in 1813. His next work was to be more ambitious. He decided that the key to the hidden wisdom of ancient Egypt lay in the Book of Genesis which, he claimed, had been reduced to nonsense by bad translation. In order to rediscover the true Hebrew language he studied 'Samaritan, Chaldean, Syrian, Arabic, Greek and Chinese'.[2] After three years of work he believed that he had not only found the true Hebrew but reconstructed a grammar which was applicable to most of the known mother languages. Hebrew, he claimed, had three different senses, or levels, corresponding to body, spirit and soul.

In his book *La langue hébraïque réstitué* (1816) he translated the first ten chapters of Genesis in the second, spiritual, sense only, claiming that he did not want to profane the mysteries of the highest sense. He added long notes for each word, proving its meaning by his analysis of its roots. This book received the distinction of being placed on the Index by the authorities in Rome. His two other main works were *l'Histoire philosophique du genre humain* (1822) and *Cain* (1823).

Fabre d'Olivet and Etteilla both, in their different ways, helped to stimulate interest in occultism, and soon the seeds of the new movement began to show a few shoots. In 1823 an author writing under the name of Lenain published at Amiens *La Science Cabalistique ou l'art de connaître les bons génies*. In the introduction Lenain declared his intention of explaining the hidden truths of occult science in a clear and comprehensible fashion, implying that he was conscious of a new public demand for less esoteric expositions of the mysteries. His treatise begins with an explanation of the Tetragrammaton, the four letters forming the sacred name of god יהוה usually transliterated JHVH. He goes on to deal with the 22 letters of the Hebrew alphabet and their various qualities and correspondences. In a further chapter he discusses the 72 attributes of God and the 72 angels of the Schemhamphorasch. The way in which he arrived at the number 72 is worth explaining as it differs from that adopted by later cabalists such as Eliphas Lévi. There are, no doubt, numerous ways of arriving at this number that are perfectly consistent with cabalistic orthodoxy. Lenain's method is to write the tetragrammaton thus:

י J
יה JH
יוה JHV
יהוה JHVH

These four lines give the following numerical values respectively: 10, 15, 21, 26, which add up to a total of 72. Lenain follows this up by giving the names of the 72 genies, each of which is given a corresponding nation of the earth and name of God. He also treats of the planets and their traditional correspondences, such as with jewels. Judging by Lenain's footnotes, he leans very heavily on Cornelius Agrippa; he also acknowledges the *Enchiridion* of Pope Leon, one of the better-known grimoires.

Another author who took advantage of the renascent interest in occultism was Eusèbe Salverte, author of *Des sciences occultes ou essai sur la magie, les prodigues et les miracles*, published at Paris in 1829. This was a two-volume historical analysis of magic, initiation and related subjects. It is a detailed and fairly scholarly work, written from an apparently non-partisan standpoint. Like the works of Fabre d'Olivet and Lenain it helped to feed the growing public demand for literature on things occult.

1. J.-B. Millet-St.-Pierre, *Recherches sur le dernier sorcier (Etteilla)*, (1859.)
2. Papus, *Les disciples de la science occulte, Fabre d'Olivet et Saint-Yves d'Alveydre* (1888).

5 Magnetisers and Mediums

Animal magnetism, which had languished somewhat in the turbulent years of the Revolution and the Napoleonic Wars, reawakened in 1815. In that year the Société de l'Harmonie was founded by the Marquis de Puységur to spread the gospel of Mesmer. Puységur was the eldest of three brothers, all of whom practised magnetism. He started magnetising at Buzancy, where he attracted such a large clientele that he resorted to the expedient of magnetising an old elm tree and linking his patients to it by a rope. Late-comers were obliged to stand on chairs and hold the lower branches. Evidently he could attend to about 300 people at a time by this method, which did not cause convulsions like those suffered by some of Mesmer's patients. One particularly good subject was a twenty-three-year-old peasant named Victor who, when magnetised, could read Puységur's thoughts. Thus the magnetiser was able to direct Victor's speech, stop him in mid-sentence and change his train of thought.[1]

One of Puységur's colleagues was the Abbé Faria, who was the son of a Hindu father and Portuguese mother and was known as 'the Brahmin'. Faria split with the other magnetisers because he did not believe that the subject's will played an important part in the process. In his sessions, the subject sat in a chair and Faria shouted 'Sleep!' in an imperative tone, after which the subject, having given a slight shake, would fall into a state called 'lucid sleep'. The magnetiser was then able to make powerful suggestions to the subject. For example, he could make water taste like milk or poor wine resemble champagne.[2] Faria enjoyed a considerable following in Paris for a time, but was ridiculed in the press and finally fell into disrepute.

Although its practitioners were often sneered at by orthodox doctors magnetism continued to be a subject of debate in the scientific world, and in February 1826 the Academy of Medicine decided to set up a permanent commission of nine members to draw up a report on the subject. The resulting report, which was read in June 1831, was favourable to magnetism, clairvoyance and precognition. The sceptics were furious at this and an uproar ensued in the Academy. Finally a curious compromise was reached: the paper was signed but not printed; it was then put away without discussion and not mentioned for ten years.

A second commission reported in August 1837, and a prize of 3000 francs was offered to anyone who could read without using his eyes. The fact that nobody was able to do this resulted in the Academy deciding to ignore in future anything to do with animal magnetism. 'The transposition of the senses', the Academy declared, 'does not exist in magnetism; thus there is nothing certain and scientific to look for in this kind of physiological experimentation.'

Magnetism has its enemies not only in the scientific community but also in the Church, and many polemics against it were published in books, pamphlets and articles written by clergymen. One such polemic was *L'Anti-magnétisme animal*, by P. H. Tissot, published in 1841. 'It is true to say', the author declared 'that the magnetisers are all, without exception, the dupes of malicious spirits.' In another passage he said: 'The company of magnetisers is composed of atheists, deists, sceptics, libertines, jugglers, and imbeciles; all the theories that they have invented or imagined to explain the phenomena of magnetism are contradictory and without foundation.' The journal *L'Apostolique*, of May 1829, is quoted with approval by Tissot as having said: 'What is animal magnetism? It is an operation by which one causes a person to be possessed by a demon.'

But opposition from scientists and clergymen did nothing to prevent the spread of magnetism. The only effect was to heighten the fanaticism of its adherents. By the 1840s it was in full swing, led by the Baron Dupotet, who had a salon near the Palais Royal.

Mesmerism is one of the cults discussed in Erdan's *La France mystique*, published in 1854. This is a highly biassed work setting out to debunk all mystical and occult groups, but the author did take the trouble to do some first-hand research in the field, and the accounts he gives are often revealing. His description of a visit to M. Dupotet makes interesting reading. Having presented himself at the salon, which overlooked the gardens of the Palais Royal, he was shown into a simply furnished room with chairs and benches forming an amphitheatre. Above a throne for the person officiating was a plaster bust of Mesmer crowned with laurel leaves.

After a short introductory lecture, M. Dupotet invited members of the audience to be magnetised. Finally three emerged as particularly suitable subjects: a young man whose hands became excessively cold under the influence of magnetism; a girl who had convulsions of the jaw; and finally 'a small woman dressed in black, of about 25, who displayed all the phenomena of second sight and of a complete subjection of the magnetised to the magnetiser'. The last of these three gave what appeared to Erdan to be a not very effective theatrical performance.

'In a second she was asleep. Pale and smiling, with eyes closed, she rose and came to the centre of the room, following the movements made by the priest with a magnestised wand... Questions were put to her and she replied with the insipid phrases one always hears in scenes of this kind. Next to her was placed the young girl with the convulsed jaw, at whose approach the magnetised woman pouted at first.

' "What is it, madame?" asked the magnetiser softly.

' "She has a bad heart. Her hand burns my shoulder."

'The magnetiser smiled:

' "Ah! She is burning your shoulder?"

'The subject, with a little-girl smile:

' "Yes, so there! It's all black."

(The smug gathering is much enlivened by this detail; their conviction deepens.)

'The magnetiser makes some passes over the young girl and then asks:

' "Now, has she still a horrid black heart?"

' "Oh no! Now its just like the heart of my little Blanche."

'And the face of the magnetiser shone.

'And the thought of Blanche brought tears to the eyes of all the mothers...'

Erdan concludes this account with some scathing remarks about the woman's incompetence as an actress.

Another cult dealt with by Erdan is spiritualism, an American import which began to be popular in France in the 1850s. The author of *La France mystique* describes a visit in the winter of

1853 to a sect of spiritualists calling themselves *frappeurs* to which he was invited by a Mme. d'Héricourt.

The lady led him to the Breda district where they traversed a 'melancholy and wintry garden' to reach as house with green shutters discreetly closed. They entered a well-furnished room with a table in the centre on which were placed cards bearing the letters of the alphabet, pencils and other utensils necessary for a séance. A curious and motley group of people were gathered in the room. They were presided over by a man of about sixty with a 'white and rapt countenance'. The medium was a healthy-looking young girl. Among the other members were an old hunchbacked woman who was there as an observer, and a young Russian who had travelled the world to visit spiritualists in many lands.

The proceedings began: 'We made a chain. We placed our hands all round the table and the mystery commenced. The young girl medium put herself into a magnetic sleep and announced, as never fails to happen, that she "had a pain in the head". The white-faced man blew and, again as always happens, the headache went away as if by enchantment. A second later the same gentleman began to shake violently on his chair as if possessed by a terrible god; he twisted his face and rolled his eyes in a strange way; then he said in a muffled voice: "Why do I tremble like this?" The young medium replied: "Because the door of the heavens has just opened and the spirits, the angels and the dead already appear in the distance." '

Having been given this assurance, the white-faced man judged that the time was right to begin evoking.

' "In the name of God," he cried "Mr. Washington, Mr. Swedenborg and Mr. Frederick Oberlin, manifest yourselves amongst us in a visible, palpable or sonorous way; I wish it! I wish it! I wish it!" '

The group waited, some of them trembling and shaking, then the white-faced gentleman addressed the medium and the following dialogue took place:

GENTLEMAN: Are the three spirits that I called present?
MEDIUM: Yes.
GENTLEMAN: Are they willing to talk to us?
MEDIUM: Yes. But they are not happy, for they knew that they were to be called this evening and they have been ready for seven hours and have been kept waiting. Mr. Swedenborg is particularly annoyed.

Apologies were made and the spirits placated. Then the group took up pencils and, under the impulses of the spirits, pointed to the letters of the alphabet in order to obtain replies to the questions that were asked. Erdan found most of the answers banal. One of the spirits evoked was St. Francis of Sales, who was asked by Erdan to describe paradise. 'Place, pretty, milk' was his enigmatic reply.

The proceedings began to take a more violent turn after the young Russian had called up three familiar spirits, one of whom attacked the old hunchbacked women. 'Oh God,' she exclaimed 'your spirit has struck me on the left shoulder and hurt me!'

Order was restored and the séance continued, Erdan finding it increasingly difficult to suppress his mirth. Finally he was obliged to make the excuse that his convulsions were due to nerves, adding that he had a cramp in his left leg.

'Can you tell us why Monsieur has a cramp?' asked the white-faced man.

The medium replied: 'It is because a spirit wanted to communicate with Monsieur, and since Monsieur was disobedient the spirit punished Monsieur by giving him a cramp.'

For Erdan this was the last straw. 'I burst out laughing and abandoned myself to the god of mirth. I was about to roll on the floor when luckily the séance came to an end. I took my respectable companion by the arm, I bowed to the group and, gritting my teeth and leaving them stupefied by my excess of hilarity, I fled to the garden as if some rapping devil were at my heels.'

The leading proponent of spiritualism in France was Allan Kardec, whose real name was Léon Hippolyte Rivail. He was born at Lyons in 1804 and studied for a time in Switzerland under the great educationist Pestalozzi. He later taught mathematics and natural science in Paris. But it was for his spiritualist writings that he was known to the world. His *Livre des Esprits* was published in 1857, and he was the founder of the first French spiritualist journal, the *Revue Spirite*.

A key part of Kardec's doctrine was the idea that spirits evolved through different grades as they acquired higher moral and intellectual qualities. There were three main grades of spirit: bad, good and pure. The bad and good were subdivided into different degrees; the pure consisted of a single class of being entirely free from material influence and displaying complete intellectual and moral superiority. The life they led was one of unadulterated happiness, but not of boredom for they were kept busy acting as messengers and ministers of God.

Even more interesting was Kardec's theory that the planets of the solar system were occupied by spirits. Mars, for example, was the domain of 'impure spirits', the lowest class of bad spirits, that is to say, those who were consciously dedicated to evil. The Earth was inhabited by bad spirits of all classes. Mercury and Saturn had a preponderance of good spirits resulting in a better social order and a happier existence. The same was true to an even greater degree of the Moon and Venus. Uranus and a planet that Kardec called 'Juno' enjoyed a still higher existence being inhabited mostly by good spirits with only a tiny proportion of bad ones of the highest class. Jupiter, however, was the most exalted planet of all and was peopled only by good spirits. These beings were not only physically but morally superior. One of the issues of the *Revue Spirite* of 1858 contains the following description of the Jupiterian:

'The conformation of the body is somewhat similar to bodies of this world, but less material, less dense and with a lower specific gravity. While we crawl painfully over the Earth, the inhabitant of Jupiter transports himself from one place to another by floating over the surface almost without fatigue, like a bird or fish.'

Kardec adds that, seductive though this picture of Jupiter is, there are other more perfect worlds unknown to us.

What a glorious and intoxicating vision! An infinity of worlds beyond the stars that might be attainable by those who could commune with the spirits. After Kardec the sky was literally the limit.

1. A. Touroude, *L'Hypnotisme* (1889).
2. Ibid.

6 The Holy King

Before looking any further at the growth of occult movements in France it would be helpful to examine the general condition of the country as it developed in the years after 1815. After the *débâcle* of that year the monarchy returned in the person of the obese Louis XVIII, brother of the luckless Louis XVI, an astute man of some personal charm, but a reactionary unaware of the real crisis that faced his country—a crisis of purpose, resulting from the events of the previous thirty-six years. The ideals of the Revolution had burnt themselves out; the brief imperial glory of the Napoleonic years had vanished with the exiled emperor. For the next half-century France was to be ruled by a series of inadequate monarchs. It was also to be haunted by ghosts. First there was the ghost of Napoleon; for, barely had he vanished to St. Helena before his legend began to grow, exercising a powerful hidden influence on the destiny of France. But there was also another legend that flourished during these years—the legend that the Dauphin, son of the decapitated Louis XVI, had not been killed during the revolution, but had survived and was now entitled to claim the throne as Louis XVII.

The movement that gathered around this legend had this in common with many of the other cults that flourished at this time: that it began as a political movement and ended as a quasi-mystical one. The same thing happened in the case of the movement based on the economic ideas of Saint-Simon, which became a religion with its own Pope.[1]

The 'Saviours of Louis XVII', as the royalist movement came to be called, was backed by a strange and powerful mythology. One of the beliefs held by its more fanatical proponents was that the Revolution and the execution of Louis XVI were a form of revenge taken by the Templars on the descendant of the King who had been responsible for the execution of the Templar Grand Master, Jacques de Molay, in the fourteenth century. According to this theory the freemasonic movement was a resurrection of the Templar order. These romantic ideas may have owed something to the Abbé Barruel.

Many candidates offered themselves as pretenders to the throne, but the most persuasive was Charles Edouard Naundorff, who styled himself the Duc de Normandie and bore a striking resemblance to his alleged father, Louis XVI. He arrived from Prussia in the early 1830s and lived in France until 1836 when he was banished by Louis Philippe. He sought refuge in England, where he lived for a time at Camberwell. He died in 1845 at Delft, in Holland, and was buried as Louis XVII. It is significant that Naundorff was also a religious visionary. He wrote a number of books allegedly under divine inspiration, one of which was entitled *The Heavenly Doctrine of the Lord Jesus Christ*. He left behind one son, Charles Guilluame, who continued the claim and lived until the end of the nineteenth century. For many years the Naundorffist cause was represented by a weekly newspaper.

The purpose of the more extreme elements in the royalist movement went beyond the mere perpetuation of the legitimate line. They saw France as the centre of a new world order based on the institution of monarchy and ordained by providence. There appeared a number of sects holding these beliefs, the two main ones being led by Ganneau and Eugène Vintras. Ganneau's sect was short-lived, but that of Vintras survived to undergo a strange metamorphosis. Vintras himself was one of the most extraordinary of the many bizarre figures of this era, and his career is worth examining in some detail.

His full name was Pierre Michel Eugène Vintras, and he was born in 1807 at Bayeux, in Normandy, to poor and devout parents. Though he acquired little education, he was endowed with great native intelligence and shrewdness which enabled him to rise from his poor background to the extent of becoming in 1839, foreman-manager of a small cardboard-box factory at Tilly-sur-Seule.

It was also in 1839 that he met the man who was to start him on the strange road that he subsequently followed. The man was Ferdinand Geoffroi, a rascally notary who was one of

Naundorff's most fervent supporters, Vintras, who already showed signs of a mystical turn of mind, was enthused by Geoffroi's elevated concept of the Naundorffist cause with its appealing philosophy promising the advent of a golden age when the true line was restored.

Vintras not only became an apostle of Naundorff, but soon began to receive supernatural intimations that he was to become leader of the cause. First the Archangel Michael appeared to him, then he had a vision of the Blessed Virgin Mary and St. Joseph in which he received the commandment to preach the new gospel, which was to be called the 'Work of Mercy'. He was to gather round him a group of disciples who would aid him in the task of saving the world from disaster and setting up a new kingdom of God.

Soon after his first vision he set up an oratory in the cardboard-box factory at Tilly, where he kept Hosts which he claimed had been sent to him by people who wished to save them from profanation by evil-minded persons. The danger of profanation was proved, Vintras claimed, by the fact that these Hosts exhibited signs of having miraculously bled real blood.

Such was the power of Vintras's personality, and the ability to persuade people of the truth of his visions, that he soon gathered about him a large following, among whom were certain members of the clergy, such as the Abbé Charvoz, Curé of Mont Louis. Charvoz was a skilful and energetic propagandist, who became the movement's theologian and whose efforts did a great deal to spread it. But Charvoz's zeal was also the cause of a great deal of embarrassment and trouble for Vintras. After the miracle of the blood-stained Hosts Vintras was anxious not to publicise the matter, but the Abbé Charvoz, lacking his master's well-founded caution, obtained sworn statements from a number of distinguished men to the effect that they had seen these blood-stained Hosts. Furthermore, a number of physicians certified that the stains were real human blood.[2] Armed with this propaganda, the Abbé Charvoz proceeded to spread the gospel, and had printed 6000 copies of a pamphlet on Vintras and his miracles.

Vintras's misgivings about publicising himself soon proved to be justified, for on 8th November 1841 the Bishop of Bayeux condemned the Charvoz pamphlet as contrary to the teachings of the Church. By this time, noises of concern were also coming from the government, whose members were alarmed that the Naundorffist cause had become associated with a mystical movement.

It was inevitable that Vintras would not be allowed to continue unmolested for long, and in August 1842 the blow fell; he and Geoffroi were arrested on a trumped-up charge of having defrauded two maiden ladies named Garnier of 3000 francs and Mlle Cecile de Cassini of 800 francs. In spite of the fact that all three alleged victims testified in favour of Vintras, the charge was carried. Vintras was sentenced to five years' imprisonment and Geoffroi to two years. An appeal was made, but the sentences were confirmed in spite of widespread public criticism of the verdict.

Vintras was a model prisoner and was allowed many privileges. He was able to receive visits and to maintain contact with his disciples. But meanwhile things were not going well for the gospel. On 8th November 1843 Pope Gregory XVI issued a brief condemning the sect. Vintras's reply shows the unshakeable confidence he had in his mission:

'If my mind is counted for anything in these condemned works, I should bow my head and fear would possess my soul. But the work is not my work, and I have had no concurrence therein, either by research or desire. Calm is within me; my couch knows no vigils; watches have not wearied my eyes; my sleep is pure as when God gave it. I can say to my God with a free heart: *Custodi animum meum, et erue me; non erubescam quoniam speravi in te.*'[3]

The Pope was not the only one to attack Vintras. A violent campaign against the movement was also waged by a disgruntled former supporter named Gozzoli, who had been expelled from the group. In a pamphlet called *Le Prophète Vintras* he accused his former master of having perpetrated gross sexual acts. Gozzoli's allegations were investigated by the police and the Bishop of Bayeux, and Vintras was found to be innocent of the charges. Nevertheless, the movement continued to antagonise the Church, and in 1848 it was declared heretical. Catholic priests were instructed to withold the sacraments from the Vintraists.

Vintras, who, up to this time, had remained loyal to Rome, retaliated by excommunicating the Pope and making himself pontiff at the head of his own ministry, which by this time included priests of both sexes. He believed himself to be carrying out a crusade against the forces of black magic.

In 1852 a new persecution opened against the sect, and Vintras was forced to flee, via Belgium, to London, where he established himself at number 33 Marylebone Road and continued to preach his gospel from that respectable, but somewhat prosaic, vantage point. His exile did not prevent him from carrying on the fight against black magic. The following is an account from Jules Bois' *Le Satanisme et la magie* of a black mass suposedly thwarted by Vintras who evidently travelled in spirit from his Marylebone lodging to the house in France where the ceremony was taking place:

'On 28th February 1855, in a little town near Paris, in the basement of a house backing on to a cemetary, a secret occult meeting was in full swing.

'Three persons were immersed in a cataleptic sleep: a girl of twenty years, an old priest and a virile man.

'Iron wires of different thicknesses were connected to their bodies which were under the control of certain spirits through fluidic action.

'These wires passed through the wall of the room and into a neighbouring chamber where three pedestal tables surrounded another table serving as an altar and raised on two steps. On this stood a cross without Christ and the statue of a nude goddess. At the foot of the cross was a piece of bread for the celebration of the Mysteries. To the right was a small cup in which blood lay coagulating; to the left a hissing snake emerged from a jar. The darkness was penetrated by an eerie light from two other vessels in which spluttering wicks were immersed in human fat.

'The three pedestals began to turn, slowly at first then with a giddy fury as they gathered momentum under the force of fourteen operators—politicians, Dominicans, ecclesiastics.

'A letter written by Vintras was intended to draw the fluidic essence of the prophet to the tables and from there to the subjects through whom he was to be evoked and dominated.

'There were two masters of ceremonies dressed in vestments of quilted silk, one of whom coated the iron wire with a poisonous oil.

'Then he cried out:

'"Omnipotent Intelligence who art about to inhabit our fluids, reveal thyself."

'The spirit appeared floating in an atmosphere imbued with

evil magic, a face of terror, swathed in bandages, with a body of mist.

'"I am Ammon-Ra," he declared, "the Ammon-Ra of Amenti; I conduct the souls of the dead in the pitiless barque.

'"I demand the sacrifice of the Great God of the Christians if you wish me to crush his last prophet.

'"All present here must consign to the brazier the cursed names of their baptisms—then I shall begin the combat."

'All came forward and wrote their names on pieces of papyrus which were then devoured by the flames.

'Then the spirit said:

'"You owe me in payment the virginal flesh of the sleeping young girl."

'"You shall have it," replied the master of ceremonies; "but make sure that we receive your active power as we abandon to you the immaculate nature of this child. Do not conceal from us any of your gifts as we make you a present of the supple virgin."

'"Possess her. We celebrate your pleasures by the immolation of the sacrifice. Raise up and excite the priest whom we have consecrated to you."

'The young girl entered, nude, still tied to the controlling wires. She sang, although still asleep. Her grace was such that a material voluptuousness emanated from her flesh.

'The master then once again coated with poisoned oil the iron wire enveloping the priest.

'The latter, at this command, and without interrupting his trance, came into the chamber and up to the pedestals. Around him, in an open circle, the assistants were grouped.

'His hairs were almost standing on end and terminated in little beads of sweat; the light of the human tallow gave to this moist bristle a strange phosphorescence. He let fall his clothes and mounted naked to the altar.

'A belligerent joy now intoxicated the operators, from now on certain of triumph.

'But the old man stared at some invisible and formidable point above his head . . . He remained inert and speechless.

'"Consecrate! Consecrate!" shouted the men.

'The priest seemed petrified, while the young girl writhed about like a white serpent; and coils of iron wire rang on the parquet.

' "What's the matter, you coward?" asked the chief, pointing to the priest.

'A cold sweat trickled from this priestly victim. "There is an invisible stranger here," he said.

'(It was Vintras, who had impeded everything from London)
' "Answer, is it He?"
' "I do not know, but I have searched his visual emanation which the fluids from that letter have conducted to me. I have caught the reflection of the intense fire that comes from him. One resists his Word of Authority in vain. His command—stronger than yours—has covered me with an imperative unction."
' "Now I am tied by his will."
' "Consecrate nevertheless."
' "You can see that my body is staggering, that my tongue is tied—I hear nothing but the magisterial unction of his word."
' "Consecrate, consecrate!"

'Again the iron wire glistened with the infamous oil. The young girl was at the point of death; the three tables began to turn dizzily again. Three of the onlookers rolled on the floor, struck by a lightning without a flash, and their heads, as though moved by furious hands, shook the walls with indefatigable blows. The priest bounded on to the table and, suddenly rejuvenated, overturned the cursed cross, the statue of luxury, the profane bread . . . All were trampled under his relentless feet.

'The second master of ceremonies said to the first:
' "Are you going to continue the struggle and will you be strong enough to enchain this hostile spirit that Vintras has launched at us?"
' "Let us try!" said the other.

'Three more people collapsed under the miraculous force, foaming at the mouth and biting themselves.
' "Let us stop," someone said.
' "No!"

'The chief operator, with a silent gesture, called the young man who was now the only one remaining in the neighbouring room. He too appeared clad in metal wires.

'Vintras's letter was made to touch the iron conductor; a circle was traced on the floor in human blood as a magnetic prison for the young man.

'In the room, those who had managed to remain standing

began to choke; the cataleptics cowered along the walls. The tables resounded with enormous blows from the inside.

'The young man remained upright.

' "Priest," he said, "come and place yourself at my feet; I am possessed by seven spirits who wish to be heard."

'Now he was in communication with the pedestal bearing the letter.

' "Struggle!" cried the assistants.

'Now his efforts became so strenuous that the blood issued from his eyes, forehead and ears. Like a damned soul who struggles against his torment, he brandished his fist.

' "Struggle!" said the master again.

'But the young man had suddenly become as quiet as a sacrificial lamb.

'Falling to his knees, his hands in prayer, extended towards the invisible will of the prophet Vintras, he cried out harmoniously:

' "You are surely he who precedes the coming of the Great Justice."

'Then, standing up again and facing the magical horde like a furious bull, he cried:

' "Cowardly assassins, ferocious beasts, impious monsters, you shall hear the truth despite your stupefaction. I am the new Balaam who prophesies for the one whom you have sent for to curse.

' "Your operations have failed, you violators of life, of the purity of the body, of the virtue of souls, of the honour of spirits.

' "Listen, princes and agents of the Roman Church and you, malevolent brutes, in league with them.

' "Hypocrites who from morning till night preach pity, prayer and faith, hiding under your honorific vestments the essential oils of prostitution and branded corpses—Shame on you and glory to your enemy the Great Prophet!"

'Silence extinguished the human candle, and the young woman whom Ammon-Ra had possessed was dead.'"[4]

If the performers of this distasteful ceremony survived the experience they must have trembled on hearing in 1863 that Vintras was returning to France. By that time the movement had secured a foothold in England and had spread to Italy and Spain. Vintras founded the centre of the White Carmel at Florence in 1867. His last two years were spent at Lyons, where he died on

The Holy King

7th December 1875. He was succeeded as head of the sect by an equally colourful and rather more sinister character, the Abbé Boullan, of whom we shall have more to say later.

Vintras was an almost exact contemporary of Eliphas Lévi. But, whereas Vintras left behind him only a comparatively small band of faithful adherents, Lévi left behind a body of writing that achieved an enormously wide influence. He appeared at a time when the borderland of occultism was very much a divided territory, with the followers of Mesmer, Vintras and Fabre d'Olivet occupying different corners. To each other their beliefs would doubtless have had little in common; yet all of the cults discussed so far had certain fundamental similarities. Lévi was able to perceive these similarities and to make out of the various elements that he brought together a highly effective mixture. His work was to give the word 'occultism' a new meaning, as we shall see.

---

1. The Saint-Simonist movement had a number of interesting offshoots. One of them was the quasi-socialist, quasi-mystical movement headed by Barthélémi-Prosper (alias Père) Enfantin (1796–1864). Auguste Comte, author of *Le Système de philosophie positive*, was also a Saint-Simonist for a time, but like Enfantin broke away to form his own movement.
2. An appendix to H. T. F. Rhodes's *The Satanic Mass* states that what the doctors saw could easily have been a species of red mould which, even under the microscope, could be mistaken for blood.
3. H. T. F. Rhodes, *The Satanic Mass*. 'Guard my soul and rescue me; I shall not feel ashamed for I have trusted in thee.'
4. Op. cit., pp. 233–40.

PART TWO

Eliphas Lévi

7   The Early Years

The man who was to become the nineteenth century's most prolific and skilful proponent of occultism was born in Paris on 8th February 1810 and christened Alphonse-Louis Constant. A baptismal register states that his parents were Jean-Joseph Constant, shoemaker, and Jeanne-Agnès Constant, *née* Beaucourt.[1] The birthplace was the Constant home at number 5 Rue des Fossés-Saint-Germain-des-Prés, now the Rue de l'Ancienne Comédie, a charming thoroughfare in the maze of narrow streets lying between the Boulevard Saint Germain and the Seine. The area has changed little since that time; the streets are still filled with the aroma from the food stalls where the Constant family must have shopped; and a little way down the street from where they lived stands the Café Procope, the oldest café in Paris, where Constant's predecessor, Court de Gébelin, doubtless discussed the occult arts with d'Alembert and Diderot in the days before the Revolution.

The boy grew up in a poor but happy family environment and seems to have cherished a deep affection for his parents. Later, in one of his poems, he glorified the satisfaction of living a virtuous and simple life such as they had led. In the poem he describes how his father had given two sous from his meagre earnings to feed a starving neighbour. 'He believed in God with all his heart', says Constant 'and taught me my prayers.'[2]

If his father set him an example of kindness and humility, his mother, with her intelligence and more fanatical piety, instilled in him self-discipline and a profoundly religious outlook. She divided her time between work and prayer and must have been a powerful personality.

In the introduction to his book *L'Assomption de la femme* (1841) Constant wrote as follows of his early years:

'My childhood was weak and dreamy; I never took part in the games of other children; I stood apart and meditated vaguely or tried to draw; I became easily enthused by a toy or picture which afterwards I broke or tore up; the need to love intensely was already tormenting me; I did not know how to explain my malaise.'

This solitary existence nourished a precocious intelligence, and Constant was fortunate in that from an early age he was placed in the hands of teachers who gave direction to that intelligence. At the age of about ten he was lucky enough to be admitted to one of the schools in Paris run by priests who gave free education to the children of the poor. These schools were known as *communautés*. The one which Constant entered was run by the Abbé J.-B. Hubault Malmaison in the presbytery of the church of Saint-Louis-en-l'Ile. He thrived at the school and became an outstanding pupil as well as showing the beginnings of a remarkable eloquence and a ready wit.

At the age of twelve Constant took his first communion, and the splendour of the Catholic religion took hold of him. 'Through the mysteries of Catholicism', he later wrote in *L'Assomption de la femme* 'I caught a glimpse of the infinite; my heart became impassioned towards a God who sacrificed himself for his children and transformed himself into bread to nourish them; the gentle figure of the immolated Lamb made me shed tears, and already the tender name of Mary made my heart palpitate.'

He confided his feelings to the Abbé Hubault, who saw in his pupil an ideal candidate for the priesthood. 'He easily persuaded a child of twelve to take up a supernatural vocation dedicated to continence and prayer . . .'

Consequently, in October 1825, Constant entered the seminary of Saint-Nicolas du Chardonnet. In doing so he put family life behind him for good. In his own words: 'I engaged on a fatal road which was to lead me to science and to unhappiness.'

A clue to Constant's later development can be found in the fact that the principal of this seminary, the Abbé Frère-Colonna, was one of France's leading authorities on animal magnetism and related subjects. For many years he carried out detailed research into these heresies—for so he considered them— and in due course published his findings in a book entitled *Examen du magnétisme animal* (1837), in which he concluded that feats of magnetism and divination were due to the intervention of the Devil. In his classes at the seminary he was fond of enlarging on his theories about these forbidden arts.

One of his most attentive pupils in these lectures was the fifteen-year-old Constant, whose thin, tight-lipped face and large pale eyes took on a look of excitement when the Abbé spoke of Mesmer and his strange skills. Had he known what was passing through the boy's mind the priest would certainly have been alarmed, for the young student was beginning to experience a curiosity about these mysterious subjects—a curiosity all the more compelling because they were being presented to him as heresies.

Constant never forgot the impression that the priest made on him, and later wrote the following passage about him:

'He was the most intelligent and sincerely pious priest I have ever known: thus it was he who was the best and the worst influence on me.

'The best, in that he broke for me the tight reins of my first Catholic education, to open before me the vast arena of progress and the future. He was inconsistent in that he taught a doctrine that was inspiring and full of movement and yet at the same time professed a blind obedience to men and ideas that belonged to the past. I did not at first see that he was in error, and leaning on his faith I walked for some time along a false route.

'The doctrine of the Abbé Frère can be summarised as follows: humanity, fallen from the bosom of God through original sin, returns towards him by a process which tears him away from matter and spiritualises him by degrees . . .

'Thus, for the Abbé Frère, the history of religion was divided into four great epochs: the epoch of penitence, or the age of the deluge and the curse of Cain; the era of faith, that of the calling of Abraham, father of believers; this era lasted, passing through the desert with Moses, until the coming of Christ, who, in dying on the cross bequeathed to his beloved apostle his Mother and hope; then, under the auspices of the Holy Spirit, the third person of God, not yet wholly revealed, there appeared a glimpse of a future century of happiness, in which Man, seated in the shade of the apple trees of the new Eden, would feel his forehead refreshed by a breath of love under the beating wings of the mysterious dove, final symbol of the Divinity.

'One can easily imagine how, under the guidance of such a master, I was able to dream of the Catholicism of ancient times and to feel myself as exalted as though I were living in those early ages. My disillusionment was all the more complete and my indignation all the greater when the disgracing of the Abbé Frère, driven out from his post by sordid intrigues, showed how little his doctrines were in line with ecclesiastical authority and made me realise above all that his austere virtues caused offence to the very people who should have encouraged and honoured them. I began to wonder if the priests really believed in God, and I shuddered—I whose religion was my only love—to see it fallen into such hands.'[3]

The episode described in this passage is of great importance, for the dilemma which it caused was to remain with Constant. His Catholicism was too deeply ingrained for him ever to abandon it; but he never lost his dislike of the authoritarian side of the Church, a dislike which the Abbé Frère's dismissal first aroused and which later experiences were to strengthen.

The Abbé Frère's ideas must have had a profound influence on the young Constant, particularly his theory about a coming golden age under the rule of the Holy Spirit. This doctrine of the Paraclete was one that became very popular in certain quarters, and Constant was to be one of its most articulate proponents.

It was at the seminary of Saint-Nicolas that Constant first began to grasp the elements of the Hebrew language, which was to stand him in such good stead as an occultist. At the age of eighteen he was already able to read the scriptures in the original.

Destined for the theological college of Saint-Sulpice, Constant was first required to take a two-year course in philosophy in a college at Issy, which he entered in 1830. It was here that he made his first sorties into literature with a biblical drama, *Nemrod*, and a poem entitled *La Petite œuvre des Savoyards à Bordeaux*.

When the time came for him to enter Saint-Sulpice, affairs at home were grim. His father had just died and his mother was in poor health. He wondered whether to abandon his priestly career, but was persuaded by the voice of his old master, the Abbé Hubault Malmaison, to continue.

He was not prepared for the disenchantment which awaited him at Saint-Sulpice. If the Abbé Frère Colonna's dismissal had shaken his faith in the Church, his experiences at the college were to give it an even sterner test. To glimpse what life was like at Saint-Sulpice—even allowing for the fact that Constant's views may have been coloured—it is only necessary to quote his own description in *L'Assomption de la femme*:

'The *sulpiciens* are cold and monotonous men for whom M. Olier's regulations and M. Carrière's theological text books take the place of spirit and heart. Custom is everything with them; progress is a word that is considered profane and ridiculous; art and poetry are regarded as puerile and dangerous things; there, one learns ignorance slowly and with difficulty. A little memory to retain ancient arguments of the school, a little subtlety to adapt them to the modern Gallic fashion, a little volubility to enunciate them and to twist their tails round reason—these are the qualities that pass for talent at Saint-Sulpice. Add to this a stiff bearing, an oily skin, greasy hair, a revolting soutane, dirty hands and furtive eyes, and you have the complete picture of what is called a good subject and a perfect seminarist . . .

'There exists between the pupils of Saint-Sulpice great mutual mistrust, extreme reserve and mortal coldness. The periods of recreation are the most exhausting ordeals of the day. Certain seminarists (always chosen from among the most fervent) are charged to report to the directors everything that they hear. The most innocent word, when interpreted and translated by them, can compromise the entire future of a young man. Thus, the more astute ones try to make these zealots, if not friends— for at the seminary friendship is unknown—at least partisans, by trying to outdo them in superstitious grimaces and puerile practices. There result from this a number of coteries or associations in which one must take part if one wishes to avoid appearing worldly or lacking in enthusiasm. One must share the sympathies and hates of the associates, one must cultivate this person and avoid that one. The directors themselves foment these dissensions among their pupils, giving to their penitents lists of people whom they must or must not associate with. By this means their domination is assured, for they exercise an absolute rule over these little opposing confraternities and easily suppress any protest on the part of those who remain isolated. These last are, in any case, rare. They are not able to withstand for long the ignominies which are constantly heaped upon them: they depart, or die, or become hypocrites in feigning to be besotted so as to be counted also among the band of elect.'

Repellent though it was to Constant, this environment did not dampen his religious ardour. 'I retreated to my cell, overwhelmed with discouragement and grief. Despite the advice of my priest I fell to praying with abundant tears which relieved me a little, then I had the thought that it was up to me to rekindle these hearts which charity had abandoned. I greatly pitied the religion that had been in the care of such children. It seemed to me that this religion was holding out its hand to me and saying: "My son, do you also wish to forsake me because you see that I am widowed and desolate?" Then, with the fervour and devotion of a young man, I cried: "No!" And I resolved to remain at the seminary and swallow all its unpleasant features.

'During the first months that I passed at the seminary I lived in my enthusiasm, possessed by an almost feverish exaltation; I addressed desperate prayers to God, such as the following, which I found among my papers of that time.

> *Devant toi, dans la nuit, mon âme se consume,*
> *Et mes désirs sont pleins d'une douce amertume.*
> *O toi que j'appelais, mais sans t'avoir nommé,*
> *Du jour que je languis de la soif d'être aimé . . .*
> *Les eaux de ton amour m'altèrent de leur source,*
> *Et l'ardeur de courir m'arrête dans ma course;*
> *Ma bouche se dessèche en voulant t'aspirer*
> *Et mon âme s'affame à toujours dévorer!*
> *Il me semble parfois que l'eternelle peine*
> *Me ronge d'un amour brûlant comme la haine:*
> *Je voudrais t'immoler à toi-même, et t'offrir*
> *A jamais les tourments que tu me fais souffrir!*
> *Etre heureux d'un enfer qui rugirait ta gloire,*
> *D'un désespoir immense exprimer ta victoire,*
> *Etre ton ennemi pour l'écraser en moi,*
> *Pour te céder mon trône, être dieu comme toi! . . .*
> *Je souffre enfin, je meurs étouffé dans mon âme*
> *Qu'appesantit la chair, que soulève ta flamme,*
> *Et qui veut à la fois grandir pour t'embrasser*
> *Et devant ta splendeur décroître et s'effacer!*
> *O néant amoureux que l'être aime et dévore! . . .*
> *O Dieu! n'étant pas toi, je souffre d'être encore . . .*
> *Donc, si je n'étais pas, pourrais-je encore aimer?*
> *Mais je veux être en toi, mais je veux m'abîmer,*

Me perdre dans ton sein, Mon Dieu! sans savoir même
Si je t'ai désiré, si je suis, si je t'aime.
Mais toi seul être heureux, seul triomphant, seul moi,
Puisque toi seul est bon, puisque tout bien c'est toi!

(Before thee, in the night, my soul burns and my desires are full of a sweet bitterness. Oh thou, whom I called, but without having named thee, from the day when I first languished from the thirst to be loved... The waters of thy love make me thirsty for their source, and the longing to run stops me in my course; my mouth becomes dry with the wish to breath thee in, and my soul becomes hungry with an eternal need to devour thee! It sometimes seems to me that the eternal pain torments me with a love burning like hate: I would like to sacrifice thee to thyself and offer thee for ever the torments that thou makest me suffer! I would be happy in a hell which proclaimed thy glory; I would be content with an immense despair if it expressed thy victory; I would like to be thine enemy so that I could crush that enmity in myself, to be a god like thee so that I could surrender to thee my throne! I suffer, stifled in my soul, which is weighed down by the flesh and raised up by thy light and which wishes to grow in order to embrace thee and at the same time to efface itself and bow down before thy splendour! Oh beneficent void which my being loves and devours! Oh God, not being thou, I suffer from continuing to exist. Yet, if I did not exist, would I still be able to love thee? But I wish to exist in thee, to be engulfed, to lose myself in thy bosom, oh God, without knowing if I have desired thee, if I exist, if I love thee. But thou art the only happy being, the only triumphant one, the only I; for only thou art good, for all goodness is thou!)

Constant's time at Saint-Sulpice cannot have been one of entirely unrelieved anguish, for, besides making his essays into poetry, he also took up singing, inspired by a group of pupils at the seminary who had formed a society to practise this art during the vacations. Evidently some of the priests attended these gatherings and encouraged the young singers.

Nor was the syllabus at Saint-Sulpice entirely barren of inspiration. Twice daily each seminarist had to make his 'examination of conscience' which was based on maxims and precepts contained in the *Golden Verses of Pythagoras*,[4] one of those non-Christian works which, like the *Meditations* of Marcus Aurelius, had been taken up by Christians for the universal morality and wisdom they contained. Whether or not Constant had at that time read Fabre d'Olivet's esoteric interpretation of the verses, they certainly must have made a deep impression on him. Each pupil had to make a translation from the verses for his own personal use and edification. Constant's extract was later quoted by him in Chapter 6 of his *History of Magic*, which is entitled 'Mathematical Magic of Pythagoras'. The quotation contained the following passage (rendered by Constant in rhyming couplets):

'I swear by him who has transmitted into our souls the Sacred Quaternion, the source of nature, whose cause is eternal. Never begin to set thy hand to any work until thou hast prayed to the gods to accomplish what thou art going to begin. When thou hast made this habit familiar to thee thou wilt know the constitution of the immortal gods and of men. Even how far the different beings extend, and what contains and binds them together . . .'[5]

This passage is pure magic, and it is rather surprising that the teachers at Saint-Sulpice did not regard such ideas as dangerous. Constant's choice of this particular part of the *Golden Verses* shows that he was already, perhaps unconsciously, being drawn towards a magical view of the universe—towards the idea of a network of hidden forces 'binding together' the elements of the visible world and capable of being controlled by the adept.

But if Constant had any dreams of becoming an adept they did not prevent him, when his time at Saint-Sulpice ended, from taking the next step in his priestly career, which was to enter the first of the three 'major orders'. These are the orders that demand irrevocable vows; they consist of sub-deacon, deacon and priest. After a few weeks' hesitation and a retreat of ten days he made his decision and was ordained sub-deacon, vowing before the Bishop total commitment to the Church and perpetual chastity. The ceremony over, he emerged from the church with a tonsure on his head and the prospect of an austere future before him.

His first task in his new capacity was giving catechism classes to the young girls of the district of Saint-Sulpice, most of whom were from rich and distinguished families. He launched himself into this work with enthusiasm. His attitude towards it is described in *L'Assomption de la femme*.

'This ministry, so sweet and so poetic, was real happiness to me. It seemed that I was an angel of God sent to these children

4 The Polish mathematician and occultist Hoene Wronski (1778–1853)

5 Saint-Yves d'Alveydre, author of many works on occultism (1842–1910)

to initiate them into wisdom and virtue. I talked freely to them, for my heart was full and needed to pour itself out. On their part these naive and tender young souls understood and loved me. In their midst I felt myself to be surrounded by my family, and I was not deceived, for I was listened to, venerated and loved like a father.'

But this happy state of affairs was interrupted by an unexpected and fateful event.

'God recomposed the sincerity of my zeal by sending me what devotees uncharitably call a *temptation*, and which I call an *initiation into life*.

'After I had been instructing these girls for two years I was one day called back to the sacristy and told that someone needed to speak to me. I beheld a poor woman, dressed in rags, with an honest expression, who presented to me a young girl with a pale and suffering face, and said; "Sir, I bring you my daughter so that you may prepare her for her first communion; other priests have rejected her because I am poor and because she is suffering, timid and awkward, but I have heard of you and I bring her to you beseeching you not only to admit her, but to protect her specially and to instruct her individually as if she were the daughter of a prince. I believe I know the kind of man I am talking to and I think that you understand me." '

Constant agreed instantly to the woman's request, promising to treat the girl 'as if she were my own'.

The girl was Adèle Allenbach. Her mother, a fervent Catholic, was the wife of a Swiss army officer, but had emigrated to France in about 1830, fearing that her daughter's religion was in danger. Since then the two had been living in Paris in the utmost poverty.

This delicate little creature, with her blue eyes and innocent expression, made an immediate impact on her teacher. Never before in his solitary existence had he experienced the sensations that she aroused in him, and they came as a disturbing revelation. At first he translated these sensations into religious language, seeing visions of the Virgin Mary with the face of Adèle. But slowly he came to realise the true nature of his feelings for the girl. Knowing what this meant for his vocation, he began a long inner struggle, but try as he might he could not banish Adèle from his thoughts.

In the midst of his torment came an announcement from his director that in a week's time he was to receive ordination into the third and final of the three major orders, the priesthood. He had already been ordained deacon on 19th December 1835, and the final ceremony was to take place in May 1836. But it was not to be. Constant's account in his book *Les Trois Harmonies* is as follows:

'My ideas were completely overturned; I realised for the first time how far I had already travelled outside Catholicism as it is understood today; the chaste love that at once troubled me and made me happy appeared an insurmountable obstacle to my sacrifice. I did not love Adèle as one loves a woman—Adèle was still almost a child—but through her I had felt awaken in me the imperious need to love; I understood that all the religion in my soul was based on this need, and I could not take my vows before the altar of a cold and egotistical cult without remorse.'

Thus Constant abandoned the priesthood at the moment when he was about to achieve the object for which he had struggled so painfully and for so long.

---

1. Paul Chacornac, *Eliphas Lévi, renovateur de l'occultisme en France* (1926).
2. 'Les Trois Harmonies', from *Chansons et poésies*, written under the name of A. Constant de Baucour (1845).
3. *L'Assomption de la femme*.
4. The authorship of the *Golden Verses* is uncertain; one suggestion is that they were written in about 388 B.C. by Lysis, an exponent of Pythagorean philosophy.
5. This is G. R. S. Mead's translation from the original. Lévi's version is rather loose; for example, he translates 'quaternion' as 'triade', probably with the Christian Trinity in mind.

8 *The Radical*

Constant emerged from Saint-Sulpice confronted by the daunting problems of adjusting to a secular life. His first thought was to avoid them by entering a monastery. 'I do not wish', he wrote to one of his friends 'to resume in the world a life of which the seminary has taken the best part, and to lead here the degrading and miserable existance of an apostate.'[1] But his friends dissuaded him, and this desperate course of action was abandoned. Constant would have to face the world as best he could.

It was not long before the world gave him his first test. His departure from the seminary had been a great shock to his widowed mother, by this time old and infirm, who had put all her hopes in her son. She appeared to have accepted the situation, but one morning a friend found her dead in her room. She had committed suicide, and it was evident that she had been planning the deed for some time.

Coming as it did so soon after the anguish of leaving the seminary, his mother's suicide affected him deeply. He wrote in *L'Assomption de la femme*: 'It seemed at that time as though all belief and all hope had abandoned me.'

But, miserable though he was, he had to face the considerable practical problem of how to earn a living. Twenty-six years old, he was still, in his habits of thought and appearance, a priest—down to the natural tonsure which precociously graced the back of his head. A drawing, (Fig 9.) made by a friend in the year he left the seminary, shows a young man with a prematurely severe expression. The cold, detached eyes and the tight lips betray little of the inner conflict that tormented him and conceal the fundamentally warm and generous character that lay behind them. There is a faint hint of the dandy in the neat moustache and beard and the slightly stiff, self-conscious way the head is carried. The receding hair accentuates a high and noble forehead. The solitary childhood years, the tribulations of the seminary, the constant forcing back on his own resources—all these show their result in an expression of ingrained resilience and toughness. The owner of such a face could never, we feel, take the escape route that Mme Constant had adopted.

The problem of earning a living was solved, for a year, by teaching in a boarding-school near Paris. But it was an unhappy year. At length, Constant says in *L'Assomption de la femme*, 'I left this school, whose masters hated me as much as the children loved me, and I found myself in the world for the first time, seeking to work and to create a future for myself.'

A friend from his very early schooldays came to the rescue. He was Aristide Bailleul, a touring actor, who offered Constant a place in the company for a tour of the provinces. The ex-seminarist accepted and evidently proved himself a skilful actor.

When the tour came to an end he returned to Paris and shortly afterwards met Flora Tristan, a woman who was to have a profound influence on him. Flora Tristan's life is summed up as follows by her grandson, Paul Gauguin, the painter, in his *Avant et Après* (1903):

'My grandmother was an astonishing woman. Proudhon said she had genius. Not having known her I believe what he says. She wrote a number of books, socialist in outlook, among them being *L'Union ouvrière*. The grateful workers had a monument erected to her memory in the cemetery at Bordeaux.

'She was probably no good at cooking. A blue stocking, a socialist and an anarchist, she was credited with having founded together with Père Enfantin the trade union movement and a certain religion, the religion of Mapa of which he was the God Pa and she was the Goddess Ma.[2]

'I cannot distinguish fact from fable and I give you all this for what it is worth. She died in 1844. There were thousands at her funeral. What is fact is that Flora Tristan was a very beautiful and noble woman. I also know that she spent all her money to further the workers' cause and travelled continually to this end.'

At the time that Constant met her Flora Tristan was thirty-four years old. Some years earlier she had left her husband, André Chazal, by whom she had three children, and had reverted to her maiden name. In September 1838 she was almost fatally wounded when her husband shot her in a desperate bid to gain custody of the children. Despite poverty and constant harassment from Chazal she was beginning to make her name as a journalist and was a frequenter of literary and artistic salons. It was at one of these that she met Constant.

Flora was a beautiful woman of magnetic personality, and Constant quickly found himself captivated by her, though it is unlikely that their relations ever became amorous. She, on her part, enjoyed Constant's company and found him a loyal and comforting friend during her periods of tribulation. It was through the influence of Flora Tristan that Constant adopted certain radical political ideas which were later to find their way into some of his writings.

Another important friend at this period was Alphonse Esquiros, who had been at school with Constant. He was a writer, who had first come to public notice with his novel *The Magician*, published in 1838. Knowing his friend's talent for drawing he invited Constant to illustrate and help to run a small monthly magazine that he had founded with some friends, entitled *Les Belles Femmes de Paris et de la province*. Constant's work for this publication and his later artistic efforts show that he had a remarkable and versatile talent for drawing. The frontispiece depicts a series of half-draped beauties, cupids, angels and elegantly dressed men, worked into a delicate pattern of flowing curves. There is a rarified sensuality about it that is hard to associate with the rather austere, priestly figure of the artist.

Among the subjects he drew for the magazine was Flora Tristan. He also drew a society woman, Mme de Girardin, at whose home he met Honoré de Balzac, who was then at the height of his fame. What they talked about is not known, but Constant later recorded his admiration for Balzac's mystical works.

It was in the company of Alphonse Esquiros that Constant had the following experience, described in *Histoire de la magie*:

'On a certain morning in 1839 the author of this book had a visit from Alphonse Esquiros, who said: "Let us pay our respects to the Mapah." The natural question then arose: "But who or what is the Mapah?" . . . "He is a god," was the answer . . . "Many thanks," said the author, "but I pay my devotions only to gods unseen." . . . "Come nevertheless; he is the most eloquent, most radiant and magnificent fool in the visible order of things." . . . "My friend, I am in terror of fools: their complaint is contagious." . . . "Granted, *dilectissime*, and yet I am calling on you." . . . "Admitted, and things being so we will pay our respects to the Mapah."

'In an appalling garret there was a bearded man of majestic demeanour, who invariably wore over his clothes the tattered cloak of a woman, and had in consequence rather the air of a destitute dervish. He was surrounded by several men, bearded and ecstatic like himself, and in addition to these there was a woman with motionless features, who seemed like an entranced somnambulist. The prophet's manner was abrupt and yet sympathetic; he had hallucinated eyes and an infectious quality of eloquence. He spoke with emphasis, warmed to his subject quickly, chafed and fumed till a white froth gathered at his lips . . .

'It will be seen that the Mapah was a successor of Catherine Theot and Dom Gerle; and yet—such is the strange sympathy between follies—he told us one day confidentially that he was Louis XVII returned to earth for a work of regeneration, while the woman who shared his life was Marie Antoinette of France. He explained further that his revolutionary theories were the last word of the violent pretensions of Cain, destined as such to ensure, by a fatal reaction, the victory of the just Abel. Now Esquiros and I visited the Mapah to enjoy his extravagances, but our imaginations were overcome by his eloquence. We were two college friends, like Louis Lambert and Balzac, and we had nourished dreams in common concerning impossible renunciations and unheard-of heroisms. After visiting Ganneau—for that was the name of the Mapah—we took it into our heads that it would be a great thing to communicate the last word of revolution to the world and to seal the abyss of anarchy, like Curtius by casting ourselves therein. Our students' extravagance gave birth to the *Gospel of the People* and the *Bible of Liberty*.'

Ganneau clearly made a powerful impact on Constant who always retained a soft spot in his memory for this quaint figure. In a letter printed in Erdan's *La France mystique*, Constant, then Eliphas Lévi, paid tribute to Ganneau's intelligence, eloquence and personal power. To what extent he was influenced by Ganneau's political views is open to doubt. It may have been that the 'impossible renunciations of unheard-of heroisms' were part of some kind of royalist mania such as Ganneau displayed; but for Constant to talk about 'sealing the abyss of anarchy' by jumping into it sounds suspiciously like a sophistical justification for the views expressed in *La Bible de la liberté*—views of which he later had good reason to repent.

For some time Constant had been discontent with the squalid lodgings in which he was obliged to live. Furthermore he was beginning to feel nostalgia for the cloister and to regret having abandoned his priestly career. Finally, in July 1839, he gave in to these feelings and entered a Benedictine abbey at Solesmes, fully intending to remain there for the rest of his life. He soon discovered, however, that the abbey was run by a man who appeared to have appointed himself abbot on very doubtful authority and was at daggers drawn with the local bishop. The inhabitants of the abbey were 'disaffected priests, incapable seminarists and bigoted peasants'.[3] Constant therefore remained at the abbey for only one year. During his stay there his first book, an anthology of hymns called *Le Rosier de mai*, was published.

Returning to Paris after his departure from the abbey, Constant became a teacher in a school run by the clergy, and it was during this period that his acquaintance with Ganneau bore fruit in the form of the social polemic which he called *La Bible de la liberté*. In spite of the efforts of the school and other members of the clergy to prevent the appearance of this inflammatory work, the book was published in 1841 by Auguste Le Gallois, the publisher of his friend Esquiros. The book was seized on the day of publication, and both author and publisher were brought to trial for producing a book that preached impiety and subversion. They were found guilty; Constant was sentenced to eight months' imprisonment and Le Gallois to three. In addition, both were fined 300 francs. The trial caused a storm of controvery in the left-wing press, as a result of which Constant found himself made famous almost overnight.

He served his sentence in the prison of Sainte-Pélagie, in Paris, where he was subjected to harsh and miserable conditions. Seeking consolation in reading, he came across the works of Swedenborg for the first time.

'This reading did not at first make the impression on me that it was to make later; I found it obscure, diffuse and strange, to say the least. It is only by a more profound knowledge of his system, and above all of his philosophical basis, that I have been able to appreciate his infinite wisdom.'[4]

There were other consolations. In the prison he met Esquiros who had also been put there for his political writings. Furthermore Constant's plight was somewhat relieved thanks to Flora Tristan who prevailed on her influential friend Mme Legrand to arrange for the prisoner to receive better food and other small privileges.

Coming out of Sainte-Pélagie in April 1842, Constant found himself the object of a kind of conspiracy of silence in the press which made it impossible for a time for him to earn his living by his pen. He was therefore forced to turn to his other gift, that of painting and drawing. The chaplain of Sainte-Pélagie, who had taken an interest in Constant, persuaded M. Lefèvre, curate of Choisy-le-Roi, to commission Constant to execute some paintings for the church. During the time that he was engaged in the work he lived in the Presbytery at Choisy, and it was here that he began to write *La Mère de Dieu*.

But probably the most important event that occurred during his stay at Choisy was his meeting with the sub-headmistress of a girls' school in the town. With this lady he established an intellectual friendship that was soon to become a closer liaison. Paul Chacornac, in his biography of Lévi, withholds her surname 'out of respect' and refers to her as Mlle Eugénie C . . .

Constant's conduct at Choisy was so exemplary and his piety so marked that the Church decided to revise its judgement on him. His cause was brought before the Archbishop of Paris, Mgr. Affre, who judged him favourably. It was not yet possible, however, to employ him in the diocese of Paris, as the scandal of his trial was still too fresh there. It was therefore decided to send him to Evreux.

At the request of Mgr. Afre, the Bishop of Evreux, Mgr. Olier, agreed to welcome Constant on condition that he changed his name to that of his mother to avoid the inflammatory memories that the name Constant aroused. Thus it was that Constant, calling himself the Abbé Baucourt, left for Evreux in February 1843. He took up residence in the seminary of that town and became an auxiliary priest with the right to give sermons.

His success at Evreux was considerable, and he soon found the local newspapers praising his sermons for their fluency and power. But it was not long before a fresh persecution began. Certain people hostile to the Bishop of Evreux, and no doubt jealous of the Abbé Baucourt's success, prevailed on the director of the *Echo de la Normandie* to publish, in the issue of 22nd July 1843, an article revealing that the Abbé Baucourt was in fact the Abbé Constant and supplying details of his past history including his trial.

There followed two letters of protest from Constant which were published in the newspaper. A few extracts from *La Bible de la liberté*, which were also published, only served to heighten the scandal which now once again surrounded the author. After a third and final letter from Constant, attempting to explain the ideas behind *La Bible*, the director decided to close the issue.

Constant, however, apparently thought that he needed to go further to clear his name, for shortly after his last letter to the *Echo* he wrote a letter to *Le Courrier de l'Eure*, the journal of the Bishop of Evreux, which constituted a sort of official retraction of *La Bible*, and appeared on 10th August 1843. Part of it read as follows:

'Now, it is to the men of peace and of religion that I must speak to make myself completely clear: or rather, it is to the holy Church, my mother, who has already received me in her mercy, and who, in the name of a beneficent God, has pardoned my faults. Prostrate before her altars, my heart broken with grief, I would like to erase with my tears all traces of this senseless book, in which in the name of the law of peace and gentleness, I was able to preach disorder and violence. I retract, brand, and condemn, with all the energy of my soul and heart, these deplorable dreams which, if they had not been follies, would have deserved to be called crimes ...'

Despite this retraction, now that the cat was out of the bag Constant was obliged to leave the seminary. The Bishop of Evreux, who had clearly taken a liking to him, found him a room in the town and provided him with the means of subsistence. He also offered him the priesthood and a post as curate in his diocese. But once again Constant refused. The priesthood was a heavy burden which he did not yet feel able to shoulder.

In 1844 Constant's book *La Mère de Dieu*, a devotional work, appeared under the imprint of his old publisher and friend Le Gallois. The appearance of this book offended the Bishop of Evreux, who evidently regarded it was doctrinally unacceptable and forbade his bookshop in the town to sell it.

Nevertheless Constant, never one to harbour a grudge if

he could help it, did not forget the Bishop's kindness to him and later wrote: 'I prefer him by far to all the other ecclesiastics I have known; in him I at least found spirit, cordiality and good sense.'[5]

After returning to Paris, Constant resumed his friendship with Flora Tristan, who was more active than ever in the cause of socialism. She had resolved to make a tour of France, preaching her doctrine of a workers' alliance, and before she left she gave Constant a mass of notes which she had made and asked him to put them in order and send them back to her with his comments. By the time he had done this Flora had reached Lyons, and he wrote to her there asking for further instructions. He never received a reply, and soon afterwards learned that Flora Tristan had died.

In due course Constant edited and annotated the manuscript that Flora had given him, and it was published in 1846 under the title of *L'Emancipation de la femme, ou testament de la paria*. Shortly afterwards, in the autumn of 1844, Constant was invited by his old benefactrice, Mme Legrand, to come and live in her house at Guitrancourt, Seine-et-Oise, in order to act as tutor to her two children, Clarisse and Adolphe. He accepted with joy, and a month after entering the household he took the important step of finally renouncing his holy orders, thus breaking the undertakings he had made to the Church and to which he had hitherto remained scrupulously faithful.

'I did not break them', he wrote 'until she had broken hers towards me, or rather I broke them because the ecclesiastical authorities have released me from my vows by refusing to judge me or even to give me a hearing, by trying to corrupt me with money and by abandoning me when I had no other resource than my work because I had categorically refused to sell my convictions to her.'[6]

Constant stayed with Mme Legrand for about a year, then returned to Paris for the publication of a pacifist manifesto he had written entitled *La Fête-Dieu, ou le triomphe de la paix religieuse*. This work was published anonymously in 1845. It was followed in the same year by two other works: *Le Livre des larmes*, an essay pleading for conciliation between the Catholic Church and modern philosophy; and *Les Trois harmonies*, a collection of songs written by Constant. The publishers of the latter work also commissioned him to execute some illustrations for two books by Alexandre Dumas, *Louis XIV et son siècle* and *Le Comte de Monte-Cristo*.

The money that these ventures sporadically brought him was immediately spent by Constant in giving gay champagne parties, for which he had a strong predilection. We can imagine the sort of people who came to these affairs. There would be his old friends Le Gallois and Esquiros as well as a selection of journalists and socialist pamphleteers. Another person who might possibly have been seen among the guests was Adèle Allenbach, the girl who had first awakened Constant's heart to love. She came to see him often and continued, throughout his life, to regard him as a father figure. She later achieved some success as an actress, and in the fullness of time became happily married. Another visitor would be Charles Fauvety, an eccentric visionary who dreamed of founding a universal religion. In October 1845 he and Constant started a monthly politico-cultural review, *La Vérité sur toutes choses*, which lasted for only four issues. In the middle of this motley gathering we can imagine the ex-Abbé himself delivering a political harangue or singing one of his own songs. But the result of his periodic extravagance was that, more often than not, he was obliged to live the life of a pauper.

From time to time Constant would go back to Evreux to visit his friend Eugénie, assistant headmistress at the girls' school. This woman had come to worship Constant, and one day, in the winter of 1845-6, they became lovers.[7] But by that time another passion had taken a fatal hold on Constant in the form of a seventeen-year-old pupil of Eugéne's named Noémi Cadiot. The unsuspecting Eugénie had taken Noémi with her on her Sunday-afternoon walks with Constant, and the impressionable young girl soon found herself under his spell. There followed a correspondence between her and Constant, which continued after she left the school. Then, in 1846, she went to live with Constant in his rooms on the Quai de l'Ecole, now the Quai du Louvre. She was then eighteen years old.

Her father reacted to this situation by demanding that they marry, and threatened that otherwise he would have Constant arrested for seducing a minor. Constant, fearing dishonour and doubtless being in love with the girl, decided to agree, and a civil wedding took place on 13th July 1846.[8]

A sad sequel occurred three months later when, as a result of his liaison with Eugénie, a son was born to her on 29th September. It may have been that after Constant's deception Eugénie had no desire to see him again; the fact was that Constant's son never saw him until after his father's death (see Appendix A).

Constant's marriage began under difficult circumstances. Noémi's parents refused to give her a dowry, and so poor were the couple on the day of their wedding that all they had to eat were a few potatoes bought at the Pont Neuf which they took home and fried. But poverty did not stem the flow of writings which came from Constant's pen. Soon after his marriage appeared a religious work, *La Dernière Incarnation*, which was followed by a political tract, *La Deuil de la Pologne*. Evidently the punishment he had suffered as a result of writing *La Bible de la liberté* had not taught him any caution, for in the same year as his marriage he published *La Voix de la famine*, a violent polemic on social inequality which once again brought him before the courts.

In February 1847 he was tried for having sought to disturb public peace by provoking scorn and hatred, first between the classes, and second against the government of King Louis-Philippe. Despite an eloquent defence on his own behalf, he was sentenced to a year in prison and a fine of 1000 francs.

Thus Constant found himself back in Sainte-Pélagie, this time with a special burden on his mind, for he had learned that his wife was pregnant. Noémi, however, showed herself to be a woman of courage and determination. She pleaded with the authorities and succeeded in having her husband's sentence reduced to six months. As a result, he was free when their daughter Marie was born in September 1847.

The following year, 1848, was one of the most troubled years of the century for France. Following the flight of Louis-Philippe and the proclamation of a republic, riots broke out in Paris during which it is estimated that 10,000 people were killed. According to Constant, the influence of Ganneau had a hand in this eruption of violence. His theory of how the trouble started is given in his *Histoire de la magie*:

'A nervous and delicate young man named Sobrier was numbered among the Mapah's disciples; he lost his head completely and believed himself predestined to save the world by provoking the supreme crisis of a universal revolution. The days of 1848 drew towards the threshold. A commotion had led to some change in the ministry, but the episode seemed closed. Paris had an air of contentment, and the boulevards were illuminated. Suddenly a young man appeared in the populous streets of the Quartier Saint-Martin. He was preceded by two street Arabs, one bearing a torch and the other beating to arms. A large crowd gathered; the young man got up on a post and harangued the people. His words were incoherent and incendiary, but the gist was to proceed to the Boulevard des Capucines and acquaint the ministry with the will of the people. The demoniac repeated the same harangue at every corner of the streets and presently he was marching at the head of a great concourse, a pistol in each hand, still heralded by torch and tambour. The frequenters of the boulevards joined out of mere curiosity, and subsequently it was a crowd no longer but the massed populace surging through the Boulevard des Italiens. In the midst of this the young man and his street Arabs disappeared, but before the Hôtel des Capucines a pistol-shot was fired upon the people. This shot started the revolution, and it was fired by a fool.

'Throughout that night two carts loaded with corpses perambulated the streets by torchlight; on the morrow all Paris was barricaded, and Sobrier was reported at home in a state of unconsciousness. It was he who, without knowing what he did, had for a moment shaken the world.'

Constant plunged into the fray with his usual gusto, composing revolutionary songs and writing articles in the left-wing press campaigning for workers' representation in the National Assembly. Mme Constant also took an interest in these affairs. She contributed an article to a short-lived journal, *Le Tribun du peuple*, and was secretary to a socialist society formed by Constant, Esquiros and Le Gallois, entitled *Le Club de la montagne*. She was also a member of a feminist organisation, *Le Club des femmes*, run by Mme Niboyet, a former Saint-Simonist.

It may have come as something of a surprise to Constant's little coterie when one of its members, Esquiros, was actually elected to the National Assembly in May 1849. In his new position Esquiros probably found that it was necessary to compromise with his former ideals; and this may have been the cause of the break in his friendship with Constant, for after the election of Esquiros the two ceased to be intimate.

In 1848 appeared Constant's last socialist treatise, *Le Testament de la liberté* which was a résumé of all his previous writings on socialism. A few quotations from this work will show how closely his political ideas were tied to his religious ones.

'Now the fourth stage of the revolution is in preparation: namely, that of love. After forms come passions; after passions, thought; after thought, love. And it is thus that the reign of the Holy Spirit, proclaimed by Christ, will be realised on earth. Already the workers of God have been to clear the ground for new constructions. The great heretics have burned the dead woods; the revolutionaries, axe in hand, have cut down and uprooted the old stumps; everywhere the socialists are sowing the new word, the word of universal association and communal property.'

This passage shows that he had not forgotten the teachings of his old schoolmaster the Abbé Frère Colonna. For Constant the new socialist Elysium had become synonymous with the reign of the Paraclete.

In another chapter he gives a hint of the way in which his religious ideas were later to develop:

'We wish to regenerate and universalise the religious sentiment by the synthesis and rational explanation of symbols, so as to constitute the true Catholic Church or the universal association of all men.'

Constant's private life at this time was as happy and tranquil as the affairs of the nation were troubled and violent. His daughter was a constant delight to him, and the bonds of his marriage seemed close and secure. His wife, whom he adored, had begun to make a name for herself in the literary world, writing articles under the name of Claude Vignon. She also began to take lessons from a distinguished sculptor named Pradier, and it was through this connection that her husband was commissioned to paint two religious pictures for the Ministry of the Interior. He also received, in 1850, a commission from ecclesiastical publisher to write a *Dictionary of Christian Literature*, which appeared the following year.

Callers at the Constant home would invariably find their host dressed in the garb of a monk, which he adopted whenever possible—a predilection that was to remain with him throughout

The Radical

his life. Indeed with his full beard and towering bald cranium, he looked more than anything like the benevolent abbot that he might have become. These were happy times for Constant, but they were not to last. Certain events were soon to alter the course of his life once more.

1. Paul Chacornac, *Eliphas Lévi*.
2. This story is incorrect. The 'Mapah' was in fact a man named Ganneau. See pages 62 and 85—86,
3. *L'Assomption de la femme*.
4. *Le Livre des larmes*.
5. *La Verité*, December 1845.
6. *Le Tribun du peuple*, No. 3.
7. Paul Chacornac, *Eliphas Lévi*.
8. *Ibid*.

9   *Enter Eliphas Lévi*

From an early age Constant had been attracted towards mysticism amd occultism. His knowledge of Hebrew had enabled him to delve into the Cabala, and he was familiar with Knorr von Rosenroth's *Kabbala Denudata*. He was attracted by Gnosticism and Christian mysticism and had read works by Boehme, Swedenborg, Saint-Martin and Fabre d'Olivet. But his study of these subjects had been unsystematic, and so far only glimpses of an interest in occultism could be found in his own writings. An initiator was needed to awaken the dormant occultist in Constant, and in 1853 such an initiator appeared in the person of a Polish *émigré* named Hoene Wronski.

The life of Wronski would occupy a volume in itself, but the main facts of it are these. The name Hoene was in fact his original surname, and he only adopted the name Wronski after his marriage. He was born of a prominent Polish family on 24th August 1778 and was educated from an early age for a military career. At the age of sixteen he became an artillery officer in the Polish Army and shortly afterwards was taken prisoner by the Prussians at the battle of Maciejowice. He was freed in 1795 when the Russians entered Warsaw and he accepted the rank of major in the Czar's army, later to be promoted to lieutenant-colonel. He continued, however, to dream of the liberation of Poland and, after serving for only a short period with the Russians, handed in his commission and departed for France with the intention of joining the Polish liberation army. He stopped off in Germany to study law, but then changed his mind and spent a year studying philosophy. In 1800 he resumed his original intention and, on reaching Paris, offered his services to General Kosciuszko, the Polish *émigré* leader. Then, having become a French citizen, he left for Marseilles to join the Polish legion.

PIERRE VINTRAS (ÉLIE-STRATANAEL)
Fondateur de l'Œuvre de la Miséricorde (dans les habits de son sacrifice)

6 Pierre Michel (Eugène) Vintras (1807–1875), visionary and founder of his own cult

L'ABBÉ BOULLAN (DOCTEUR JOHANNÈS)
Exorciste, mort en 1893.)

7 Joseph-Antoine Boullan (1824–1893), self-appointed successor to Vintras and friend of J.-K. Huysmans

Enter Eliphas Lévi

In Marseilles, however, a more tempting opportunity arose. Hoene had become acquainted in Paris with the astronomer Lalande and had suggested some rectifications to Lalande's treatise on the subject. On Lalande's instructions Hoene was given the use of an observatory at Marseilles, and he remained there from 1803 to 1810 conducting astronomical researches and developing an extraordinarily complex mathematical theory of the universe. During this period he was in contact with all the leading astronomers, geometers and physicists of the time. But this happy period came to an end when he published the first fruits of his researches; these evidently offended the orthodoxy of the Institute of Marseilles which disowned him and forced him to leave the observatory.

Back in Paris he was plunged into poverty which throughout his life became steadily worse. His wife, who was the adopted daughter of a wealthy newspaper proprietor, the Marquis de Montferrier, fell ill, and their young daughter died in 1811. By this time he had adopted the name of Wronski.

For a while he scraped a living by teaching in a small boarding-school in Montmartre. Then, in 1812, he was employed to teach mathematics to a rich young banker from Nice, named Arson. After several months Arson refused to pay him the agreed sum. Wronski took the case to court and lost. Nevertheless, he had already extracted enough money from Arson to pay for the publication of some of his mathematical work.

After this episode Wronski spent thirty-seven years of unrelieved poverty. In such circumstances it was amazing that he was able to sustain his intellectual life, but during those years he poured forth a stream of philosophical and mathematical writings. He died in 1853 and was buried in the cemetery at Neuilly where his friend, the Comte de Durette, erected a modest memorial to him. He left behind seventy manuscripts, of which a catalogue was drawn up by his widow with the help of Montferrier, Constant and others.

Constant met Wronski in 1852 and conceived a tremendous admiration for him. After Wronski's death Constant wrote: 'A man whose mathematical discoveries would have intimidated the genius of Newton has placed, in this century of universal and absolute doubt, the hitherto unshakeable basis of a science at once human and divine. First and foremost, he has dared to define the essence of God and to find, in this definition itself, the law of absolute movement and universal creation.'[1]

The effect of Wronski's influence was to reconcile a number of opposing elements in Constant's thinking. Hitherto the staunch Christian in him had conflicted with the socialist, the rationalist with the mystic. Wronski's writings were to show him the possibility of a glorious synthesis of rationalism, religion and a belief in human progress. Hence Wronski's influence on Constant is of the utmost importance.

Wronski's most significant work was *Messianisme, ou réforme absolue du savoir humain*, which appeared in 1847. The publisher's imprint was given as the *'bureau de messianisme'*, which indicates that Wronski probably published the book at his own expense. If so, it is something of a mystery how he managed it, as the book was issued in three enormous and beautifully printed folio volumes. It is dedicated to France 'as a mark of gratitude for the long hospitality that the author has received in this noble country'.

He defines *'messianisme'* as the union of philosophy and religion, and declares that it will produce the following seven results in mankind:

1. The foundation of truth on earth and the realisation of absolute philosophy.

2. Following the Holy Scriptures, revealed religion will be accomplished and absolute religion—namely paracletism—will be realised.

3. Following *a priori* principles, the sciences will be reformed and definitively established.

4. History will be explained, in conformity with the august laws of liberty.

5. In order to stop the present political torment of nations the supreme purpose of states will be revealed.

6. The absolute purpose of man will be fixed by means of reason.

7. In view of this august purpose the destinies of nations will be revealed.

This quasi-scientific, quasi-religious utopianism appealed strongly to Constant.

Another work of Wronski's which throws some light on his thought is a *Secret letter to His Highness Prince Louis-Napoleon, President of the French Republic on the destinies of France and of the civilised world in general*, published at Metz in 1851. In this letter he sets out the Platonic idea that if only certain supreme laws were recognised and acted upon nations would realise their true aims and all problems and strife would disappear. Wronski evidently believed that these laws could be expressed mathematically. To seek for this supreme law without knowing what one was doing was to fall into the chaos of revolution. 'Napoleon' says Wronski, 'attempted to realise this aim, in so far as that was possible with his new political authority, that potent authority which, under the false name of despotism, remains generally misunderstood.' The rediscovery of this supreme aim belonged 'as a providential mission to Prince Louis-Napoleon'.

Having outlined the mission of Louis-Napoleon, Wronski goes on to say that there is an obstacle, an unknown cause of revolutionary disorder, and the purpose of this 'secret' letter is to reveal it. The cause arises, he says, from the mis-comprehension of 'our holy religion', and it is necessary to go back to the scriptures to rediscover the true nature of religion. He talks of a 'superior science that Christ has promised us by the advent of the Paraclete, that Spirit of Truth who, according to this sacred and infallible promise, will reveal to us all truths.'

One of Wronski's main preoccupations was the construction of strange machines for perpetual motion. 'Unfortunately', wrote Constant in a letter, 'these wretched machines would never work; because the copper and steel, not understanding any algebra, failed to conform to the evidence of his original designs.' Another of his inventions was a prediction machine which he called a 'prognometre'. This machine passed through a number of hands after Wronski's death, and was eventually acquired by Constant from a second-hand dealer. He described it in his correspondence as follows:

'The form is that of the letter Shin ש. The double branch which stems from the base of the machine ends in two copper balls surmounted by two triangular pyramids; one represents divine knowledge, the other human knowledge, coming from the same base and functioning together, but always opposed to one another in order that harmony may result from the interplay of contraries.

'Man can explore the entire sphere of the sciences; but never will he meet God, who always seems to retreat before his researches and who is always hidden by the globe, that is to say by the thickness of material things.

'The globe symbolising divine knowledge can be dismantled, and on it is written:

ALL THAT SHOULD BE HAS BEEN, IS AND WILL BE

'Around this globe are fixed four cut-out letters A.B.X.Z. ... From the globe emerge two articulated branches to which are fixed two small compasses showing the proportion of that which is above to that which is below, and of the turning globe to the immobile Zodiac.

'The globe of human knowledge carries a pyramid on the apex of which the sign of Solomon is visible from all sides; the arrow pointing towards the main globe terminates in the pentagram, the sign of initiative and of human autonomy.

'The main globe, which is composed of two spheres, one inside the other, has two alternative movements of rotation, one around its vertical axis, the other around its horizontal. To change from one axis to the other it is only necessary to alter a screw.

'This philosophical machine is an entire encyclopaedia, and the inner globe is covered with long equations which the best mathematicians of the Academy of Sciences would no doubt have difficulty in deciphering.

'On the wheel, which bears the signs of the zodiac, doors are constructed which open and close. On these doors are written the fundamental axioms of each science. There are thirty-two doors, and on each door is the name of three sciences.'

Under Wronski's influence all Constant's latent occult inclinations came to the surface and he began to write his first magical treatise, the *Dogme de la magie*. While he was engaged in this task a sad event took place in his personal life. Mme Constant had for some time been associating with the Marquis de Montferrier, for whose paper, the *Revue progressive*, she had been writing under the name of Claude Vignon. Her husband, engrossed in his work, had not noticed the way that the liaison was developing and was shattered when one day in 1853 Noémi disappeared never to return.

To escape the pain of this betrayal he immersed himself in his writing, and in due course the *Dogme* appeared. It bore the name that he was to use for the rest of his life: Eliphas Lévi,

Enter Eliphas Lévi

the Hebrew equivalent of his two Christian names. He also sometimes added the third name of Zahed. The Abbé Constant was no more, and it is by his new name that we shall henceforth call him.

In the spring of the year after his wife's desertion Eliphas Lévi was still suffering from the anguish it had caused him. He decided on a change of scene and set out for London where he put up in a hotel at number 57 Gower Street.

It seems that on arrival in England Lévi had immediate access to some of the most important English occultists. This could hardly be explained by his embryonic reputation in the field. But he carried with him letters of introduction, and this suggests that an international network of occultists was well established by this time.

He was on the whole disappointed with his English colleagues, whose attitudes he found superficial and frivolous. There were, however, two exceptions. One was Dr. Ashburner, a distinguished physician and scholar; the other was Sir Edward Bulwer-Lytton, later Lord Lytton, one of Britain's most popular novelists and also a successful politician. Lytton's knowledge of occultism was apparent from certain of his writings, particularly the novel *Zanoni*, in which a number of magical themes are woven together. The title is the name of an adept around whom the story centres. From the heights of magical achievement he falls into the snare of earthly love and finally perishes having sacrificed himself for his beloved. There is an interesting account of how Zanoni's spiritual master Mejnour attempts to initiate a young aspirant who overreaches himself and drinks the magic elixir before he is ready, thus laying himself bare to the perils lying on the threshold of the other world. Lytton recognised in Lévi a fellow adept, and the two became friends.

The most important event, however, in Lévi's visit to London was his famous evocation of Apollonius of Tyana. This is described in full in his *Dogme de la magie*, and is worth quoting extensively:

'... returning one day to my hotel, I found a note awaiting me. This note contained half a card, divided transversely, on which I immediately recognised the seal of Solomon. It was accompanied by a small sheet of paper on which these words were pencilled: "Tomorrow, at three o'clock, in front of Westminster Abbey, the second half of this card will be given you." I kept this curious assignation. At the appointed spot I found a carriage drawn up, and as I held unaffectedly the piece of card in my hand, a footman approached, making a sign as he did so, and then opened the door of the equipage. It contained a lady in black, wearing a thick veil; she motioned to me to take a seat beside her, showing me at the same time the other half of the card. The door closed, the carriage drove off, and, the lady raising her veil, I saw that my appointment was with an elderly person, with grey eyebrows and black eyes of unusual brilliance, and strangely fixed in expression. "Sir," she began, with a strongly marked English accent, "I am aware that the law of secrecy is rigorous among adepts; a friend of Sir B— L—,[2] who has seen you, knows that you have been asked for phenomena, and that you have refused to gratify such curiosity. You are possibly without materials; I should like to show you a complete magical cabinet, but I must exact beforehand the most inviolable silence. If you will not give me this pledge, I shall give orders for you to be driven to your home." I made the required promise, and faithfully keep it by divulging neither the name, position, nor abode of this lady, whom I soon recognised as an initiate, not exactly of the first order, but still of a most exalted grade. We had a number of long conversations, in the course of which she invariably insisted upon the necessity of practical experience to complete initiation. She showed me a collection of magical vestments and instruments and lent me some rare books, which I needed; in short, she determined me to attempt, at her house, the experiment of a complete evocation, for which I prepared during a period of twenty-one days, scrupulously observing the rules laid down in the thirteenth chapter of the *Ritual*.

'The probation terminated on 24th July; it was proposed to evoke the phantom of the divine Apollonius, and to question it upon two secrets, one which concerned myself and one which interested the lady. She had counted on taking part in the evocation with a trustworthy person, but this person proved nervous at the last moment, and, as the triad or unity is indispensable for magical rites, I was left to my own resources. The cabinet prepared for evocation was situated in a turret; it contained four concave mirrors and a species of altar having a white marble top, encircled by a chain of magnetised iron. The sign of the pentagram, as given in the fifth chapter of this work, was carved and gilded on the white marble surface; it was drawn

Enter Eliphas Lévi

also in various colours upon a new white lambskin stretched beneath the altar. In the middle of the marble table there was a small copper chafing-dish containing charcoal of alder and laurel wood; another chafing-dish was set before me on a tripod. I was clothed in a white garment, very similar to the vestments of our Catholic priests, but longer and wider, and I wore upon my head a crown of vervain leaves, intertwined with a golden chain. I held a new sword in one hand, and in the other the *Ritual*. I kindled two fires with the required and prepared substances, and I began reading the evocations of the *Ritual* in a voice at first low, but rising by degrees. The smoke spread, the flame caused the objects on which it fell to waver, then it went out, the smoke still floating white and slow about the marble altar; I seemed to feel a kind of quaking of the earth, my ears and my heart beat quickly. I heaped more twigs and perfumes on the chafing-dishes, and as the flame again burst up I beheld distinctly, before the altar, the figure of a man of more than normal size, which dissolved and vanished away. I recommenced the evocations and placed myself within a circle which I had drawn previously between the tripod and the altar. Thereupon the mirror which was behind the altar seemed to brighten in its depth, a wan form was outlined therein, which increased and seemed to approach by degrees. Three times and with closed eyes I invoked Apollonius. When I again looked forth there was a man in front of me, wrapped from head to foot in a species of shroud which seemed more grey than white; he was lean, melancholy and beardless, and did not altogether correspond to my previous notion of Apollonius. I experienced an abnormally cold sensation, and when I endeavoured to question the phantom I could not articulate a syllable. I therefore placed my hand on the sign of the pentagram, and pointed the sword at the figure, commanding it mentally to obey and not alarm me, in virtue of the said sign. The form thereupon became vague, and suddenly disappeared. I directed it to return, and presently felt, as it were, a breath close by me, something touched my hand which was holding the sword, and the arm became immediately benumbed as far as the elbow. I divined that the sword displeased the spirit, and I therefore placed its point downwards, close by me, within the circle. The human figure reappeared immediately, but I experienced such an intense weakness in all my limbs, and a swooning sensation came so quickly over me that I made two steps to sit down, whereupon I fell into a profound lethargy accompanied by dreams of which I had only a confused recollection when I came again to myself. For several days my arm remained benumbed and painful. The apparition did not speak to me, but it seemed that the questions I had designed to ask answered themselves in my mind. To that of the lady an interior voice replied—Death!—it was concerning a man of whom she desired information. As for myself, I sought to know whether reconciliation and forgiveness were possible between two persons who occupied my thoughts, and the same inexorable echo within me answered—Dead!...

'Am I to conclude from all this that I really evoked, saw and touched the great Appollonius of Tyana? I am not so hallucinated or so unserious as to believe it.... I do not explain the physical laws by which I saw and touched; I affirm solely that I did see and that I did touch, that I saw clearly and distinctly, apart from dreaming, and this is sufficient to establish the real efficacy of magical ceremonies.'

Lévi repeated the evocation of Apollonius on two other occasions and each time experienced similar phenomena. Cautioning his readers who might be tempted to try similar experiments, he mentions as a conclusion to his account that 'great fatigue' results from such procedures.

He returned to Paris in August 1854. The verdict of Apollonius on his marriage proved correct, for shortly after his return his wife applied for, and was granted, a decree of separation. The marriage was finally to be declared null and void in 1865.

1. *Revue progressive*, 1st September 1853.
2. Sir Edward Bulwer-Lytton.

10   *The Magician*

The autumn of 1854 found Eliphas Lévi living in a first-floor apartment at 120 Boulevard du Montparnasse, consisting of a single modest room. Besides the scanty pieces of furniture there was an easel, for once again he had fallen back on his talents as an illustrator when times were hard. A Carmelite community in the Rue d'Enfer had commissioned him to paint a series of tableaux. Another plan he had conceived—to illustrate the works of Rabelais—was forestalled when Gustave Doré's illustrations of the work appeared. Skilled as he was, Lévi could hardly hope to compete with the great Doré, and he had to abandon the project.

But soon literary work began to take precedence again. In 1855 he founded, in collaboration with Charles Fauvety and Charles Lemmonier, a monthly called *La Revue philosophique et religieuse*, to which he contributed poetry and articles on the Cabala. This periodical lasted for only three years, but it helped to spread his reputation. In addition, his *Dogme* and its companion volume the *Rituel de la magie* continued to enjoy a large demand and went through edition after edition.

Attracted by his growing reputation, an increasing number of visitors made the pilgrimmage to his door. One of these callers came in his eagerness at an early hour of the morning and his knock awakened Lévi from his sleep. He opened the door to an unknown person. 'It was a man with white hair, entirely clothed in black; his physiognomy that of an extremely devout priest; his whole air, in short, was entirely worthy of respect.' Lévi continues the story as follows in the *Clé des grandes mystères*:

'This ecclesiastic was furnished with a letter of recommendation conceived in these terms:

Dear Master,
This is to introduce to you an old savant who wants to gabble Hebrew sorcery with you. Receive him like myself—I mean as I myself received him—by getting rid of him in the best way you can.

Entirely yours, in the sacrosanct Quabalah,
AD. DESBARROLLES'

'Reverend sir,' said Eliphas, smiling, after having read the letter, 'I am entirely at your service, and can refuse nothing to the friends who writes to me. You have then seen my excellent disciple Desbarrolles?'

'Yes, sir, and I have found him a very amiable and very learned man. I think both you and him worthy of the truth which has been lately revealed by astonishing miracles, and the positive revelations of the Archangel St. Michael.'

'Sir, you do us honour. Has then the good Desbarrolles astonished you by his science?'

'Oh, certainly he possesses in a very remarkable degree the secrets of cheiromancy; by merely inspecting my hand, he told me nearly the whole story of my life.'

'He is quite capable of that. But did he enter into the smallest details?'

'Sufficiently, sir, to convince me of his extraordinary power.

'Did he tell you that you were once the vicar of Mont-Louis, in the diocese of Tours? That you are the most zealous disciple of the ecstatic Eugène Vintras? And that your name is Charvoz?'

It was a veritable thunderbolt; at each of these three sentences the old priest jumped in his chair. When he heard his name he turned pale and rose as if a spring had been released.

'You are then really a magician?' he cried; 'Charvoz is certainly my name, but it is not that which I bear; I call myself La Paraz.'

'I know it; La Paraz is the name of your mother. You have left a sufficiently enviable position, that of a country vicar, and your charming vicarage, in order to share the troubled existence of a sectary.'

'Say, of a great prophet!'

'Sir, I believe perfectly in your good faith. But you will permit me to examine a little the mission and the character of your prophet.'

'Yes, sir; examination, full light, the microscope of science, that is all we ask. Come to London, sir, and you will see! The miracles are permanently established there.'

'Would you be so kind, sir, as to give me, first of all, some exact and conscientious details with regard to the miracles?'

'Oh, as many as you like!'

And immediately the old priest began to recount things which the whole world would have found impossible, but which did not even turn an eyelash of the Professor of Transcendental Magic.

Here is one of his stories:

One day Vintras, in an access of enthusiasm, was preaching before his heterodox altar; twenty-five persons were present. An empty chalice was upon the altar, a chalice well known to the Abbé Charvoz; he had brought it himself from his church of Mont-Louis, and he was perfectly certain that the sacred vase had neither secret ducts nor double bottom.

'In order to prove to you,' said Vintras, 'that it is God Himself who inspires me. He acquaints me that this chalice will fill itself with drops of His blood, under the appearance of wine, and you will all be able to taste the fruit of the vines of the future, the wine which we shall drink with the Saviour in the Kingdom of his Father . . .'

'Overcome with astonishment and fear,' continued the Abbé Charvoz, 'I went up to the altar, I took the chalice, I looked at the bottom of it: it was entirely empty. I overturned it in the sight of everyone, then I returned to kneel at the foot of the altar, holding the chalice between my two hands . . . Suddenly there was a slight noise; the noise of a drop of water, falling into the chalice from the ceiling, was distinctly heard, and a drop of wine appeared at the bottom of the vase.

'Every eye was fixed on me. Then they looked at the ceiling, for our simple chapel was held in a poor room; in the ceiling was neither hole nor fissure; nothing was seen to fall, and yet the noise of the fall of the drops multiplied, it became more rapid, and more frequent . . . and the wine climbed from the bottom of the chalice towards the brim.

'When the chalice was full, I bore it slowly around to that all might see it; then the prophet dipped his lips into it, and all, one after the other, tasted the miraculous wine. It is in vain to search memory for any taste which should give an idea of it . . .

And what shall I tell you,' added the Abbé Charvoz, 'of those miracles of blood which astonish us every day? Thousands of wounded and bleeding hosts are found upon our altars. The sacred stigmata appear to all who wish to see them. The hosts, at first white, slowly become marked with characters and hearts in blood . . . Must one believe that God abandons the holiest objects to the false miracles of the devil? Should not one rather adore, and believe that the hour of the supreme and final revelation has arrived?'

The Abbé Charvoz, as he thus spoke, had in his voice that sort of nervous trembling that Eliphas Lévi had already noticed in the case of M. Madrolle.[2] The magician shook his head pensively; then, suddenly:

'Sir,' said he to the Abbé; 'you have upon you one or two of these miraculous hosts. Be good enough to show them to me.'

'Sir . . .'

'You have some, I know it; why should you deny it?'

'I do not deny it,' said the Abbé Charvoz; 'but you will permit me not to expose to the investigations of incredulity objects of the most sincere and devout belief.'

'Reverend sir,' said Eliphas gravely; 'incredulity is the mistrust of an ignorance almost sure to deceive itself. Science is not incredulous. I believe, to begin with, in your own conviction, since you have accepted a life of privation and even of reproach, in order to stick to this unhappy belief. Show me then your miraculous hosts, and believe entirely in my respect for the objects of a sincere worship.'

'Oh, well!' said the Abbé Charvoz, after another slight hesitation; 'I will show them to you.'

Then he unbuttoned the top of his black waistcoat and drew forth a little reliquary of silver, before which he fell on his knees, with tears in his eyes, and prayers on his lips; Eliphas fell on his knees beside him, and the Abbé opened the reliquary.

There were in the reliquary three hosts, one whole, the two others almost like paste, and as it were kneaded with blood.

The whole host bore in its centre a heart in relief on both sides; a clot of blood moulded in the form of a heart, which seemed to have been formed in the host itself in an inexplicable manner. The blood could not have been applied from without, for the imbibed colouring matter had left the particles adhering to the exterior surface quite white. The appearance of the phenomenon was the same on both sides. The Master of Magic was seized with an involuntary trembling.

Eliphas Lévi was even more shocked when the Abbé showed him an album containing pictures of other miraculous hosts, three of which particularly caught his attention because of the signs that they bore. The first was stamped with the star of the microcosm, or the magic pentagram. 'It is the five-pointed star of occult masonry, the star with which Agrippa drew the human figure, the head in the upper point, the four limbs in the four others. The flaming star, which, when turned upside down, is the hieroglyphic sign of the goat of Black Magic, whose head may then be drawn in the star, the two horns at the top, the ears to the right and left, the beard at the bottom. It is the sign of antagonism and fatality. It is the goat of lust attacking the Heavens with its horns. It is a sign execrated by initiates of a superior rank, even at the Sabbath.'

The appearance of the diabolical inverted pentagram on a holy object would certainly be a sacrilege, but, as Aleister Crowley points out in a footnote to his translation of the *Clé des grandes mystères*, if the sign were on a circular host, how could it be upside down?

The second host bore the sign of the two intertwined hermetic serpents. 'But the heads and tails, instead of coming together in two similar semicircles, were turned outwards, and there was no intermediate line representing the caduceus. Above the heads of the serpents one saw the fatal V, the Typhonian fork, the character of hell. To the right and left, the sacred numbers III and VII were relegated to the horizontal line which represents passive and secondary things.'

Finally, the third host bore the cabalistic monogram of Jehovah, the Jod and He, but upside down. 'This, according to the doctors of occult science, is the most frightful of all blasphemies, and signifies, however one may read it, "Fatality alone exists: God and Spirit are not. Matter is all, and spirit is only a fiction of this matter demented."'

Charvoz also gave Lévi a description of the vestments worn by Vintras. 'They are red in colour. He wears upon his forehead a cross in the form of a lingam; and his pastoral staff is surmounted by a hand, all of whose fingers are closed, except the thumb and little finger.

'Now, all that is diabolical in the highest degree. And is it not a really wonderful thing, this intuition of the signs of a lost science? For it is transcendental magic which, basing the universe upon the two columns of Hermes and Solomon, has divided the metaphysical world into two intellectual zones, one white and luminous, enclosing positive ideas, the other black and obscure, containing negative ideas, and which has given the synthesis of the first, the name of God, and to that of the other, the name of the devil or of Satan.'

Occupied as he was with occultism, Eliphas Lévi had not lost his taste for meddling in politics. Once again he found himself in trouble with the police because of a satirical poem he had written entitled *Caligula*, in which he drew an obvious parallel between the reign of the decadent Roman emperor and that of Napoleon III, criticising the latter's vanity, the extravagance of his court and his vain military adventures. As a result of the poem, Lévi found himself condemned to a term of imprisonment at Mazas. But this time Lévi was in no mood to make a martyr out of himself. From the prison he composed another poem, entitled *L'Anti-Caligula*, addressed to the Napoleon III, in which he wittily apologised for having compared the Emperor to 'a monster of antiquity', but pointed out that, in view of the inhumane way in which he had been seized and imprisoned by the imperial police, it was small wonder that people mistook the Emperor for Caligula. Napoleon III was touched by the poem and promptly pardoned Lévi who was set at liberty.

At the beginning of 1856 the *Dogme* and *Rituel de la magie* appeared together as one volume. Eliphas Lévi had ceded the copyright to the publisher, Mme veuve Germer-Baillière in return for a fee of 500 francs for each new edition. The following year he began to write for Alexandre Dumas's periodical, *Le Mousquetaire*, to which he contributed a number of poems.

The year 1857 opened with a bizarre and grisly event. On 3rd January the Archbishop of Paris, Mgr. Sibour was inaugurating the festival of St. Geneviève at the church of Saint-Etienne-du-Mont. Eliphas, who was present at the ceremony, describes in the *Clé* what happened:

'The head of the procession had already returned to the choir, the Archbishop was arriving at the railing of the nave: there the passage was too narrow for three people to walk in file; the Archbishop was in front, and the two grand-vicars behind him, always holding the edges of his cope, which was thus thrown off, and drawn backwards, in such a manner that the prelate presented his breast uncovered, and protected only by the crossed embroideries of his stole.

'Then those who were behind the Archbishop saw him tremble, and we heard an interruption in a loud and clear voice; but without shouting, or clamour. What had been said? It seemed that it was: "Down with the goddesses!" But I thought that I had not heard aright, so out of place and void of sense it seemed. However, the exclamation was repeated twice or thrice; then someone cried: "Save the Archbishop!" Other voices replied: "To arms!" The crowd, overturning the chairs and barriers, scattered, and rushed towards the doors shrieking. Amidst the wails of children, and the screams of the women, Eliphas, carried away by the crowd, found himself, somehow or other, out of the church; but the last look that he was able to cast upon it was smitten with a terrible and ineffaceable picture!

'In the midst of a circle made large by the affright of all those who surrounded him, the prelate was standing alone, still leaning on his cross, and held up by the stiffness of his cope, which the grand-vicars had let go and which accordingly hung to the ground.

'The head of the Archbishop was a little thrown back, his eyes and his free hand raised to Heaven. His attitude was that which Eugène Delacroix has given to the Bishop of Liège in the picture of his assassination by the bandits of the Wild Boar of the Ardennes; there was in his gesture the whole epic of martyrdom; it was an acceptance and an offering; a prayer for his people, and a pardon for his murderer . . .

'Before the Archbishop, a lifted arm, sketched in shadow like an infernal silhouette, held and brandished a knife. Policemen, sword in hand, were running up.'

The assassin, a young priest named Louis Verger, was brought to trial a few days later. Reading about the trial in the press, Lévi was suddenly struck by a disturbing memory touched by a description of the accused. Soon afterwards he saw a sketch of the assassin and all possible doubt was removed. The Archbishop's murderer was a young priest who had come to Lévi a year earlier asking how he could obtain a copy of a rare magical work known as the *Grimoire of Pope Honorius* and had explained mysteriously how he was 'seeking the realisation of a thought' and had 'something to do'. Desbarrolles, who had been present at the interview, had examined the palm of the young man, who refused to give his name, and had concluded that he had a vivid imagination which he indulged freely and which might overflow in a dangerous manner. As the mysterious visitor was leaving he had turned and said: 'Before long, you will hear something . . . You will hear me spoken of.'

As a postscript to this incident, Lévi relates how, several weeks after the trial, he had visited a bookseller specialising in the occult and he got on to the subject of the *Grimoire of Pope Honorius*.

' "Nowadays it is impossible to find it," said the merchant. "The last that I had in my hand I sold to a priest for a hundred francs."

' "A young priest? And do you remember what he looked like?"

' "Oh, perfectly, but you ought to know him well yourself, for he told me he had seen you, and it is I who sent him to you."

'No more doubt, then; the unhappy priest had found the fatal *Grimoire*, he had done the evocation, and prepared himself for the murder by a series of sacrileges.'

Six months after this unhappy affair, Lévi, now slightly better off, moved to a more spacious lodging in the Avenue de Maine, where he was to live for seven years. Here he worked on his *Histoire de la magie*, which was published in 1859. He also continued to give lessons in occultism, but was always careful to warn his pupils in advance that he did not indulge in the performance of spectacular magical feats. Nevertheless, despite these warnings, his pupils sometimes had difficulty in keeping their magic within reasonable bounds. The following incident is related in Lévi's correspondence.

'A worker named Maurice, who was fond of evocations, had received from me a prayer which he had been instructed to read before going to bed in the evening in order to drive away the spirits of darkness and to bring himself closer to the spirits of light. One evening he had inadvertently put out his candle and was holding this prayer in his hand when the paper lit up by itself, and he was able to read distinctly what I had written . . . The following night there appeared beside his bed a light so bright that he woke up, and in the middle of this light he recognised my silhouette . . . holding a hand out to him. Taking me for a god or a devil, the poor man began to pester me to obtain from me communications, revelations etc. etc., and I was obliged to show him the door.'

One of Lévi's pupils at this time was Dr. Fernand Rozier (1839–1922), who was destined to become one of the leaders of French occultism. After qualifying as a doctor, Rozier had developed a passion for travel and had spent seven years as a ship's doctor. On his return he had established a practice in Paris. He later became one of the founders of the movement created by the occultist Papus in 1885.

Rozier and Lévi together carried out experiments in alchemy, one of which is described in the following account by Rozier:

'As far as I can remember it was in 1859 or 1860, the exact date is of little importance; let us just say that it was a long time ago. Eliphas Lévi had been struck by the resemblance between pyrites and certain hermetic figures. This mineral is composed of crystals of ferrous sulphur grouped together so as to imitate, to a fault, an apricot; everything is there, even the stalk. This resemblance of a mineral to a fruit seemed to him to be a signature.

'There was also something even more suggestive: gold is often found in this mineral.

'Finally, there was the motto: *Visita Interiora Terrae Rectificando Invenies Occultum Lapidem Veram Medicinem*,[3] whose initial letters spell out the word *Vitriolum*. This was the crowning piece of evidence: pyrites could be nothing else but the *first matter*, the substance on which one had to work to obtain the *philosopher's stone*.

'Another observation added a new possibility. Pyrites, left in humid air, deteriorates, producing a white powder which is a mixture of ferrous sulphate and free sulphuric acid; I cruelly discovered this when I noticed, one fine day, that my supply had leaked into a drawer where I kept my linen. The latter was completely ruined, reduced to shreds by sulphuric acid, oil of *vitriol*.

'Nevertheless, this property made Eliphas Lévi suppose that this *first* matter must also be capable of creating FIRE. In fact, all combustions emit heat; here was a type of combustion, which must give a weak heat; this weak heat must be *gentle fire*.

'Following all these reasonings, and on the instructions of Eliphas Lévi, I procured a fairly large quantity of pyrites; I pulverised part of it which I then enclosed in a glass sphere *hermetically*(?) sealed. The hermetic sealing consisted of a cork stopper with a covering of sealing wax . . . It would have been better to seal the neck of the vessel with a glazier's lamp, but I was not equipped for that. The sphere was buried up to the neck in a mass of pyrites, broken up into thin pieces, then the whole thing was left to itself until the pyrites had been reduced to a magma composed of ferrous sulphate, sulphuric acid and a residue of pyrites, not yet attacked; all this took several months.

'At the end of this time I removed the sphere with a justifiable feeling of curiosity, and inside I found . . . the powder of pyrites which I had put in: it had undergone no change. Once again the philosopher's stone had failed to be discovered.

'I repeated this experiment several times, varying the conditions, but I never obtained any result—which I am bound to say did not astonish me in the least.

'One day, however, Eliphas Lévi believed that he saw a light tint of black; the powder had taken on a darker colour. This could have meant that we had touched the Raven's Head.[4] I owe it to truth to say that I did not have this joy; I saw no indication of the Raven's Head.'[5]

Eliphas Lévi himself preferred the theoretical side of alchemy, but he did claim to know the secret of transmutation. 'I possess', he stated in a letter, 'some very curious manuscripts of the hermetic art, and I have a profound knowledge of the mysteries of that science. I have seen the secret fire produced, I have seen how two metallic sperms are formed, the white which resembles mercury, and the red which is a viscous oil resembling molten sulphur. I know what can be done with gold, but believe me when I say that I will never do it.' One of Lévi's close friends was Louis Lucas (1816-1863), a leading alchemist and author of the *Roman alchemique*.

The late 1850s were a happy time for Lévi. He was well established as an occultist and now basked in the affection and esteem of a lively circle of friends. His genial, monk-like figure was to be seen at gatherings all over Paris. Among the regular salons which he attended were those held by his friend the religious writer, Charles Fauvety (1813-1894), and his wife at their house in the Rue de la Michodière. To these affairs came a curious selection of philosophers, littérateurs and occultists. Fauvety himself had once been a Saint-Simonist and had been involved in a number of radical publishing ventures including *La Vérité*, in which he had collaborated with Lévi.

One of the regular attenders at the Fauvetys was Dr. Henri Favre (1827–1916). Besides being a physician and the author of a number of scientific and medical books, Favre was also an occultist and a skilled astrologer. His occultism was Christian in orientation, and one of his works was a vast treatise on the Bible. He was also a literary critic and had written a study of Balzac.

Another frequent guest was the palmist, Adolphe Desbarrolles. He had once been a pupil of Lévi, but he had irritated the master by his concern for worldly success, and the two had ceased to be friends. In his book, *Les Mystères de la main*, Desbarrolles included an analysis of Lévi's palm.

In 1861 a significant event took place in Lévi's life. Persuaded by Fauvety and another friend named Caubet, he became a freemason. On 14th March he was initiated into a lodge called the Rose of Perfect Silence, of which Caubet was Worshipful Master.

Caubet recalls that during his reception speech Lévi made the following declaration:

'I come to bring back into your midst lost traditions and the exact knowledge of your signs and emblems, and consequently to show you the purpose for which your association was formed.'

He subsequently made efforts to convince his fellow masons that the symbolism of masonry was derived from the Cabala. But evidently they were not persuaded by his theories. He later left the society and gave his reason for doing so in *Le Livre des sages*, written in 1870.[6] The book consists of a series of imaginary dialogues between the author and a number of people representative of different creeds. In the dialogue with 'a cleric' occurs the following interchange:

CLERIC: Courage, monsieur, unmask yourself at last. You are without doubt a freemason and you know perfectly well that the freemasons have just recently been excommunicated by the Pope.

ELIPHAS LÉVI: Yes, I am aware of that, and since then I have ceased to be a freemason because the freemasons excommunicated by the Pope believe they should no longer tolerate Catholicism. I have therefore broken away from them to retain my freedom of conscience and to avoid associating myself with their reprisals which, although perhaps excusable, are not legitimate and are certainly illogical. For the essence of masonry is the tolerance of all cults.

In 1861 Lévi made a second visit to London, this time in the company of his friend Count Alexander Braszynsky, a practising alchemist who had a laboratory in the Château de Beauregard at Villeneuve-Saint-Georges, Mme de Balzac's home. The count was, like Lévi, a friend of Bulwer-Lytton, and the two men went to stay with Lytton at his home, Knebworth, in Hertfordshire. Lytton's reputation as an occultist had grown, and ten years after Lévi's second visit he was made Grand Patron of the Societas Rosicruciana in Anglia.

Another person whom Lévi went to see in England was the exiled prophet, Eugène Vintras. Lévi called on Vintras several times at his lodgings in the Marylebone Road, and on one occasion, together with Count Braszynsky, took part in Vintras's 'sacrifices'. Lévi's impressions of Vintras's personality are given in one of his letters:

'Vintras is an illiterate labourer, but gifted with a singular fluidic power. He reflects immediately the spirit of any person who comes to him and reproduces on the spot the thoughts of people he is seeing for the first time. Thus, when I called on him, I saw a man with a twisted neck and a pious manner . . . As soon as he heard my voice his whole body underwent a transformation; he drew himself up, lifted his head, looked me straight in the face, took on my tone of voice and appearance and talked to me as though he had an exact knowledge of everything that I knew. He then spoke under my influence like a perfect somnambulist.'

Soon after his return to Paris, Lévi's novel *Le Sorcier de Meudon* appeared. This work, despite its title, has little to do with sorcery. It is a light-hearted and partly autobiographical story. It begins in a monastery where a young novice, Lubin, is about to take his vows, but is having second thoughts. His fellow monk, François, who is studying medicine, comes to the rescue. François, who clearly represents the author, arranges a 'miracle' by pretending to be a living statue of St. Francis. In this guise he relieves Lubin of his vows and marries him into the bargain to a nubile girl called Marjolaine. François's pranks and his mockery of the pompous clergy finally result in his expulsion from the monastery, after which he travels round solving people's problems, beginning by curing his sick father. The novel is dedicated to Mme de Balzac in memory of the charming evenings spent at the Château de Beauregard.

In December 1861 a young Englishman named Kenneth Mackenzie, who was a member of the Societas Rosicruciana in Anglia, paid a call on the Professor of Transcendental Magic at his apartment in Avenue de Maine. His account of the meeting which appeared in the journal *The Rosicrucian and Red Cross* of May 1873, is worth quoting at length:

'On the morning of the 3rd December, 1861, I therefore repaired to the residence of Eliphas Lévi, situated at No. 19, Avenue de Maine. The building proved to be a handsome and well arranged structure of brick, with a square garden in front, handsome gate, porter's lodge, and generally good approaches—the building being three stories high. Upon enquiring of the porter, I found that Eliphas Lévi resided upon the second floor, the first floor, probably, being offices of some kind. There I found a narrow passage in which there were four doors to my right, apparently opening upon a number of small rooms. On the fourth door I perceived a small card about three inches long, upon which were inscribed some Hebrew characters equivalent to Eliphas Lévi (Alphonse Louis); in each corner was one of the four letters forming the sacred word INRI, and the whole of this Hebrew inscription was written in the three primitive colours—viz: red, yellow, and blue.

'It was about ten a.m. when I knocked, and the door was opened by Eliphas Lévi himself. I found him a short burly man, with a rubicund complexion, very small but piercing eyes twinkling with good humour, his face broad, his lips small and well compressed together, nostrils dilating. The lower part of his face was covered with a thick black beard and moustache, and I noticed that his ears were small and delicate. In person he was lusty, and his dress was plain and quiet. Upon his head he wore a kind of felt hat turned up in front. On his removing his hat to salute me, I observed that his head was partially bald, his hair dark and glistening, and that portion of his skull, which had been submitted to the tonsure, was partially overgrown with hair.

'He apologised for wearing his hat, stating that he was compelled to do so by an affection of his head, which rendered it dangerous for him to remain uncovered.

'Having briefly stated my name and presented my credentials, I proceeded to express my gratification at the information I had derived from the perusal of his works, and I told him that my mission to him was to learn the state of his studies, insofar as he might feel disposed to inform me, and at the same time to give him the latest intelligence of the condition of occult studies in England. He replied, in French, that language, Latin and Hebrew, being the only languages known to him, that he was highly pleased to receive any stranger whose studies were akin to his own, and that he had the satisfaction of knowing that his works upon Philosophical Magic had obtained for him the sympathy of many inquiring minds in all parts of Europe.

'Among his disciples, Eliphas Lévi especially mentioned, the Count Braszynsky, the Polish millionaire, to whom, he said, he was indebted for a variety of the manuscripts then in his possession. I said that I had been, for some time, making collections in reference to the occult game of Tarot, and that I wished particularly to learn whether he proposed to carry out the intention expressed in the "Rituel et Dogme de la Haute Magie" of issuing a complete set of Tarot cards.

'He replied that he was very willing to do so—and took from among his manuscripts a small volume in which were depicted the twenty-one cards of the Tarot with the Zero or Fool, according to the earliest authorities. Those cards were drawn by his own hand, and the little volume contained a large number of the symbols of Theurgia and Goetia, a medley of collections from the Key of Rabbi Solomon and similar occult repertories.

'This little work (he told me) had cost him twenty years to put together. He was kind enough to state that if I had any intention of publishing, in England, any set of Tarot cards, I might count upon him for all assistance, and that he would supply me with all drawings and instructions for their use.

'After this preliminary conversation our discourse became general, and then, for the first time, I ventured to take a glance at his apartment.

'The room is small and irregular in shape, and its dimensions appear all the less from the fact of its being crowded with furniture. In a recess behind his usual writing table, was a species

The Magician

of altar, with a set of gilt vessels such as are usually used in Roman Catholic Churches in the celebration of the Mass. Sumptuous drapery of yellow and drab covered this piece of furniture, in the centre of which lay a Hebrew roll of the Law; above it was a gilt triangle bearing the name of Jehovah; on the right side of this altar was a species of sideboard, also hung with drapery. Under a glass case I noticed a manuscript of talismans, as I perceived from the pages that were open.

'Next to this came the window, having a northern aspect, and close to it was placed the ordinary writing table of Eliphas Lévi—a large and substantial piece of furniture, with shelves in front, covered with books and manuscripts. Behind, on the wall, next to the writing table and close to the window, hung a life-size picture representing a female, her hands clasped to her bosom, adoring the Sacred Word, which appeared in a kind of glory.

'Eliphas then informed me that the female represented the Holy Cabbala. Underneath the picture was an antique sofa, with red velvet cushions. At the end of the room was the fire-place, before which a curiously contrived screen was placed. The mantle-shelf was loaded with a series of massive looking vases, in which were coins, medallions, and talismans. On the other side of the fire-place, opposite the picture was a smaller cabinet with glass doors, hung with red drapery, with shelves above, on which were ranged books not of an occult character. Within the cabinet I saw a number of manuscripts, printed books, talismans, a glass water vessel of a blue colour, two skulls, and a variety of other magical apparatus.

'Next to this cabinet came the door upon which was suspended a large cabbalistical diagram, of which Eliphas Lévi informed me that only one hundred impressions had been taken. Upon the walls were suspended many engravings and paintings having reference to the Cabbala. The whole room was profusely decorated with hangings of every kind, and presented an effective theatrical appearance. Upon one of the sideboards I noticed an Egyptian figure of Isis, upon which I commented as being very perfect, at which Eliphas Lévi laughed, and told me it was an article of commerce in Paris, being, in fact, a very large tobacco jar.

'We conversed upon the subject of Theosophy considerably, and Eliphas Lévi did me the favour to remark that the form of my head was evidently that of a person greatly given to such studies. Eliphas Lévi informed me that if there were any truths to be discovered in his books—as he believed there were—they were not to be attributed to his own wisdom, but that he had arrived at the various inductions there published by means of the combinations presented by the twenty-two cards of the Tarot. He also mentioned that those works had been prepared for the press by a friend, he himself not possessing the requisite literary ability.

'Altogether my impression upon my first visit was highly favourable; his manner was simple, sincere and straight-forward. He spoke to me of his visit to England, stating his inability to speak English, a language he had in vain endeavoured to acquire —he rendered a tribute to the versatile knowledge of Lord, then Sir Edward Bulwer, Lytton, with emphasis. I asked him, among other questions, whether he recognised the existence, as a fact, of means of communication with departed spirits. His reply was this:

'"Break a bottle of oil under water, at however remote a distance from the surface, the mass of oil will ascend to that surface, while the remains of the bottle will sink to the bottom. Thus" he continued, "do I conceive that the soul, upon quitting the body, by its spiritual specific gravity, ascends to the sphere for which it is destined. Like the oil, it remains ever uppermost, and returns not to earth."

'I then urged upon him that spirits might, by refraction, or reflection, communicate with earth, but I found him an utter materialist upon this question. Time was now drawing on. I therefore bade him adieu, fixing the next morning for a resumption of our converse.

'On my second interview, the following morning, he reiterated all his friendly expressions, and proceeded with great kindness to show me a variety of manuscripts of his own and of other persons. One work he laid before me was a photographic copy of a printed book, the title-page of which was unknown to him. Having been torn off; it was, however, a prophecy by the celebrated Paracelsus, illustrated with symbolical figures, and predicting, in unmistakable language, the first French revolution, the rise of Napoleon, the downfall of the Papacy, the restoration of the kingdom of Italy, the abrogation of the temporal power of the Pope, the downfall of the clergy, and the ultimate ascendancy of the occult sciences, as a means of restoring general harmony in society.

'The work is an octavo, containing thirty-two chapters, and the copy I saw was one of six taken by the Count Braszynsky from the imperfect original, which the possessor, a gentleman residing in Warsaw, would not sell to the Count, although he offered him any money he wished to ask for it. Some portion of the work has been quoted by Eliphas Lévi in *La Clé des grandes mystères*, pp. 378 and 99. . . .

'From his numerous receptacles he produced a remarkable Cabbalistic plate, which he had bought upon one of the quays. Respecting this plate, he informed me that in a manuscript record, in the possession of his friend, the Count Braszynsky, and attributed to the renowned Cagliostro, a prediction had been made that a certain person would arise in the nineteenth century, who should be able clearly to express the meaning of this plate, and in the manuscript the name of the person was given as Alphonse; this Eliphas Lévi attributed to himself.

'Eliphas Lévi and myself also conversed respecting the Urim and Thummim, and the breast-plate of Aaron. Upon this Eliphas Lévi referred to the small hand-book formerly named, and there showed me a drawing of the Ark of the Covenant, with the four symbolic figures at the corners. He then bade me notice that the top of the ark was a plane surface, and that it was large enough to allow the rectangular breast-plate of the High Priest to turn freely round in any direction. He then told me he had discovered the method of using the Urim and Thummim to be as follows:

'The breast-plate of the High Priest, it is known, contained twelve stones, each cut into six facets or sides; upon each was engraven one of seventy-two names of God. Thus the Urim and Thummim contained the whole Cabbala. Upon its being placed at the top of the ark, the High Priest, offering up a prayer for enlightenment, turned the breast-plate round upon itself, and, upon its ceasing to revolve, the High Priest watched the reflection of the four animals in the stone of the tribe whom the question concerned, and, combining them with the Divine Name, drew his conclusions.

'I finally parted with Eliphas Lévi, with the greatest assurances of good feeling on his part, and his testimony of satisfaction at being informed of the present condition of magical and other studies in England; he reiterated to me his offers of service, and requested me to correspond with him upon any topics that might seem of interest to both.'

One of the most remarkable stories that this British disciple took back with him was as follows. One evening Eliphas Lévi was sitting at his desk thinking of Paracelsus and wondering why, in the works of the sixteenth-century sage, he had been unable to find any mention of the Tarot, for he was convinced that the great man must have been familiar with the 'Book of Hermes'. In the midst of these contemplations he fell asleep and awoke in his dreams in an alchemist's laboratory. A majestic figure appeared; it was none other than Paracelsus himself.

Lévi told the apparition of the question in his mind, and Paracelsus replied by reaching into a little purse hanging from his belt and extracting a copper medallion which he handed to Lévi. On the outside of the piece was represented what appeared to be the juggler or magus, the first key of the Tarot; on the other side was an alphabet.

Having shown him the coin, Paracelsus beckoned Eliphas to follow him. Traversing the streets of Paris they came at last to a point near the Pont Neuf where the sage pointed to a spot on the pavement.

The following day Lévi, remembering the dream, went in search of the coin. Passing along the Quai Conti, near the Pont Neuf, he came to the place that Paracelsus had indicated, now occupied by a stall selling medallions and coins. He searched through the merchandise and there, among a quantity of miscellaneous pieces, he came upon the very one that he had seen in his dream.

Such an experience would be enough to convert most people to a belief in spiritualism. Yet Lévi refused to accept any irrational explanation. As he explained to Mackenzie: 'I have no doubt that upon purely natural causes the whole of this singular vision may be explained. I had fallen asleep with the work of Paracelsus in my hand—what more natural than that my mind should recur to such circumstances as I knew connected with him?' As for the question of the coin, 'I was well acquainted with the fact that the coin dealer habitually exposed his wares on the quay beside the bridge. I had often passed the stall, yet I confess I had never seen the coin. The matter is inexplicable to me.'

The Magician

This ingrained scepticism was one of the qualities that lifted Eliphas Lévi out of the class of most dabblers in occultism. The magical universe, he realised, is not to be entered by gazing open-mouthed at perfectly explicable phenomena. The true magus needs common sense as well as faith.

1. The palmist Adolphe Desbarrolles, see page 115.
2. Another disciple of Vintras whom Lévi had met.
3. 'Visit the inner regions of the earth and by rectifying you will find the occult stone, the true medicine.'
4. According to the alchemical tradition the transformation of matter takes place in three stages, represented by three different colours, black, white and red. The 'Raven's Head' was an allegorical term used to refer to the first, or black, stage.
5. *L'Hyperchimie*, No. 10, October 1900.
6. Unpublished during his lifetime, this book was issued by the firm of Chacornac in 1912.

11 *The Pundit*

In July 1861 an Italian nobleman of occult leanings was walking past a bookshop in Marseilles and noticed in the window a copy of Lévi's *Dogme et rituel de la haute magie*. He bought the book and was soon eager to get in touch with its author. The correspondence which ensued was later to result in his becoming one of Lévi's closest disciples.

This man was Baron Nicolas-Joseph Spedalieri, born in Sicily in 1812 of an old and distinguished family. In his twenties he had become interested in magic and mysticism and had read the works of Saint-Martin. Later he had joined a Martinist society at Naples. At the age of about thirty he had come to live in France.

Lévi must have been impressed by Spedalieri for one of the first things he sent to the Baron was a copy of his manuscript work, the *Clés majeures et clavicules de Salomon*, written in 1860. This work was published posthumously in 1896, but as the original consists largely of hand-coloured illustrations, most of its value is lost in the printed edition, which contains no colour plates.[1] At the end of the book is a note stating that the manuscript was 'copied for the exclusive and personal use of Monsieur le Baron Spedalieri in October and November 1861'. The work contains some important evidence about Lévi's doctrines, and I shall later discuss it in detail.

In one of his letters to the Baron, Lévi wrote: 'I have twelve disciples, but they are not all in Paris. Of the twelve, four, counting you, are my devoted friends. One of these four is a doctor in Berlin; the two others are great Polish noblemen. Of these four, you are the most advanced in Theosophy; the Berlin doctor has made great progress with the Cabala, one of the Polish nobles is a first-rate scholar of hermetic philosophy, the other is enamoured of science; and science has turned him from the man of pleasure, which he was, into a man of duty and reason.'

The two Polish noblemen referred to were Count Alexander Braszynsky and Count Georges de Mniszech. The Berlin doctor was a man of Polish origin named Nowakowski who had been led to occultism through an interest in the dervishes.

In another letter to Spedalieri, Lévi gives his recipe for a well-ordered life. 'A great calmness of spirit, a great cleanliness of body, a constantly even temperature, rather on the cold side than too hot, a dry and well-aired lodging, where nothing is incongruous and there is no reminder of the base needs of life (I would be just as ashamed to display a wash-basin in my apartment as to go out into the street without my trousers), well-regulated meals proportional to the appetite which should be satisfied but not over-stimulated. Simple and substantial food; stop work before one becomes tired; take moderate and regular exercise; never allow yourself to become over-excited in the evening, to ensure that the greatest possible calm precedes sleep.'

The sober life recommended by Lévi was in contrast to the general mood of Paris in the 1860s. The Second Empire was at its extravagant zenith. Napoleon III and his beautiful Empress Eugénie set the tone for the gay life in which Paris revelled. Yet there was a hint of desperation in this revelry, as though the country were trying to shut out the ominous rumblings from abroad, such as the Russian suppression of the Polish uprising, in which the Braszynsky brothers lost most of their estates. Many people must have sensed that the golden years of Napoleon III's reign could not continue for long and sought to distract themselves from the future in any way they could. One of the symptoms of this mood was a growth of interest in spiritualism, and in the early 1860s all of Paris was talking of the exploits of the American medium Daniel Dunglas Home, whose book, *Revelations of my Supernatural Life*, was published in a French edition in 1863. Home was the illegitimate son of the 11th Earl of Home and a Southampton chambermaid; Sir Alec Douglas-Home is therefore his great-nephew.

Eliphas Lévi regarded Home with scorn and included a long attack on the medium in *La Clé des grandes mystères*. The following anecdote is given as one indication of the bogus nature of Home's claims:

'Mr. Home ... was once more about to leave Paris, that Paris where even the angels and demons, if they appeared in any shape, would not pass very long for marvellous beings, and would find nothing better to do than to return at top speed to Heaven or to Hell, to escape the forgetfulness and neglect of human kind.

'Mr. Home, his air sad and disillusioned, was then bidding farewell to a noble lady whose kindly welcome had been one of the first happinesses which he had tasted in France. Mme de B— treated him very kindly that day, as always, and asked him to stay to dinner; the man of mystery was about to accept when, someone having just said that they were waiting for a cabalist, well known in the world of occult science by the publication of a book entitled *Haute magie*, Mr. Home suddenly changed countenance and said, stammering, and with a visible embarrassment, that he could not remain, and that the approach of this Professor of Magic caused him an incomparable terror. Everything one could say to reassure him proved useless. "I do not presume to judge the man," said he; "I do not assert that he is good or evil, I know nothing about it; but his atmosphere hurts me; near him I should feel myself, as it were, without force, even without life." After which explanation Mr. Home hastened to salute and withdraw.'

The 'Professor of Magic' was, of course, Lévi himself. After recounting this story Lévi adds, by way of explanation: 'This terror of miracle-mongers in the presence of the veritable initiates of science is not a new fact in the annals of occultism.'

Continuing his attack on Home, Lévi says; 'Far be it from us, however, to denounce Mr. Home as a low-class sorcerer, that is to say, as a charlatan. The celebrated American medium is sweet and natural as a child. He is a poor and over-sensitive being, without cunning and without defence; he is the plaything of a terrible force of whose nature he is ignorant, and the first of his dupes is certainly himself ...

'Mr. Home is subject to trances which put him, according to his own account, in direct communication with the soul of his mother, and, through her, with the entire world of spirits. He describes, like the sleep-walkers of Cahagnet, persons whom he has never seen, and who are recognised by those who evoke them; he will tell you even their names, and will reply on their behalf, to questions which can be understood only by the soul evoked and yourselves.'

Lévi goes on to describe some of the strange phenomena that occurred at Home's séances:

'Visible and tangible hands came out, or seem to come out, of tables; but in this case the tables must be covered. The invisible agent needs certain apparatus, just as do the cleverest successors of Robert Houdini.

'These hands show themselves above all in darkness; they are warm and phosphorescent, or cold and black. They write stupidities, or touch the piano; and when they have touched the piano it is necessary to send for the tuner, their contact being always fatal to the exactitude of the instrument.

'One of the most considerable personages in England, Sir Bulwer-Lytton, has seen and touched those hands; we have read his written and signed attestation. He declares that he has seized them, and drawn them towards himself with all his strength, in order to withdraw from their incognito the arm to which they should naturally belong. But the invisible object has proved stronger than the English novelist, and the hands have escaped him.

'A Russian nobleman who was the protector of Mr. Home, and whose character and good faith could not possibly be doubted, Count A. B—, has also seen and seized with vigour the mysterious hands. "They are," says he, "perfect shapes of human hands, warm and living, *only one feels no bones.*" Pressed by an unavoidable constraint, those hands did not struggle to escape, but grew smaller, and in some way melted so that the Count ended by no longer holding anything.

'Other persons who have seen them and touched them say that the fingers are puffed out and stiff, and compare them to gloves of india-rubber, swollen with a warm and phosphorescent air. Sometimes, instead of hands, it is feet which protrude themselves, but never naked. The spirit, which probably lacks footwear, respects (at least in this particular) the delicacy of ladies, and never shows his feet but under a drapery or cloth.'

Lévi himself attended spiritualist séances, as is proved by an anecdote in a letter to Spedalieri:

'I must tell you quite a recent story of medio-mania. I had gone incognito to a circle of table-turners; a young man with a look of ill-health was holding a pencil and writing as if by a convulsive movement, divining thoughts and answering difficult questions. I approached him, and he wrote that I did him harm. I ordered him to calm himself and answer me. "What do you want of me?" said he at last. "Tell me my name." His hand hesitated for a few moments, then he wrote in large, slightly tremulous letters: Rivoel. I was strangely struck by this coincidence with the name given me by another evoker, who could not have had any collusion with this one. I asked the medium what this name might mean, and he wrote rapidly:

' "Don't you know how to read, you fool?" And below, he wrote the signature: "Osphal".

'It was for me a ray of light. I reversed the word in reading it and read: Leo vir. Now Lavater's engraving representing Alphos, the Maphon of Gablidom, has for its chief emblem an initiate seated and leaning upon a lion. I took good care not to explain all this to the worshippers of Ob, and in their eyes I remained crushed under the weight of the insult that the pretended spirit had addressed to me. From that moment the so-called spirit wandered hopelessly and only dictated to the medium phrases devoid of meaning and utter follies.'

Evidently the spirit had detected in Lévi the presence of a true magician and had been disconcerted by the experience in the same way that Home had been. The story illustrated Lévi's total inability to resist any kind of symbol, even if it came from the despised pen of a medium. Whatever the word that the spirit had communicated Lévi would have found some anagram or translation that was full of significance for him.

If 'miracle-mongers' like Home took care to avoid the company of the Professor of High Magic, more genuine seekers after esoteric wisdom continued to place themselves under his instruction. One such was a pupil named Jean-Baptiste Pitois, the political editor of the *Moniteur Parisien*, who came to Lévi in about 1852. Pitois was to become one of the leaders among the host of occultists who followed in the wake of Lévi. The world was to know him by his pseudonym of Paul Christian.

He was born at Remiremont, Vosges, of middle-class parents and, like Lévi, was guided from an early age towards the priesthood. At the age of eighteen he entered a Trappist monastery and after a year's novitiate was ready to take his vows. At the last minute, however, he changed his mind and resumed a secular life, becoming a student at Strasbourg under the direction of his uncle who was rector of the academy there.

8 Alphonse-Louis Constant in 1836; a drawing by one of his friends

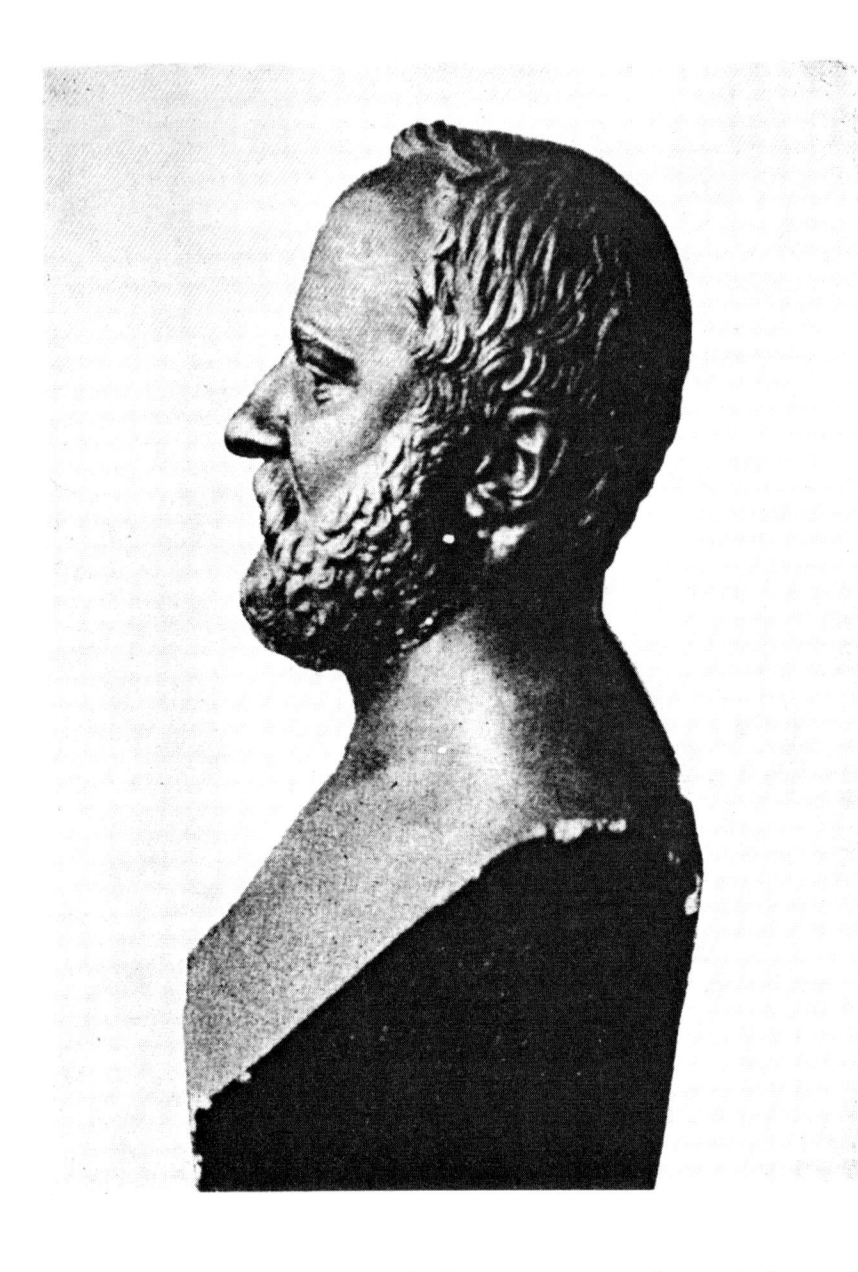

9 A bust by F.-F. Rouband of Constant in 1852, the year before he adopted the name of Eliphas Lévi

In 1846 Christian left for Martinique where he remained for three years. On his return to France in 1839 he was given a post in the library of the Ministry of Public Instruction where he was entrusted with the task of putting in order a conglomeration of books and manuscripts originating from the suppressed monasteries. As he worked his way through this collection, a number of strange writings on forbidden subjects of an occult nature caught his eye. Their esoteric language first puzzled, then fascinated him, as curiosity led him to acquire an ever-deepening knowledge of their content.

He was soon reading avidly anything he could obtain on the subject of occultism, and it was not long before he was ready to make his own contribution to occult literature. His early works appeared under a variety of colourful pseudonyms: Hortensius Flamel, Une Sybille, Frédéric de la Grange, Lusidès. Finally he settled on the more credible name of Paul Christian.

He dabbled for a time in left-wing politics, presiding over the Central Jacobin Club and founding the *Journal des Jacobins*, which had a short life. In 1853 he married an Italian woman related to the family of Sir Walter Scott.

In 1854 he published an astrological work entitled *Carmen Sybillum*. Two years later a prediction he had made in the book was fulfilled when the Prince Imperial was born to Napoleon III and the Empress Eugénie. This made his name, and he soon found himself much sought after as an astrologer in the salons and at the court. He was for a time a neighbour of Lévi and took a number of lessons from him in the Cabala and the Tarot.

Christian's best-known works are *L'Homme rouge des Tuileries* (1863) and *Histoire de la magie* (1871). The title of the former refers to a legend concerning a demon who haunted the Tuileries Palace in the form of a little red man and who was supposed to have advised Napoleon Bonaparte and been responsible for his victories. He is also referred to by clairvoyant Mlle Le Normand in her book *Le Petit Homme rouge des Tuileries*.

Christian's book is in the form of a story concerning an eccentric old man living in a dilapidated house in Paris and advertising himself as a '*Professeur des Mathématiques célestes*'. His treasured possession is a manuscript which he claims to be 'fragments of a lost book' of secret wisdom. The manuscript, which purports to be quoted in full, forms the bulk of the text and serves as the vehicle for Christian to explain his peculiar and highly unorthodox system of astrology.

The document propounds a kind of cabalistic astrology according to which 'the seven spirits who have as their thrones the planets Saturn, Jupiter, Mars, the Sun, Venus, Mercury and the Moon, are the agents by which the universal Intelligence exercises its dominion over men and things'. The manuscript goes on to explain that under these seven there are thirty-six inferior demons corresponding to the decans; these in turn rule over 360 intelligences which govern the degrees of the zodiac. The planets and signs are linked to the cabalistic angels and keys of the Tarot.

Christian's system for individual divination is onomantic, that is to say it uses the person's name as the starting point for deducing his future. A horoscope is worked out by using the letters of his name and the digits of the year in which he was born.

Christian, with his unorthodox system, was one of the few astrologers practising in France at this time. The traditional type of astrology, using careful calculations to determine the positions of the heavenly bodies at the time of a person's birth, had been temporarily lost sight of, mainly because very little had been published on the subject for a century or more, except in England where a revival was taking place. Lévi's knowledge of astrology was slight, as his references to the subject reveal.

In *L'Homme rouge des Tuileries* appears the following passage:

'Only two men in Paris read the future like an open book.

'For these two men there was no invisible world. The invisible exists only in proportion to the sensitivity of our organs.

'The first of these men, taciturn as an eagle in his eyrie, contemplated, in the light of his genius, the plans dictated by his mission of glory.

'The second, a solitary magus, grew older in the study of the infinite and meditated on the algebra of the skies.'

The 'eagle' in this passage was Christian. The 'solitary magus' was Lévi.

In 1864 Lévi moved to number 155 Rue de Sèvres, where he was to remain for the rest of his life. He had a pleasant three-room apartment on the second floor, overlooking some gardens and filled with books, pictures and esoteric trappings. There was a bed set in an alcove, surmounted by a sumptuous canopy on columns and mounted on a velvet-covered step; there were

The Pundit

portraits of Rabelais, Voltaire, Rousseau and St. Sophia; and in a place of honour, on a table next to his desk, stood Wronski's prognometre.

Though, as has been mentioned before, Lévi was somewhat averse to practical magic, he nevertheless seems to have effected a number of feats of quasi-magical healing. One of them is described in a letter to Spedalieri.

'You know how much I adore children; I have a little neighbour of eleven years called Marie, blond, pink-cheeked, who loves me more than her doll. This dear little thing has a weak chest and often coughs during the night. Well, during the cold period that we have just been through her mother, who had put the girl to sleep next to her, heard her cough. The mother was not completely awake; she believed that she saw me beside the bed and said to me: "You, who cure those who are ill, prevent my little one from coughing." I replied (in my dream of course): "Very well. I wish her to stop coughing." At this the mother woke up completely: The little girl was no longer coughing; she did not cough any more that night, nor any subsequent nights, and she is now as fresh as a rose and as happy as a squirrel...

'A few days later I instantly cured of a headache this same lady (the mother of little Marie), by blowing lightly on her forehead and taking her two feet in my hands.

'I am moved by these phenomena, and I would very much like to cure in this way all those who are ill, but I well know that this power does not come from me.'

One of Eliphas Lévi's pupils at this time was a Mrs. Hutchinson, wife of the English Consul in Paris, who took lessons from the Professor of High Magic twice a week for a year. She wrote as follows of her teacher:

'Eliphas Lévi is the only man I have known to have arrived at a state of profound peace. His good humour was indestructible, his gaiety and liveliness inexhaustible. His brilliant, Rabelaisian wit, profound for those who understood the philosophical sense of his words, was equally pleasing to humbler people who only detected amusing jokes in them and succumbed to the charm of this amiable man. Whatever were the faculties of the souls who approached his soul, he put himself within their reach while at the same time elevating them as much as possible without deceiving himself as to the degree to which they could attain. Talking much, without ever venturing an indiscreet word, he displayed at the same time a complete frankness and an extreme reserve; his conscience was a priestly sanctuary.

'Profoundly attached to the Catholic religion, he told me many times: "Catholicism is the only religion whose sacraments are efficacious."

'He initiated me into holy Science without revealing to me what he considered my level to be and without making me experience any fatigue or tension of mind. As soon as he saw my enthusiasm for an idea he led me to consider the opposite idea, thus producing equilibrium. Equilibrium was his aim to such a degree that I sometimes revolted against apparent contradictions. He kept his smiling gravity, making me oscillate between Reason and Faith, knowing well that the seed thus deposited in my mind would bear fruit of its own accord.'

Lévi's reputation brought him not only pupils, but also some very strange visitors. One such is described in a letter from Lévi to Spedalieri:

'Between three and four o'clock in the afternoon I heard someone knock at my door by giving seven little raps, spaced out like this: oo-o-oo-oo. I opened, and a young man, well-dressed and with a distinguished-looking face, entered the room with a slightly sardonic smile and said to me in a familiar tone of voice: "My dear Monsieur Constant, I am delighted to find you at home." Having said this, he went on into my study as though he were in his own house, and sat down in my armchair. "But, Sir," I said "I do not recognise you at all." He laughed "I can well believe it; this is the first time you have seen me, at least in this form. But as for me, I know you well. I know your entire life, past, present and future; it is regulated by the inexorable law of numbers. You are the man of the pentagram, and the years marked by the number five are always fateful ones for you. Look back and judge for yourself: In 1815 your moral life begins, because your memory does not extend further back than that. In 1825 you enter the seminary. In 1835 you leave the seminary and enter into freedom of conscience. In 1845 you publish *La Mère de Dieu*, your first essay in religious synthesis, and you break with the clergy. In 1835 you are free, having left a woman who absorbed you and subjected you to the binary. Mark that, if you had remained together, she would have destroyed you completely or else lost her reason. Then you went to England; well, what is England? It is the *jod* of present-day Europe; you went there to steep yourself again in the virile and active principle. It was there that you saw Apollonius, sad, chafed and tormented as you were then, for this Apollonius that you saw was you yourself; he came out of you and re-entered you, and he is there still.

"You will see him again in this year of 1865, but this time beautiful, radiant and triumphant. The natural end of your life is marked (barring accident) for the year 1875, and if you pass that date you will carry on until 1885. Apollonius, when you saw him, feared the points of swords, and you fear them like him, for at this moment you take me for a madman, like the one who came one time with the intention of assassinating you;[2] you are wondering anxiously if I am going to terminate my extravagant behaviour with some similar action (and here he began to laugh)."'

Startled by these revelations, Lévi asked the man if he was a spirit. To which the visitor replied:

'Spirits are scorpions who pump a cadaverous venom under tombstones. They draw the dead to them, but do not resuscitate them. Soon the earth will be covered with walking corpses. We are in the epoch of death. Louis-Philippe was a Mercury without wings on his temples—he only had them on his feet and he fled. —Napoleon III is a Jupiter without a Sun; after him will come the lame Saturn, the king of dotards and priests,—M. le comte de Chambord . . .'

It transpired that the name of Lévi's visitor was Juliano Capella. In appearance, 'his face resembled portraits of Lord Byron, with less corrections in the lines; he had very white hands, laden with rings, a confident gaze, full of irony, red lips and regular teeth'.

Capella asked if he might come again, but Lévi, who felt a certain antipathy towards this curious individual, showed him politely to the door, and Capella departed, as he said, for a perilous journey. He never reappeared.

In June 1865 appeared *La Science des esprits*, the last of Lévi's books to be published during his lifetime. This book consolidated his reputation among occultists throughout Europe.

August of 1865 found him convalescing from a severe attack of influenza as a guest of Mme de Balzac at the Château de Beauregard. While he was there he gave some lessons in the

Cabala to Mme de Balzac's son-in-law, the Comte de Mniszech.

As he grew older, Lévi began to suffer from violent headaches which rendered him completely inactive while the attacks were on. Nevertheless he still continued to welcome the many people who flocked to his apartment in search of teaching or advice on occult matters.

One day in 1867 he received a visit from two Jersey farmers, a father and son, who claimed that they were victims of attacks by black magic perpetrated by three hostile neighbours. As a result of these attacks animals had died, crops had perished, and the two victims had suffered various personal misfortunes. Lévi did not disappoint them. He gave them a talisman bearing the sign of the microcosm and inscribed with sacred letters, as well as a magnetised photograph, presumably of himself. The two farmers thanked him profusely and promised to write to him and report on the efficacy of his cure.

About two weeks later he received a letter from the son, stating that, after they had left Lévi's presence, his father had sensed that two opposing forces were working on him. He had invoked the aid of Lévi and immediately the good force had triumphed. Other good effects had been noticed, but he complained that they were still afflicted by evil forces on certain days when the moon was full, and asked Lévi for further assistance, which he presumably gave, possibly in the form of another talisman.

At the beginning of 1868 Lévi conceived the idea for a new book on magic and related subjects, to be called *Le Grande Arcane*. The first two parts were finished in June 1868, by which time his headaches and dizzy spells were worsening and forcing him to close his door, even to disciples. By the end of 1868, however, his condition had improved.

Towards the end of 1869 Lévi had a visit from an old friend, the actor Bailleul, who had come to his rescue years ago by offering him a place in a touring company when he was destitute and out of work. Bailleul had read Lévi's work and become an ardent disciple. But his enthusiasm had led him into trouble. He had attempted to read Lévi's verses in the theatres of Rouen and Elbeuf, but had been forbidden to do so and had taken to declaiming them in the cafés. This had aroused the antagonism of the clerical authorities, and he had soon found himself the object of wild accusations, such as that he was an agitator protected by the Jews (on account of the name of his hero). Finally he had come to Paris in the hope of finding a better reception there.

Bailleul is one of the more tragic among the many strange people who passed in and out of Lévi's life. What became of him is a mystery, for Lévi records that one day he simply disappeared without trace.

1. I have not seen the original, but I have examined what I understand is a faithful copy made by one of Eliphas Lévi's disciples. This copy was formerly in the library of Wynn Westcott, a distinguished English occultist and one of the founders of the Hermetic Order of the Golden Dawn. At the time of writing it is in the private collection of Mr. Geoffrey Watkins.
2. This was true. In 1862 a man came to see Eliphas Lévi; he carried under his arm a copy o fthe *Dogme et rituel* and had a dagger in his sleeve. The master spok to him with quiet persuasiveness, and the man went away trembling.

12 The Last Years

The Franco-Prussian War of 1870 and the humiliating defeat of France came as a bitter blow to Eliphas Lévi, who saw France as the future saviour of civilisation. Sitting in his little book-lined refuge in the Rue de Sèvres while the war raged outside, he wrote:

'The palace of Louis XIV has become the home of the king of vandals. Our countryside is devastated, our villages burned, our young men massacred or about to be, our soldiers crushed by Prussia. Paris, once the centre of the world, no longer seems part of it. There is silence in the streets and squares, but for the occasional boom of a cannon. Armed men pass through, some sad and silent, others singing or armed with the happiness of dying. Watching them pass by, one's eyes fill with tears, for most will not return.'[1]

Yet this despair is mixed with a kind of fatalistic optimism. 'All this had to happen', he writes. 'Anybody with any judgement or wisdom could see it coming, and only the short-sighted are surprised. The people are like blind flocks pushed by fate.' And in another passage he says: 'Prussia tells us: "It is force which must prevail over right." And France replies: "No, it is right which must prevail over force."

'If everything is but force and matter, as Dr. Buchner would have it, then Prussia is right. But if force is only the manifestation of the universal intelligence, right exists over and above force, and France is right.

'Force can for a time be put to the service of stupidity, but real and lasting power belongs to reason alone, for complete reason is the same word as God.'

During the siege of Paris, Lévi lived a painful existence. His

The Last Years

disciples in the provinces, who might have sent him supplies, were prevented from doing so by the total isolation of the capital. But in spite of his plight, he did his best to help raise the morale of the city. He addressed public meetings and went out in the evenings to mingle with the crowds and encourage the patriotism of his fellow citizens.

No sooner was the siege of Paris over than the Commune began, which pleased Lévi even less, as he had by this time lost most of his sympathy for revolutionary political activity. After the Commune had collapsed and the Versailles troops had entered the city someone thought they saw a shot fired from Lévi's window. An officer burst into his apartment and threatened to have him shot. The Professor of High Magic greeted him calmly, explaining that he was a philosopher and not an assassin and inviting him to search the apartment. Nothing was found, and the officer, impressed by Lévi's calm sincerity, ordered his men to withdraw.

By then Lévi had no resources whatever, but he was saved from starvation by one of his pupils, Mary Gebhard, who invited him to stay with her at her home in Germany. He stayed there for about two months in the summer of 1871. Frau Gebhard was of Irish parentage and was the wife of a rich German Industrialist.

On his return to France, Lévi learned of the death of Mme Spedalieri, which had caused the Baron such bitter grief that he had become disillusioned with all his former religious beliefs. In spite of a long poem of consolation written by Lévi, Baron Spedalieri remained plunged in profound despair, and from then on his communications with Lévi were rare.

By now Lévi's periods of illness were becoming increasingly frequent, but in between them he continued to entertain his followers and to write. *L'Evangile de la science* was finished in 1873, and was the only work that he ever re-read and corrected. It was followed soon afterwards by a short work called *La Religion de la science*.

His main cause of grief at this period was the behaviour of Baron Spedalieri, whose mind had been poisoned by the death of his wife and whose friendship with his former teacher had turned to open aversion. Nevertheless he was consoled by the continuing devotion of such close disciples as Frau Gebhard and Jacques Charrot. The latter, who had originally been introduced to Lévi by Spedalieri, was later to form a Rosicrucian group at Lyons.

Lévi also received accolades from the literary world. One day he was visited by Mme Judith Mendès, wife of the novelist Catulle Mendès and daughter of Théophile Gautier. Like her father she had made a reputation in literature and wrote poetry and novels under the name of Judith Gautier.

Catulle Mendès had read the works of Lévi and was enthused by them. He invited Lévi to his house and there introduced him to Victor Hugo, who was also familiar with the writings of the magus.

The year 1874 saw the completion of Lévi's book *Le Livre d'Abraham le Juif*, composed for Count Georges de Mniszech in gratitude for the material help that the Count had given him. In the same year Lévi made a final attempt at a reconciliation with Spedalieri. The Baron had, however, departed for a long voyage abroad and did not return until after Lévi's death. The loss of Spedalieri's material help was to some extent compensated for by the generosity of Mniszech. The following year, 1875, Lévi finished his last manuscript, *Le Catéchisme de la paix*.

As the year 1875 wore on, his condition became steadily worse. From March he was forced to stay in his room. Dropsy had also developed, and gangrene had begun to attack his feet. He could not tolerate being in bed and spent the long painful nights in an armchair, in which he was to die.

His friends were constantly with him. His physician, Dr. Wattelet, did everything possible to relieve his condition, and an old friend, Mlle Anna Bornet, acted as a devoted nurse, until an attack of bronchitis removed her and her place was taken by Edouard-Adolphe Pascal, son of Mme Legrand who had helped Lévi years earlier during his imprisonment at Sainte-Pélagie.

Eliphas Lévi faced these last agonising days with stoicism and courage, and preserved his mental faculties to the last. Mrs. Hutchinson, who visited him towards the end, left the following account:-

'He was seated near his bed. On the wall, which was hung with beautiful tapestries, there stood out a beautiful Christ which he looked at often . . . He was very calm and full of serenity. He knew for certain that he was going to die, for his eyes took on an ecstatic expression that I had never seen in them before, when, pointing to the Christ, he said to me: "He told me that he would send the Consoler: the Spirit, and now I wait for the Spirit, the Holy Spirit!" Nothing can describe the religious radiance, the profound faith that his look expressed.[3]

And so Lévi waited confidently for the Paraclete. In May he made his last will and testament. To the Comte de Mniszech he left his manuscripts, books and scientific instruments, incliding the prognometre. Furthermore he stipulated that no one was to touch the manuscripts but the Count, his wife, the Count Braszynsky and Mme Gustaf Gebhard. Pascal was given the right to take his pick of Lévi's non-scientific books, curios and *objets d'art*. To his sister, Mme Pauline Bousselet, he gave all his pictures and devotional objects, explaining that he was unable to leave her anything of greater value 'because of my brother-in-law', with whom he presumably had had some difference. His clothes and linen were given to a community of nuns in the Rue Saint-Jacques. What remained of his belongings was to be sold and the proceeds divided between the friends who had cared for him in his last hours.

An old pupil, Mme Jobert, visited him on 29th May and, judging the end to be near, went off to find a priest. After being refused at one church she went to a Jesuit chapel in the Rue de Sèvres and persuaded a priest by the name of Father Lejeune to come. He came the next day, but was unable to gain entry and returned the day after, 31st May, when he had a long talk with Lévi and, in all probability, gave him absolution.

The priest's visit was timely for, shortly after his departure, at two o'clock in the afternoon, Eliphas Lévi died.

M. Pascal arranged for him to be photographed on his death bed, and the funeral service was held two days later at the church of Saint-François Xavier, in the Boulevard des Invalides. The burial took place at the cemetery of Ivry. A small group of devotees was gathered round the grave, and a speech was given by Lévi's friend Henri Deyrolle. He spoke of Lévi's courage in renouncing the priesthood, of his personal charity, of his efforts to unite science and religion, and of the great writings he had left. The panegyric ended with these words:

'Farewell Constant! Honest and loyal soul who never knew charity and yet practised it with dignity; rest in peace and may the sincere grief of your friends be the proof of the void which you have left among them.

'Adieu! Adieu! And perhaps *au revoir!*'[4]

---

1. *Les Portes de l'avenir. Dernières paroles d'un voyant* (1870). This unpublished manuscript formerly belonged to Wynn Westcott and at the time of writing is in the possession of Mr. Geoffrey Watkins.
2. Ibid.
3. *L'Initiation*, Vol. XVI, No. 11, August 1892.
4. Paul Chacornac, *Eliphas Lévi*.

13 Eliphas Lévi: An Assessment

The generation of occultists that followed Lévi regarded him as its guide and master. And it was not only in France that his name was revered. Kenneth Mackenzie, as we have seen, came to Paris to sit at his feet, MacGregor Mathers called him a 'great qabalist', and Aleister Crowley believed himself to be a reincarnation of Lévi. All of these men were involved, at various times, in the Hermetic Order of the Golden Dawn which had a profound influence on the development of occultism in the West. Lévi, therefore, can be considered as one of the key figures in the history of modern occultism.

There must, however, be many people who, knowing of Lévi's position in the occult pantheon, have read his works with a feeling of extreme disappointment. Much of what he wrote is turgid, confused and naive. The reader who braves the chaos of Lévi's writing soon finds himself baffled by the contradictions which beset the man and his work. He succeeded in being at the same time a radical and a traditionalist, a rationalist and a believer in the supra-rational, an occultist and an orthodox Catholic. His writings teem with apparent inconsistencies. To attempt to extract a coherent teaching from Lévi's books is like trying to fit together a jigsaw puzzle whose pieces are constantly changing shape and colour. A. E. Waite, one of Lévi's main exegetists and also a Golden Dawn member, eventually gave up in despair, concluding that his writings represented 'the shifting moods of a brilliant mind which had no certain anchorage, outside a hypothesis for explaining certain phenomena.'[1] But in order to evaluate Lévi it is necessary to understand that he did not develop his occult philosophy suddenly; he evolved towards it, navigating his way through misty regions and across perilous seas—it is not surprising that he changed course several times. Finally he did succeed in finding, if not an anchorage, then a method and a point of view. But before assessing his contribution to occultism we must also consider in turn two other aspects of Lévi: the radical polemicist and the literary stylist, both of whom deserve modest recognition.

As a radical thinker Lévi introduced no very original ideas. But he was in many ways ahead of his time and he differed from many of his fellow socialists in adhering firmly to Catholicism and in attempting to base his political philosophy on Christian principles. Though he was not capable of constructing a profound political theory he did have the ability to see certain truths and to point them out in a succinct and pithy way. For example, in *Les Portes de l'avenir*, he says: 'Liberty, Equality, Fraternity! Three words which seem to shine and are in fact full of shadow! Three truths which, in coming together, form a triple lie! For they destroy one another. Liberty necessarily manifests inequality, and equality is a levelling process that does not permit liberty, because the heads that rise higher than others must always be forced down to the mean. The attempt to establish equality and liberty together produce an interminable struggle . . . that makes fraternity among men impossible.'

When, however, it comes to drawing up any kind of political programme, Eliphas Lévi becomes naive and extravagant. In *Les Portes de l'avenir*, he recommends a series of reforms, including the following:

'That public scandals be no longer tolerated.

'That women without estate who live idle and luxurious lives be taught to work in houses of correction.

'That honest women be protected by law and be admitted to any job which they can do as well as a man, so they no longer have to resort to prostitution.

'That men who live off prostitutes be imprisoned.

'That the death penalty be replaced by a longer, harder punishment: life imprisonment in a dark hole without human contact and only bread and water to eat and drink.

'That there be a federation of all peoples and that disagreements between nations be settled by arbitration, not war.

'That men reduced to begging be judged: if it is through their own fault they should be imprisoned, if through the fault of others, Society should make amends.'

Apart from the somewhat inhumane suggestion about replacing the death penalty, most of these ideas would be totally impossible to put into effect. Some of his recommendations are, however, more sensible and far-seeing. He suggests, for example, that primary education be free and obligatory. He also says that the election of Church dignitaries should be by universal suffrage—a very revolutionary proposal coming from one who professed strict obedience to the Pope.

Les Portes de l'avenir was, of course, written towards the end of his life. His earlier political writings such as *Le Testament de la liberté* contain very little constructive political thought and a great deal of rhetoric. They represent impassioned reaction to injustice rather than a coherent political philosophy. Nevertheless they helped to stir up movements for reform at a time when they were much needed, and the fact that he went to prison three times for his views shows that he was sincere.

The quality of his literary style is as erratic as that of his political thought; it ranges from empty verbosity to passages of power and simplicity. There is no doubt that he is at his worst when trying to write in a sensational manner about occult matters. The following passage, from chapter 18 of the *Rituel de la haute magie*, is an example:

'Let us now adventure in Thessaly, the country of enchantments. Here was Apuleius beguiled, like the companions of Ulysses, and underwent a humiliating metamorphosis. Here all is magical—the birds that fly, the insects humming in the grass, even the trees and flowers. Here in the moonlight are brewed those potions which compel love; here spells are devised by stryges to render them young and lovely like Charites. O all ye youths, beware!'

This kind of turgid outpouring contrasts with some of the passages in his later philosophical works in which a genuine piety is reflected in a clear and unaffected prose, marked by the skilful use of paradox. In *Libres pensées sur des idées nouvelles*[2] he writes:

'Pious men can commit faults and even crimes, for they know how to expiate them with grandeur: impious men do everything fruitlessly and basely. There are a myriad vile honest men who are not worth a single noble rogue.'

But these flashes of insight and literary quality are not enough to earn Lévi any lasting importance as a writer. It is as an occult philosopher that he will be remembered, and it is here that he becomes most difficult to assess. Was he, as Waite said, 'an occult philosopher for whom there is no occultism'?[3] Or did he have a genuine teaching?

One of the things that perplexed Waite was Lévi's repeated insistence that his occult philosophy was based on faith, science and reason—a combination which seemed incompatible to Waite. But Lévi, in *La Clé des grandes mystères*, Part I article 3, explains his position quite clearly:

'Faith, being the aspiration to the unknown, the object of faith is absolutely and necessarily this one thing—Mystery.

'In order to formulate its aspirations, faith is forced to borrow aspirations and images from the known.

'But she specialises in the employment of these forms by placing them together in a manner which, in the known order of things, is impossible. Such is the profound reason for the apparent absurdity of symbolism . . .

'The formula of a mystery excludes necessarily the very intelligence of that formula, so far as it is borrowed from the world of known things; for, if one understood it, it would express the known and not the unknown.

'It would then belong to science, and no longer to religion, that is to say, to faith.

'The object of faith is a mathematical problem whose x escapes the procedures of our algebra.

'Absolute mathematics prove only the necessity, and, in consequence, the existence of this unknown which we represent by the untranslatable x.'

In Lévi's system, therefore, there is room for both science and faith, provided that each recognises its true province.

Waite was equally puzzled by Lévi's professed obedience to the Catholic Church, but here again Lévi has a sophisticated defence of his position. In his introduction to Part I of *La Clé des grandes mystères*, he argues that there will always be a gap between the known and the unknown which science cannot bridge. Mankind needs an act of faith to bridge the gap in a meaningful way. But faith must be directed so as to give human life a moral meaning and purpose, and for this 'it is necessary to have the absolute and invariable affirmation of a dogma preserved by an authorised hierarchy. It is necessary to have an efficacious cult, giving, with an absolute faith, a substantial realisation to the symbols of belief.' The priest-

10 Eliphas Lévi in 1862

11 Frontispiece to Lévi's *Clés majeures et clavicules de Salomon*, depicting the Apocalyptic angel. This is a copy made from Lévi's own hand-illustrated original

hood, Lévi says, who are the guardians of this dogma, must be respected.

'The priest, *qua* priest, is always the representative of God. Of little account are the faults or even the crimes of man. When Alexander VI consecrated his bishops, it was not the poisoner who laid his hands upon them, it was the Pope . . . At all times and in all places there have been liars and criminals, but in the hierarchical and divinely authorised Church there have never been, and there never will be, either bad popes or bad priests. "Bad" and "priest" form an oxymoron.'

This is, of course, a highly dangerous doctrine, and it seems likely that Lévi did not believe in it wholeheartedly. Throughout his writings he gives the impression of presenting certain opinions for public consumption and withholding certain others which might be dangerous to the uninitiated. In certain of his manuscript writings he criticised the Church and also expressed his respect for other religions. The key to his real point of view is to be found in *Libres pensées sur des idées nouvelles* where he says that there is an exterior and an interior morality. The exterior morality is the observance of laws and customs; the interior morality is piety which, he declares, 'is absolutely independent of religious formulas and priestly prescriptions'. Observance of the exterior forms is no use without interior piety.

But Lévi was always very cautious when it came to ideas that might conflict with Catholicism, and he had a peculiar trick of appearing to bow to orthodoxy but in fact leaving the way open for whatever opinion he wished to profess. An example is the following passage in chapter 2 of the *Rituel*.

'I am aware that Christianity has for ever suppressed Ceremonial Magic, and that it proscribes the evocations and sacrifices of the old world. It is not therefore our intention to furnish a new basis for their existence by revealing their antique mysteries after a lapse of so many centuries . . . From the standpoint of the tribe of Lévi, the exercise of High Magic must be considered as a usurpation of the priesthood; and the same reason has caused the proscription of Operative Magic by every official cultus. To demonstrate the natural foundation of the marvellous and to produce it at will is to annihilate for the vulgar mind that convincing evidence from miracles which is claimed by each religion as its exclusive property and its final argument.'

This passage is equivocal in the extreme. A priest reading it

K

would probably be reassured that the author shared the orthodox view in outlawing ceremonial magic. But in fact what Lévi seems to be saying is this: all so-called miracles are caused by perfectly explicable phenomena. And these phenomena can be manipulated by anyone who knows the techniques of magic. Therefore, to the initiated, magic is a marvellous demonstration of the unity of all religions; but for an uninitiated person it could merely lead to rejection of his own particular creed. Therefore it is prudent for the adept not to reveal the innermost secrets of magic to the public.

In his letters to Spedalieri, he is less guarded about expressing his views on orthodox religion and the Catholic Church. The following letter is especially revealing:

'I fail to understand how our talk the other day could make you fear a whirl of reactionary Catholicism, nor, above all, what relation there is between that grand book the *Zohar*, which I read to you, and the rosary, which you are almost afraid to use. I ought to have a rosary somewhere or other; it is a respectable child's toy. The Church gives it instead of a book to those who cannot read and to those who are afraid to think. Are you among the latter? But why should you be? The rosary is the little turning-table of prayer; it represents the indulgence and indulgences of the church for the little ones, the aged, the idiots who do what they can and who only know just enough to be always stammering out to God the perpetual syllables of childhood; papa, mamma. Without blushing, nay, even with a certain tenderness of tears, I could join myself to the almost baa-ing prayer of this flock of invalids and little ones. A rosary had no greater terrors than a *grimoire*, and I do not think these are old-fogeyish or reactionary opinions.'

For Lévi, the trappings of orthodoxy played a part in that they supplied the religious needs of the masses. But they could be dispensed with by the elect who had the intelligence and boldness to wish to go beyond the narrow confines of dogma.

How much Lévi himself knew of the magical tradition has often been disputed. Judging by his published works one might easily conclude that he knew next to nothing and covered up his ignorance by pretending that he was holding back secrets through caution; but an examination of what he wrote for his disciples and a careful reading of his published writings show that he did have a teaching of sorts.

Much of what Lévi wrote was based on ideas that were common currency in western occultism as expounded in the works of such writers as Trithemius, Paracelsus and Cornelius Agrippa. All the traditional notions on which magic is based are to be found in his work: that man is a microcosm of the universe; that all things are bound together by a network of inner correspondences; that there are entities on a different plane which can be evoked and manipulated by the use of signs and talismans. But Lévi did not adhere very strictly to traditional magical doctrine. He was quite willing to change the accepted scheme where it suited his ideas. For example, traditional cabalism holds that there are four worlds emanating from God in the following order of descent: first comes Atziluth, the world of emanations; second, Briah, the world of creation; third, Jetzirah, the world of formation; and fourth, Assiah, the world of action in which we live. In chapter 3 of the *Doctrine* he gets the order right: 'The Jews term these three series or degrees in the progress of spirits [advancing from lower to higher], ASSIAH, YETZIRAH, BRIAH ... The supreme circle was named ATZILUTH.' But in a frontispiece to the *Clés majeures et clavicules de Salomon*, Lévi shows Briah as the lowest world with Jetzirah above it and Atziluth on top, leaving out Assiah altogether. This must have been a deliberate departure from orthodoxy, because Lévi's letters to Spedalieri show that he was very familiar with the main cabalistic texts. Another interesting point on which he departs from traditional cabalism is revealed in a letter to Spedalieri containing the following passage:

'The word you could not read in one of my previous letters is the word *science*—knowledge. It is the first of the gifts of the Holy Spirit, and corresponds to faith in the enumeration of the seven Christian virtues.

'You know that Knowledge is not one of the Sephiroth, but is the mirror wherein are concentrated the rays from them all. It is named Daath.'

The letter contains a diagram of the tree of life showing Daath placed in the middle of the abyss between the first and second triads. What is interesting about this passage is that Daath is not stressed by the old cabalistic writers and plays little part in the traditional system, being regarded as a 'false sephira'. Modern occult groups using the Cabala, however, lay great emphasis on it, and this may date from Lévi.

But Lévi's most startling innovation was in connecting the Cabala with the Tarot. Modern occultists take this connection so much for granted that it tends to be forgotten that there is absolutely no historical evidence that the two were in any way related. Court de Gébelin does not mention the Cabala in his section on the cards; and Etteilla, though he was a practitioner both of the Cabala and the Tarot, did not make any systematic attempt to relate them. Lévi, therefore, appears to have been the first to do so. In his *Doctrine et rituel de la haute magie* he connects the twenty-two trumps with the twenty-two letters of the Hebrew alphabet and the four suits with the four letters of the tetragrammaton or Name of God and the ten numbered cards of each suit with the ten Sephiroth. In chapter 22 of the *Rituel* he pours scorn on the superficiality of Etteilla's works, then goes on:

'The true initiates who were Etteilla's contemporaries, the Rosicrucians for example and the Martinists, were in possession of the true Tarot, as a work of Saint-Martin proves, where the divisions are those of the Tarot, as also this quotation from an enemy of the Rosicrucians: "They pretend to the possession of a volume from which they can learn anything discoverable in other books which exist now or may be produced at any future period. This volume is their criterion, in which they find the prototype of everything that exists by the facility which it offers for analysing, making abstractions, forming a species of intellectual world and creating all possible things. See the philosophical, theosophical, microcosmic cards." (*Conspiracy against the Catholic Religion and Sovereigns*, by the author of *The Veil Raised for the Curious*. Paris, Crapard, 1792).'

None of this constitutes evidence for the antiquity of the Tarot as an occult system, much less its connection with the Cabala. The mere fact that Saint-Martin divided his book up along the lines of the Tarot proves nothing at all and was almost certainly coincidence. The quotation from the anti-Rosicrucian polemic is interesting, but also proves nothing as it dates from after the appearance of Court de Gébelin's *Monde primitif* from which the Rosicrucians attacked by the writer could well have derived their claims about the Tarot.

Clearly Lévi was in possession of no pre-Court de Gébelin material connecting the Cabala and the Tarot. The connection was his invention. It is of course an attractive idea which lends itself to endless refinements, such as the supposed resemblance between the figures on the cards and the Hebrew letters. Lévi states, for instance, that the first of the trumps, the Juggler, is based on the shape of the letter Aleph to which it corresponds. The myth of the cabalistic Tarot was taken up by Papus, Oswald Wirth and most of the later writers on the Tarot. But it was Lévi who started it off.

In addition to changing parts of the magical tradition, Lévi also brought in certain new ideas, one of the most important being his theory of the 'Astral Light' or 'Universal Agent', which he probably derived from Mesmer. He used this to explain all magical workings and apparitions.

'The primordial light,' he wrote, 'which is the vehicle of all ideas, is the mother of all forms . . . Hence the Astral Light, or terrestrial fluid, which we call the Great Magnetic Agent, is saturated with all kinds of images and reflections.'[4]

This Astral Light, he says in another passage, is a plastic medium upon which thoughts and images can be imprinted. 'The soul, by acting on this light through its volitions, can dissolve it or coagulate it, project it or withdraw it. It is the mirror of the imagination and of dreams. It reacts upon the nervous system and thus produces the movements of the body . . . It can take all forms evoked by thought, and, in the transitory coagulations of its radiant particles, appear to the eyes; it can even offer a sort of resistance to the touch.'[5]

Since thoughts can be imprinted on the Light, it follows that by the use of the imagination the Light can be manipulated. The omnipotence of the imagination, says Lévi 'belongs exclusively to the domain of magic'.[6] He continues: 'Imagination is in effect like the soul's eye; therein forms are outlined and preserved; thereby we behold the reflections of the invisible world; it is the glass of visions and the apparatus of magical life. By its intervention we heal diseases, modify the seasons, warn off death from the living and raise the dead to life, because it is the imagination which exalts the will and gives it power over the Universal Agent.'

But in magic, imagination has to operate according to established rules. Otherwise the magician will not make contact with the forces already implanted in the Astral Light. Hence he uses well-known signs. 'The empire of will over Astral the Light, which is the physical soul of the four elements, is represented in Magic by the Pentagram . . . The elementary spirits are subservient to this sign when employed with understanding.'[7]

But the purpose of Lévi's magic is not to take the magician into an agreeable realm of fantasy, nor to give him control over spirits. The basic function of magic, according to Lévi, is to enable the magician to direct his will more effectively. 'Would you reign over yourselves and others? Learn how to will. How can one learn to will? This is the first arcanum of magical initiation . . .'[8]

In order for the will to act freely it must master the Astral Light instead of being influenced by it. The Astral Light consists of two opposing currents respresented, in one sense, by the masculine and feminine poles; and human being are unwittingly swayed by the ebb and flow of these currents. As a first step, therefore, to gaining control over the Light, the magician must attain equilibrium between the two. He must strike a balance between masculine and feminine, positive and negative, dark and light. This is the meaning of the strange figure illustrated at the beginning of the *Rituel*, a creature with a goat's head and legs, a woman's breasts and a male phallus.

The idea of equilibrium runs through all magical operations. The magician is always seeking for the points where opposing forces counterbalance each other. He seeks to balance not only the two currents of the Astral Light, but also the forces of the four elements by making obeisance to the entities that govern them, represented by Salamanders, Gnomes, Sylphs and Undines, who correspond respectively to Fire, Earth, Air and Water. All magical operations, says Lévi, must begin with a consecration of the four elements. Formulae for carrying out this ceremony are given in chapter 4 of the *Rituel*. Balance is also represented by the Cabalistic Tree of Life, which has a masculine pillar, a feminine pillar and a central, mediating pillar.

A magical operation acts on the magician himself, using outward signs to bring about inner changes. Astrological symbols, for example, can be used for this purpose. 'The seven planets are, in fact, the hieroglyphic symbols of the keyboard of our affections. To compose talismans of the Sun, Moon or Saturn, is to attach the will magnetically to signs corresponding to the chief powers of the soul . . . The analogous metals, animals, plants and perfumes are auxiliaries to this end.'[9]

Lévi always professed to discourage his pupils from performing practical magical evocations. Evidently he had discovered the dangers of such procedures when he himself had called up Apollonius of Tyana in London. When, therefore, he taught his pupils to make talismans and perform cabalistic rituals it was to enable them to manipulate forces within themselves.

One other aspect of his teaching must be mentioned and that is his preoccupation with prophecies. When he wrote *Le Testament de la liberté* he believed that the reign of the Paraclete was about to begin, but he later became attracted towards the prognostications of Trithemius as set out in his book *De Septem Secundeis*. Trithemius's theory was that the world is ruled successively by seven Archangels, each of whom governs for 354 years and 4 months. The seven angels are: Orifiel, Anael, Zachariel, Raphael, Samael, Gabriel and Michael. According to Trithemius's calculations, the reign of Michael would begin in 1879. Writing in 1855, Lévi declared: 'We see therefore, according to this calculation, that in 1879—or in twenty-four years' time—a universal empire will be founded and will secure peace to the world. This empire will be political and religious; it will offer the solution of all the problems agitated in our own days, and will endure for 354 years and 4 months, after which it will be succeeded by the return of Orifiel, an epoch of silence and might. The coming universal empire, being under the reign of the Sun, will belong to him who holds the keys of the East, which are now being disputed by the princes of the world's four quarters. But intelligence and activity are the forces which rule the Sun in the superior kingdoms, and the nation which possesses at this time the initiative of intelligence and life will have also the keys of the East and will establish the universal kingdom. To do this it may have to undergo previously a cross and a martyrdom analogous to those of the Man-God; but, dead or living, its spirit will prevail among nations; all peoples will acknowledge and follow in four-and-twenty years the standard of France, ever victorious or miraculously raised from the dead.'[10]

Later Lévi seems to have discarded this scheme in favour of a different system of rulerships. In his *Clés majeures et clavicules de Salomon*, he sets out the theory that the earth is ruled over by a succession of beings who are called Mitatron-Sarpanim.[11] Enoch, he says, was the first of these, then came Elias, then Jesus.

Each Mitatron, according to this theory, has two reigns, returning to earth after traversing all the planets of the solar system. The return of Enoch and Elias, therefore, will precede the second coming of Jesus.

At times of decomposition and corruption, Lévi says, inferior spirits appear, always announcing and preceding the arrival on earth of a regenerating spirit in the form of the solar Mitatron. He continues with the following interesting passage:

'Talking tables and rapping spirits have announced the return of Enoch. He will return when the papacy has lost all authority in the world and the Kabbalistic sciences are flourishing once again. The advent of Elias will closely follow that of Enoch, then Jesus, the Saviour of the World, will come to the earth a second time.

'He will be preceded by the Anti-Christ whose mission will be to prepare the great temporal empire revealed in the Gospel.

'The astral light will provide elementary spirits. A new creation is being prepared.

'Already the keys of Solomon have been rediscovered and the mysteries of high masonry explained.

'A school, whose beginnings are still obscure and almost invisible, will form in the Slavic world, in Germany and in France.

'In a century this school will have 7000 adepts, and its last grand master will be Enoch.

'Enoch will appear in the year 2000 of the Christian world, then the Messianism of which he will be the precursor will flourish on the earth for 1000 years.'

Readers of this passage will no doubt be tempted to read their own theories into these prophecies. The statement about the mysterious school which was to have 7000 adepts must, in particular, have been the subject of much speculation.

What then is Lévi's significance in the history of occultism? It is this: that he helped to change the popular concept of magic. Whereas magic had hitherto been regarded by most people as a means of manipulating the forces of nature and by many as a dangerous superstition, Lévi presented it as a way of drawing the will through certain channels and turning the magician into a more fully realised human being. This has, of course, always been the real purpose of theurgy as opposed to the cruder forms of magic, and Lévi was not the first to express it in writing, but he was the first to popularise it on a large scale.

An assessment of Lévi would not be complete without a mention of his personal qualities. Apart from his rather shabby treatment of his mistress Eugénie, the mother of the son he never saw, there seems to have been little that was ignoble in Lévi's life. All testament points to his having been a man of courage, honesty, warmth and compassion. It was these qualities, as much as his teaching, that endeared him to his pupils.

1. Biographical Preface to *Transcendental Magic, Its Doctrine and Ritual*.
2. I examined this unpublished work in the form of a handwritten copy taken by an unknown person from a manuscript which belonged to Wynn Westcott in the Golden Dawn library.
3. Biographical Preface to *Transcendental Magic, Its Doctrine and Ritual*.
4. *Doctrine*, ch. 5.
5. *Clés des grandes mystères*, Part II.
6. *Doctrine*, ch. 1.
7. *Doctrine*, ch. 5.
8. *Rituel*, ch. 1.
9. *Doctrine* ch. 7.
10. *Rituel*, ch. 21.
11. Lévi uses this spelling instead of the normal one, which is 'Metatron'.

PART THREE

Towards the Kingdom of the Paraclete

14 The Heirs of Eliphas Lévi

One of the topics of conversation in occult circles in 1884 was an interesting phenomenon which had appeared in Paris in the form of the ample frame of Mme Blavatsky, whose Theosophical Society was by now well established in America and who had come to preach her gospel in France. By the time of her arrival a French branch of the society had already been formed and was run by Lady Caithness, Duchesse de Pomar, a rich woman who believed that she was a reincarnation of Mary Queen of Scots. Bringing theosophy to France was rather like taking coals to Newcastle, and the society never met with much success among the French. Nevertheless, it gained enough adherents to hold regular meetings and publish a journal.

In 1888 the *Petit bulletin Théosophique* carried a report of a speech that had been given to the Isis lodge of the society by none other than Colonel Olcott, the co-founder and Mme Blavatsky's right-hand man. In his address the Colonel announced that he had taken the unusual step of designating two Isis members as delegates to the headquarters of the society at Adyar, in India.

'The election of M. Thurmann and M. Encausse to the General Council of the Theosophical Society,' he said 'is simply a personal distinction which confers on neither the right to interfere in the affairs of Isis, nor the right to interfere in those of the 150 present branches of the Theosophical Society . . .

'I profit by the occasion to confirm that M. Encausse is a good and regular member of the Theosophical Society. His application, dated October 1887 and countersigned by M. Dramard and M. Gaboriau, was agreed by me on 2nd November of the same year.'

This M. Encausse was later to leave the Theosophical Society and to become one of the leaders of a new occult movement and a prolific author on esoteric subjects. The world was to know him under his pen-name of Papus. At the time of Colonel Olcott's speech he was a young medical student. Because of his importance as an occultist, some account of his life is called for here.

He was born on 13th July 1865 at Corogna in Spain, the son of a French father and Spanish mother. After leaving school he enrolled in the faculty of medicine at Paris and in 1884 published his first written work. Entitled *Hypothèses*, it was an entirely down-to-earth piece of writing and contained no hint to his later occult interests.

His conversion away from a materialistic view of life is described in a short memoir entitled *Comment je devins mystique*, from which I quote the following revealing passage:

'They told me: "These mineral salts, this earth, having slowly decomposed and been assimilated by the root of the vegetable, will *evolve* and become the cells of the vegetable. This vegetable, in turn, transformed by the secretions and fermentations of the animal's stomach . . . will be transformed into the cells of this animal." But reflection soon caused me to understand that they had forgotten one of the most important factors in the problem.

'Yes, the mineral does evolve, and its essential principles become the material elements of the vegetable cell. But on one condition, which is that the physico-chemical forces and the sun itself come to the aid of this phenomenon, that is to say, on condition that the superior forces by their evolution *sacrifice* themselves to the evolution of the inferior forces.

'Yes, the digested vegetable soon becomes the material basis of the animal cell, but on condition that blood and the nervous force (that is to say, the superior forces in the ladder of evolution) come to sacrifice themselves for the evolution of the vegetable cell . . .

'In short, each step in the series, each evolution demands the sacrifice of one, and more often of two, superior forces. The doctrine of evolution is incomplete. It represents only one side of the facts and ignores the other. It brings to light the law of *the struggle for life*, but it forgets *the law of sacrifice* which dominates all phenomena.

'Possessed by this idea which I had just brought to light and to which I held firmly, I resolved to deepen my discovery as best

The Heirs of Eliphas Lévi

I could and I passed my days in the Bibliothèque Nationale . . . To the study of alchemical works, old magical grimoires and the elements of the Hebrew language, I devoted the years that my colleagues spent in studying for their examinations, and from then on my future was mapped out. This discovery which I believed I had made, I rediscovered in the works of Louis Lucas, then in the Hermetic texts, then in Indian traditions and the Cabala. Only the language was different; where we write HCL, the alchemists would depict a *green lion*, and where we write

$$2\ HCL + Fe = Fe\ CL_2 + H_2$$

the alchemists would portray a warrior (Mars, Iron) devoured by a green lion (acid).

'In short, these famous grimoires were as easy for me to read as the much more obscure works of our pedantic chemists of today. And, what was more, I learned to wield that marvellous *analogical method*, so little known to modern philosophers, which allows all sciences to be grouped into a single synthesis and which shows that the ancients were purely and simply libelled from the scientific point of view by the infinite historical ignorance of the professors of today.'

This passage eloquently expresses the excitement of any young man or woman when catching first glimpse of the magical universe. Such experiences often lead the discoverer to lose himself in fantasy, but Encausse, in spite of his occult studies, perhaps because of them, presented a brilliant thesis for his Doctorate of Medicine, and was accordingly given the degree in 1894.

By that time he had already achieved a certain fame as an occult writer under the pseudonym of Papus. In 1891, at the age of twenty-six, he had published a weighty volume entitled *Traité méthodique de science occulte*, which became a classic of late-nineteenth-century occultism. In the speech accompanying the conferring of the degree Professor Mathias-Duval of the Faculty of Medicine paid the following tribute to his student:

'M. Encausse, you are no ordinary student. On philosophical and medical subjects and above all on difficult matters which I cannot dwell upon here, under your name or under a pseudonym that you have made famous, you have written works of high value, and I am proud to be the examiner of your thesis.'[1]

Having qualified as a doctor, Papus, following the example of

Paracelsus, declared that he knew nothing and decided to remedy his ignorance by a tour of Europe. Having visited England, Holland and Belgium, studying homoeopathy and other unorthodox medical systems, he made his way to Russia where he was already famous enough for a Russian edition of his *Traité méthodique* to be published. He was introduced to the Imperial family and enjoyed a certain notoriety which is brought out in a story related by M. Paléologue, the French Ambassador, and published in the *Revue des deux mondes* of 15th March 1922, though the piece must have been written shortly after Papus's death in 1916.

'Newspapers, which have recently arrived from France via Scandinavia, announce that Papus died on October 25.

'I swear that this news did not draw my attention for one instant; but it caused great consternation, I was told, among people who had formerly known the "spiritual master", as his enthusiastic disciples called him between themselves.

'M. R . . . , who is both an adept of spiritualism and a devotee of Rasputin, explained this consternation to me as being due to a strange prophecy which is worth noting: namely, that the death of Papus presaged nothing less than the imminent ruin of Tsarism. And this is the explanation.

'At the beginning of October, 1905, Papus was summoned to St. Petersburg by certain of his faithful, highly placed, who had great need of his brilliance in the formidable crisis that Russia was passing through at that time. The disaster of Manchuria had provoked, in all corners of the empire, revolutionary troubles. bloody strikes, and scenes of pillage, massacre and arson. The Emperor lived in a state of cruel anxiety, unable to choose between contradictory pieces of advice with which his family, his ministers, his dignitaries, his generals and all his court plagued him daily. Some impressed upon him that he had no right to renounce the ancestral autocracy and exhorted him not to flinch from employing the necessary rigours of an implacable reaction; others counselled him to recognise the exigencies of modern times and to inaugurate loyally a constitutional regime.

'The same day that Papus disembarked at St. Petersburg a riot spread terror in Moscow, while a mysterious syndicate proclaimed a general railway strike.

'The magus was immediately called to the Imperial Palace. After a quick conversation with the Emperor and Empress he organised for the next day a grand ritual of incantation and necromancy. Besides the sovereigns, only one person was present at this secret liturgy, a young aide-de-camp of His Majesty, Captain Mandryka, who is today a Major-General and the governor of Tiflis. By an intense condensation of his will and by a prodigious exaltation of his fluidic dynamism, the "spiritual master" succeeded in evoking the ghost of the very pious Tsar Alexander III; unquestionable signs attested to the presence of the invisible spectre.

'Despite the emotion which rung his heart, Nicolas II gravely asked his father whether or not he should react against the current of liberalism which threatened to engulf Russia. The phantom replied:

'"You should, cost what it may, crush the Revolution which is beginning; but it will revive one day, and the degree of its violence will be greater in proportion as the repression of today will have been more rigorous. It does not matter! Courage, my son! Do not cease to struggle!"

'While the dazed sovereigns considered this overwhelming prediction, Papus affirmed that his magical power permitted him to exorcise the predicted catastrophe, but that the efficacy of his exorcism would cease as soon as he himself was no longer "on the material plane". Then he solemnly executed the rites of exorcism.

'Well, since 25th October last, the magus Papus has been absent from "the material plane"; the efficacy of his exorcism is abolished. Therefore the Revolution is at hand . . .'

This story drew the following hot denial in the October 1922 issue of *Le Voile d'Isis*, the journal Papus himself had founded in 1890. 'In the opinion of people very *au courant* with Russian affairs, this article teems with errors. The scene of incantation is pure imagination, as is the report that Papus claimed to possess the power to exorcise the menace that hovered over Russia and the court . . .'

Nevertheless, the fact that the story, true or false, had gained such wide currency is in itself interesting. A man who could become the subject of such a legend could not have been a run-of-the-mill mystery-monger, especially in a country which had bred a magus of the stature of Rasputin.

At the outbreak of the First World War, Papus entered the army medical corps with the rank of captain and was attached

L

to a hospital. A photograph of 1915 shows him, by now grey-haired and distinguished looking, dressed in a dapper uniform and carrying a swagger stick. Later he was sent to the front and promoted to the rank of major. While caring for his companions he contracted tuberculosis and was demobilised and sent back to Paris for treatment. He recovered sufficiently to resume medical duties, but in 1916 the disease, combined with a brain seizure, caused his death.

Papus left behind him not only a large volume of writing on occultism, but also a considerable number of medical works. The latter are probably largely forgotten today, but his occult works are still widely read, particularly *Le Tarot des Bohémiens*, in which he produced an ingenious theory of the correlation between the Tarot and the Cabala, linking the four suits with the four letters of the Tetragrammaton. This work has probably done more than any other to perpetuate the idea of a connection between Cabalism and the Tarot—an idea which plays such a major part in modern occultism.

Another reason why Papus's career may be considered significant is that he was responsible for a number of occult groups which, in the late nineteenth century gave a new spirit or organisation to occultism.

One of Papus's chief mentors in his early years was a certain Saint-Yves d'Alveydre, whose real name was Joseph-Alexandre Saint-Yves (1842–1910), another strange and colourful character. Saint-Yves, who styled himself 'Marquis', was a disciple of Fabre d'Olivet and the author of a number of works mixing politics and occultism, in which he proposed ian ideal society ruled by an intellectual élite. His best-known works are his *Mission de ouvriers* (1883) and *Missions des Juifs* (1884).

Jules Bois, in his *Le Monde invisible*, includes an account of his meeting with Saint-Yves d'Alveydre.

'He lived at that time in a charming house in the Rue Vernet. Never, even in the houses of the most ancient patrician families, have I seen so many solemn ancestral portraits, with their wigs and heraldic insignia. He was in the habit of sitting against the light to give a more profound impression . . . He had beautiful grey hair, a sly smile, hands loaded with rings, and was dressed in a frock coat. He told me, with the appearance of serious conviction, that he had written 400 pages in three days and that he communicated by telepathy with the Grand Lama of Tibet . . .

The Heirs of Eliphas Lévi

'Certain of his friends whispered that he had made gold. "Is it true?" I asked the Marquis de Saint-Yves . . . Staring at me, he said: "Would you like to visit my laboratory and become my disciple?" I had the imprudence to say yes . . . However, I did not see the Marquis de Saint-Yves again, I did not penetrate into his laboratory, which perhaps does not exist. I never would learn to make gold—for was I not indiscreet to put him in an awkward position by interpreting literally a simple formula of alchemical politeness?'

Saint-Yves claimed to have received initiation from a Brahmin who had fled from his country during a revolt and had established himself at Le Havre as a bird merchant and teacher of oriental languages. Saint-Yves took lessons from him, but antagonised his teacher by his penchant for spiritualism and other Western phenomena of which the Brahmin disapproved. Relations came to an end when, Saint-Yves claimed, the Brahmin threatened him with a knive.

Towards the end of his life he developed an obsession about his dead wife. The room in the house at Versailles where she had died was transformed into a chapel, and he obtained permission from the Pope to celebrate masses there. The deceased continued to have her place laid for her at table, and Saint-Yves claimed that he was in constant communication with her.

Papus met Saint-Yves soon after leaving the Theosophical Society in 1888 to set up his own Groupe Indépendant d'Etudes Esotériques. Papus was impressed by Saint-Yves's claim to be Grand Master of the Martinist Order, that is the order composed of the followers of Pasqually and Saint-Martin, and was soon actively promoting the Martinist cause with the help of his friend Augustin Chaboseau. The lodges began to multiply, and in 1891 a meeting was held at No. 29 Rue de Trevise, in Paris, to establish a Supreme Council, whose members would be elected in perpetuity. Papus was elected Grand Master.

Meanwhile Papus had become involved in another order which was to become one of the leading occult societies of the time. This was the Cabalistic Order of the Rosy Cross, headed by two curious characters, the Marquis Stanislas de Guaita and Joséphin Péladan.

It has been suggested that these two men were the recipients of a genuine Rosicrucian initiation dating back to the original brotherhood. Robert Ambelain, in his *Templiers et Rose-Croix*

(1955), states that Eliphas Lévi received the initiation from the English Rosicrucians on his trip to London in 1853 and, on his return to France passed it on to the Abbé Lacuria who passed it on to Dr. Adrien Péladan, a distinguished homoeopath and hermetic scholar, who in turn passed it on to his brother Joséphin. It is true that Edward Bulwer-Lytton for a time was honorary Grand Patron of the Societas Rosicruciana in Anglia, and he may have given Lévi some sort of initiation, but all this is speculation, and it is extremely doubtful whether the Cabalistic Order of the Rosy Cross was part of any such chain of initiation.

Nevertheless, de Guaita, who died suddenly at the early age of thirty-six in 1897, was an important figure in French occultism and the main facts of his short and romantic life are worth recording.

The de Guaitas were an old Lombardy family. Stanislas's great-great-grandfather had married the daughter of a French baron and had thus inherited an estate at Alteville, in Lorraine. It was here that Stanislas de Guaita was born, on 6th April 1861. He received his schooling from the Jesuits, first at Dijon and later at Nancy. In 1878 he entered the Lycée at Nancy where one of his companions was Maurice Barrès, later to become a prolific writer, distinguished politician and French Academician. Barrès was one of the early members of the Cabalistic Order of the Rosy Cross, but left because it conflicted with his strict Catholicism.

Stanislas was an alert, but somewhat idle pupil, who applied himself only to the subjects that interested him—literature, Latin and science. He was intrigued by chemistry and also developed a passion for poetry and a particular admiration for Baudelaire.

With the intention of taking a law degree, he went to Paris and soon became friendly with the poets of the Latin Quarter. In 1881 he published his own book of poetry, *Oiseaux de passage*, which was followed by two other volumes, *La Muse noire* (1883) and *Rosa Mystica* (1885). One of his poetic mentors was Catulle Mendès who told him about Eliphas Lévi. 'Read him,' advised Mendès; 'it is worth the trouble; he is a thinker of singular ideas and uneven style, but a prodigious artist.'[2]

De Guaita followed this advice and found Lévi's works a revelation. From that moment, as he says in a letter of 30th August 1893, 'I devoted myself entirely to occultism, and I set about researching and reading everything that had been written on the occult sciences. Shortly afterwards I made the acquaintance of Péladan, then of Barlet and Papus.'[3]

Péladan (1858-1918) was a character who would have been quite at home in one of the more bohemian enclaves of twentieth-century California. An ex-bank clerk, he had set himself up as an occult propagandist and called himself Sar Mérodack Péladan; Sar is the Assyrian word for king; the name Mérodack was based on Merodach Baladan, the king of Babylon mentioned in Isaiah xxxix, and also on Marduck, the Chaldean god associated with the planet Jupiter.

The Sar was a striking-looking man, with a thick, black beard, an enormous mop of curly hair and huge, dark, slightly protruding eyes staring from beneath bushy brows. He cut a quaint figure in the cafés of Montmartre where he was to be seen in a variety of exotic costumes. Sometimes he appeared in a monk's robe, sometimes in a medieval doublet with velvet breeches fringed with white lace. Péladan was a versatile character and, among other things, produced a series of extraordinary novels in which occultism and eroticism are mixed and in which the author himself figures as Mérodack, the magician who has read 'all carnal literature from Martial to de Sade'. The series of novels was called *La Décadence latine*.

One of the chief obsessions apparent in these novels is the figure of the hermaphrodite, already seen in Balzac's *Séraphita*. In Péladan's work the idea of the androgyne possesses a special occult significance, which probably owes a great deal to Eliphas Lévi. Péladan saw the androgyne as the perfect fusion of voluptuousness and intelligence, of the active and contemplative faculties. One of the novels in which this idea is emphasised is *Curieuse* (1886), which inspired de Guaita to write, in his *Essais des sciences maudites*:

'*Curieuse* is reminiscent of *Séraphitus-Séraphita*, but this, mystery, which Balzac stammered out through intuition, M. Péladan formulates with the serene boldness and authority of one who knows, not with the feverish enthusiasm of one who divines.'

The heroine of *Curieuse* is the Princess Paule Riazan, who has a love affair with an individual called Nébo, a painter-aesthete who is a disciple of Mérodack. It is conceivable that Nébo was to some extent modelled on de Guaita, who also adopted the name Nébo when writing to Péladan. Nébo at first resists advances of the Russian princess, but finally succumbs after preparing his studio for the occasion. The room is lit with dazzling copper lamps, and perfumed by the aroma from substances burning on a tripod. The walls are painted with Hebrew-Phoenician phallic symbols. In this exotic setting Nébo, wearing a Chaldean tiara and swinging a censer, approaches the princess who, titillated by the smell of the incense, imagines herself to be 'the great Ishtar, the aphrodite of Chaldea'.

The first volume of *La Décadence latine* was *Le Vice suprême*, which appeared in 1884. It made a strong impression on de Guaita, who wrote as follows to Péladan.

'It is your *Vice suprême* that revealed to me (me, a sceptic, though respectful to all holy things) that the Cabala and High Magic can be more than just a mystification. I knew Eliphas Lévi by name; I immediately obtained his complete works and have been meditating on them—too superficially—during my rustic exile with my mother (at the château of Alteville) ... Permit me to tell you again, my dear Sir, that I shall never forget this fact: that it was owing to your book that I undertook the study of Hermetic science which seems to me, at first sight, so beautiful and fecund in sublime symbols.'

This slightly conflicts with the letter quoted earlier in which he says that Eliphas Lévi's works gave him his occult awakening. It seems likely that he was anxious to impress and flatter Péladan, for he concludes the letter by saying:

'In a fortnight, Sir, I shall be back in Paris. If you will be so kind as to permit me, I shall come to ask for some advice to guide the researches which I hope to make.'[4]

Evidently Péladan wrote back inviting his young admirer to come and see him, for in a subsequent letter de Guaita said:

'You do me a great kindness in offering to let me have a chat with you about Hermetism, something which I have wanted to do for a long time. I do not claim until now to have been anything more than a mere admirer of the higher sciences, who has studied them attentively and perseveringly; it will therefore be a great joy for me to be able to talk with a true initiate—who is greatly my senior in cabalistic studies.'

After his interview with Péladan, de Guaita wrote:

'I am grateful to you for having sacrificed several precious hours ... you have pleased, interested and obliged me.'

The Heirs of Eliphas Lévi

The correspondence from which these passages are quoted is extremely interesting as it shows the master and pupil relationship between the two men, a relationship which was played down by certain writers on de Guaita and doubtless by de Guaita himself after the two broke up.

Meetings between Péladan and his disciple became frequent, and the tone of the correspondence became more intimate. In one letter de Guaita said:

'I am very uneasy about you and would be greatly comforted to see you again. You are becoming very seldom seen.'

In another, he waxed eloquent in praise of Péladan:

'I know, I sense, that you are an intelligence superior to mine . . . you have the genius of spontaneity and synthesis; I have the talent for patience and analysis.'

Later the friendship came to be more like one between equals, and de Guaita eventually considered himself close enough to Péladan to be able to criticise him. One characteristic to which de Guaita objected was Péladan's extreme hatred of Germany and things German, a hatred which was exacerbated by the death of his brother Adrien owing to an erroneous prescription by a German doctor. In a funeral oration which he wrote for the occasion he castigated the German nation. When de Guaita was sent a copy he wrote to his friend reminding him that there were good things about the Germans and telling him not to forget Mesmer, Goethe and Albrecht Dürer.

De Guaita also took Péladan to task for his amorous excesses. 'Your soul', he wrote 'is perpetually haunted and obsessed by ridiculous sentimental cravings. Can you not live for one week without your spirit being preoccupied with these futilities?'

They also disagreed over astrology, which was coming back into vogue under the influence of Ely Star's *Les Mystères de l'horoscope* (1887); this taught an onomantic, cabalistic astrology similar to that of Paul Christian. Péladan laid great stress on astrology in his works and made frequent allusion to the doctrine of 'signatures' according to which all earthly things have their celestial counterparts. De Guaita's attitude was made clear in a letter:

'. . . I do not believe in astrology for the reasons I have given, though I do believe completely in the possible virtue of talismans and in the odic medicine of Paracelsus, because here there is a direct action of the doctor on the sick person, an application of the will to cure, a will which is formulated by a corresponding sign.'

But in spite of his scepticism, de Guaita still expressed a desire to have his horoscope cast by the occultist and clairvoyant Eugène Ledos, though he was reluctant to pay the fee required by Ledos when, as he wrote to Péladan, he doubted whether the result would be as accurate as a handwriting analysis.

At a certain point in the friendship de Guaita began to address his letters to 'Mérodack' and to sign himself 'Nébo' (a reference to Nabu, the Babylonian god associated with Mercury). In some cases these names are companied by the planetary sigils. Many of the letters are also dotted with other esoteric signs: there are Hebrew letters, Chi-Rho monograms and in one case an Indian lingam and yoni symbol, signifying sexual union. This is accompanied by the question: 'What news? Daphne? Linga-Yoni?'—another jibe at Péladan's sexual activities.

In another letter de Guaita wrote to Péladan warning him of some impending danger.

'. . . A very definite, though avoidable, peril is on the way; A TRAP; the Tarot will tell you as it told me if you illuminate your consultation with prayer—Les lucides idem. I have positive confirmation of it from three different sources, each of which confirms the other. In this struggle—for there will be a struggle—I am with you in Spirit. Cave, Cave . . . Do not take this matter lightly.

'Immerse yourself in the ספר יצירה (Sepher Jetsirah). I do not know if you fully realise its significance. It is extremely revealing.

'Heartfelt greetings to you in יהוה אלהים צבאות (Jehovah Elohim Sabaoth=Jehova God of the armies).

'The living God of Triumph (ז) (Zayin=7).
Nébo

Evidently Péladan survived the danger, for de Guaita was soon writing again full of enthusiasm after his re-reading of *Le Vice suprême*.

De Guaita soon felt able to make his own contribution to occult literature, and in 1886 he published an article in *L'Artiste* entitled *Au seuil du mystère*, which was announced as the first of a series called *Essais des sciences maudites*.

The French branch of the Theosophical Society did not attract de Guaita, who preferred the Western occult tradition to the Mahatmas of Mme Blavatsky. He did, however, write approvingly of the Theosophists in an article in *La Jeune France* of December 1887:

'Let it be permitted to a child of the Occident, humble heir to the Judaeo-Christian tradition to address . . . a fraternal and distant homage to the adepts of the Himalayas—not forgetting also to send his felicitations and good wishes to this valiant Theosophical Society which spreads, with the shade of its growing branches, the doctrines of truth, justice and peace.'

In the same year, 1887, de Guaita met the man who was later to become his secretary and most devoted disciple. This was a young Swiss named Oswald Wirth, who practised as a hypnotic healer. In his memoirs[5] Wirth recalls how he first made the acquaintance of de Guaita.

'Practising at that time curative magnetism, I was treating a sick woman who went to sleep under my influence and imparted her visions to me . . . I was struck by the tone of exceptional conviction with which she said: "I see a letter with a red seal carrying armorial bearings. You will receive it; it is very important for you."

'I wanted to know who was planning to write to me and with what intention.

' "It is a young man of your age, but shorter than you, blond, clear-skinned, with blue eyes. He is very learned and is interested in the same things as yourself. He has told me about you and is anxious to make your acquaintance." '

A few weeks later arrived the predicted letter with the red heraldic seal:

'Sir, My excellent brother, Canon Roca, has talked to me about you in terms which make me extremely anxious to make contact with you.

'If it would please you to come and visit me tomorrow, Saturday, at six o'clock, we can dine together informally and that will give me the opportunity to make your acquaintance.'

The letter was signed Stanislas de Guaita, and the address was given as No. 24 Rue de Pigalle. Wirth accepted the invitation and was greatly impressed by his host's knowledge of magnetic healing. De Guaita, for his part, inquired how much his guest knew about occultism. Wirth, although he had dabbled in Theosophy and had been initiated as a freemason in 1884, knew little about the subject and was grateful when de Guaita drew his attention to the Tarot as a magical system. Relations between the two men soon became close, and in due course Wirth undertook his own study of the Tarot, which he submitted for de Guaita's approval and which was published in 1889 under the title of *Les Vingt-deux clés kabbalistiques du Tarot*.

Meanwhile de Guaita had conceived the idea of forming his own occult order. In 1888 he called together a group of friends in Paris, and the Cabalistic Order of the Rosy Cross was born. It was headed by a supreme council of twelve. The names of six of these were known; the other six remained unknown with the idea that the order could be secretly resurrected if circumstances ever conspired to destroy it. It is likely, however, that the 'unknown' six never existed.

The main participants in the order were: de Guaita, the supreme chief; Péladan; Papus; Marc Haven; the Abbé Alta, whose real name was the Abbé Mélinge and who was a curate in the diocese of Versailles and a religious author; the writer Paul Adam; and François-Charles Barlet, whose real name was Alfred Faucheux. The last-named, who was to succeed de Guaita as head of the order, was a minor civil servant who lived in a tiny lodging near the Seine filled with alchemical trappings; he was also the author of a large number of books on occultism.

Members of the order passed through three grades of initiation: baccalauréat, licentiate, and doctorate of the Cabala. Each stage required the passing of examinations. The purpose of the order was threefold: first, to study the classics of occultism; secondly, to enter into spiritual communion with the Divine through meditation; thirdly, to spread the word among the uninitiated.

But if de Guaita dreamed of uniting occultists into a glorious universal brotherhood under the banner of the Rosy Cross he was soon to be disillusioned. The occult world in France was soon to become the scene of a series of spectacular battles between warring factions.

1. Philippe Encausse, *Papus (Dr. Gerard Encausse), sa vie, son œuvre* (Paris, 1932).
2. Oswald Wirth, *Stanislas de Guaita, souvenirs de son secrétaire* (Paris, 1935).
3. Ibid.
4. *Lettres inédites de Stanislas de Guaita au Sar Joséphin Péladan, une page inconnu de l'histoire de l'occultisme à la fin du XIXe siècle*. Intr. by Dr. E. Berthelet (1952).
5. *Stanislas de Guaita, souvenirs de son secrétaire* (Paris, 1935).

15 The War of the Roses

Péladan, like Eliphas Lévi, combined his occultism with a strong adherence to Catholicism, and he soon found himself affronted by some of the more pagan activities of de Guaita's order. He was, in any case, too big a fish to swim for long in the same pond as de Guaita, and the inevitable split became public when he published an article in *L'Initiation* of June, 1890, announcing his departure from the Cabalistic Order.

'. . . My adherence, fruitful until now, would henceforth become sterile. My absolutist nature isolates me from your eclectic work. I could not take occultism in its entirety with me to Mass, and I refuse to rub shoulders with spiritualism, masonry or Buddhism.'

In stating his aversion to masonry, Péladan was no doubt thinking particularly of Oswald Wirth. Between the two men there was clearly no love lost, for Wirth in his memoirs is scathing about Péladan and gives the entirely erroneous impression that de Guaita was contemptuous of the Sar from the beginning.

Péladan stated in his article that his intention was to establish a new 'triple intellectual order for Romans, Artists and women'. The new group was to be called the Order of the Catholic Rose Cross, the Temple and the Grail. Soon after the appearance of this announcement, Péladan departed for Nimes, having drawn up an impressive document on parchment appointing his friend Gary de Lacroze as his second-in-command with instructions to look for recruits. The document was headed with drawings of a tiara, a chalice, a standard and crosses of three different designs. The message, written in a flowery, archaic style in Péladan's decorative handwriting, read as follows:

Under the Tau, the Greek cross, the crux ansata and the Tiara of Chaldea, before the Grail, the Standard and the Rose Cross,

We, Grand-Master of the Order of the Catholic Rose Cross, the Temple and the Grail, detained in Barbary to elaborate the constutution of the order, do hereby designate to you our friend Commander Gary de Lacroze as Archwarden of the Province of Paris for the reception and preliminary selection of candidates . . .

Do not forget, friend Commander, that only science or genius can compensate in our order for the absence of worldly position.

Given at Paris under our seal this day of . . . etc.

Sar Péladan[1]

Through his order Péladan hoped to bring occultism back under the wing of Catholicism. The stated aim of the Catholic Rose Cross was the accomplishment of works of mercy, with a view to preparing for the reign of the Holy Spirit. The coming kingdom of the Paraclete was by now a familiar theme among occult groups.

Every candidate for initiation had to appear before the Grand Master, who put to him the following ten questions:

1. Who are you?
2. What is your void?
3. To what does your will tend?
4. How do you realise yourself?
5. By what force?
6. Declare your attractions and repulsions.
7. Define your glory.
8. State the hierarchy of beings.
9. Name happiness.
10. Name sorrow.[2]

If, having passed through this interrogation satisfactorily, the candidate was judged to be suitable, he entered the lowest rank of the society which was divided, in ascending order, into the following grades: servants of work, equerries, knights and commanders. The commanders were assigned to the various Sephiroth of the cabalistic Tree of Life. De Lacroze, for example, was Commander of Tiphereth, while Comte Léonce de Larmandie was Commander of Geburah.

Péladan received his initiates in the large room in which he lived in the Rue Notre-Dame-des-Champs. He dressed in a monk's robe with a Rose Cross on his chest and addressed the faithful in a musical voice, gesturing energetically with his ring-laden hands.

When de Guaita heard of these antics he immediately appealed to Péladan to cease his schismatic activities. His tone was at first conciliatory, and on 13th August 1891, he wrote to Péladan the following letter, on paper headed with the symbol of the Cabalistic Order, a cross with four roses at the corners and a pentagram in the centre (see plate 15b).

My dear friend,

I hope that my book gives you as much pleasure as the androgyne gave to me: the reading of it reminded me of some of the most picturesque years of my life at college, apud patres jesuitas. Thank you also for so graciously sending me your *Gynandre*. Everything that comes to me from you reminds me of a past which is a precious memory to me.

I only regret that the provocations, more or less indirect of your R+C+C+ force us to protest energetically against it. It is important to make known to the students of occultism that its doctrines are the very opposite of all the rosicrucian traditions, and that we can have nothing to do with the acts of wilful madness which you have been perpetrating in increasing numbers for a year under the label of the Rosy Cross. Furthermore, your *Letter to Papus* and your Declaration of 'Exodus' contain errors of fact which it is necessary for us to deny, remembering the principal events of your breaking away and subsequent founding of your R+C+C+.

I strongly regret that the provocations of your attitude have driven us to such explanations, which always have an unfortunate effect.

Yours
Guaita

It seems that Péladan must have written back accusing de Guaita of making an unnecessary fuss and suggesting that they should meet and have a talk to smooth out their differences. De Guaita's next letter was more brusque than his last.

My dear friend,

A conversation would not smooth out anything: for it is not a question of a misunderstanding between us; it is a question of proclaiming solidarity before the public, who believe all of us to be involved in your acts. As to your final statement: 'you desire aggression for the sake of aggression', let me tell you that I find that strange, when what you refer to is a very belated response to a series of gratuitous aggressions on your part.

Yours, and *bon voyage*.

Guaita

After this de Guaita seems to have given up hope of bringing Péladan to heel. Meanwhile the Sar was attracting increasing attention to himself. In 1892 he published *Comment on devient mage*, which is a curious mixture of occultism and Catholic dogma. At the beginning of the work Péladan states that he proclaims the truth of the Catholic Church, recognises the infallibility of the Pope and is ready to burn the book if it is judged by St. Peter to be bad or untimely. The text of the book includes a section on the different planetary types of human being, giving advice on how to make use of one's planetary abilities. He attempts to tie up his theories with Catholic doctrine.

Péladan envisaged his Rose Cross as much more than an occult society. He sought to establish a nucleus from which would emanate a whole set of religious, moral and aesthetic values. To propagate his aesthetic ideas he began a series of annual salons of the pictorial arts as well as instituting an 'idealist theatre' and promoting concerts of 'sublime music'. The first of the 'Salons de la Rose Croix' took place in March 1892 and, surprisingly enough, met with considerable success.

The Rosicrucian salons became quite an institution, and by 1894 Péladan was able to write, in *L'Art idéaliste et mystique*: 'From year to year the Rosicrucian idea wins over both artists and the public. Aesthetically the cause is won.' In the same book he discusses his theories of how artists ought to work.

'The work should be conceived in our own image, as man was created in the image of the Elohim; that is to say, it should be conceived on three planes: plastic, organic, intellectual.

'The artist should begin with the abstraction of his subject, that is to say by fixing the abstract plane which it occupies; then he will imagine the soul most consistent with this abstract plane; finally he will choose the forms most characteristic of this soul.'

Péladan was no less active as a theatre impresario, playwright and director. He claimed to have discovered two missing plays by Aeschylus, *Prometheus, Bearer of Fire* and *Prometheus Delivered* which formed a trilogy with *Prometheus Enchained*. Having failed to persuade the Comédie Française to take the plays, Péladan arranged his own performance of the trilogy. His company, the 'Théâtre de la Rose+Croix', also performed a number of other plays with an occult or mystical message. An advertisement, reproduced in *L'Art idéaliste et mystique* announced the performance at the Champ-de-Mars of: '*Babylone*, a Wagnerian tragedy in four acts, refused by the Comédie Française, performed on the 11th, 12th, 15th, 17th, 19th March 1893 at the Rose Cross. M. Hattier played the Sar Mérodack; M. Dammebie, the Archmagus; and Mlle Mellot, Samsina.' The titles of some of the other plays performed were: *Orpheus, Le Mystère du Graal, Le Mystère des + Rose Croix* and *Les Argonautes*.

De Guaita, who had hitherto made only private protests about Péladan's activities, decided that the time had come for a public denunciation of the rival Rose Cross. In 1893 his order issued the following proclamation:

We, Brothers of the Rose+Cross, considering that Joséphin PÉLADAN, former member of the council of twelve, having, in 1890, attempted to monopolise the order for the sake of a papism injurious to the Pope himself; having, in his 'Declarations' issued on behalf of the 'Catholic Rose Cross', poured forth in the name of the Brotherhood and without consulting a single Rosicrucian, various fantastic accusations of a wildly ultramontanistic tone; and this when he knew, with complete certainty, that he was in flagrant contradiction, not only with the traditional spirit of the Order, but also with the dearest convictions of his colleagues—considering, we say, that M. Joséphin Péladan resigned, afterwards to establish, independently from us and against our wishes, a 'Triple Intellectual Order', called the 'Catholic Rose Cross', in conformity with the letter of his declarations;

That, in doing so, he shamelessly usurped the title and emblem of the Rose Cross, to drag this revered name and symbol through every contradiction and ridicule;

> We, Brothers of the Rose Cross, declare the said M. Péladan to be a schismatic and apostate Rosicrucian;
> We denounce him and his so-called Catholic Rose Cross before the tribunal of public opinion;
> And we solemnly affirm, should he prepare to manifest himself again, that the title under which he operates was knowingly and groundlessly usurped by him.
> Paris, 25th March, 1893.
>
> By order.
> For the Supreme Council
> of the Rose Cross,
> The Director
> Stanislas de Guaita
> The Arbiter   The Delegate General
> F.-Ch. Barlet   Papus.[3]

Although Papus was one of the signatories of this pompous and turgid document he later repented somewhat and wrote in an article in *Les Sciences maudites* in 1900:

'For his part, Joséphin Péladan—that admirable artist to whom the future will render justice at the final reckoning, in judging him apart from the perhaps too original aspects of his work—took the head of a movement to spiritualise aestheticism, whose fruits are only beginning to be apparent and which will have profound repercussions on contemporary art.'

---

1. Pierre Geyraud, *Les sociétés secrètes de Paris* (Paris, 1939).
2. Ibid.
3. Wirth, *Stanislas de Guaita*.

12 Figures from a copy of Lévi's *Clés majeures et clavicules de Salomon*. Top left, the Juggler of the Tarot, superimposed with the Hebrew letter Aleph; bottom left, the 'pentacle of Eden', so-called prototype of all the Hebrew letters; top right and bottom right, two sides of a talisman, each one representing one of the Names of God from the Schemhamphorasch

13 Josephin Péladan (1858–1918), prolific writer and leader of his own Rosicrucian movement

16 The Magical Quest of J.-K. Huysmans

A favourite rendezvous of Paris occultists was Edmond Bailly's bookshop in the Rue de la Chausée d'Antin, where the review *La Haute Science* was published. It was a place frequented by representatives of every kind of cult, and among its habitués were de Guaita, Papus and Paul Adam. One of the people who could sometimes be seen browsing in the shop was a neatly dressed man with close-cropped hair and a jutting beard named J.-K. Huysmans who occupied a flat in the Rue de Sèvres, the same street in which Eliphas Lévi had died. He worked as a minor official at the Ministry of the Interior, but he was known to the public as a novelist. With his book *A Rebours* he had caused a sensation in literary circles by overturning the realist doctrines of his former master, Zola, and glorying in a world of artificiality and fantasy. The hero of the book, Des Esseintes, weary of the world and its banal pleasures, shuts himself away in a house on the outskirts of Paris where he surrounds himself with every kind of device for stimulating the imagination—a keyboard in which liqueurs take the place of notes and on which he plays subtle melodies of taste, a dining-room fitted out like a ship's cabin so that he can imagine himself at sea, a collection of perfumes on which he experiments endlessly, concocting new and evocative smells. As these pleasures slowly begin to pall, Des Esseintes goes from one extravagant scheme to another in a desperate search for titillation.

A Rebours was one of those books that capture a widespread mood among a whole generation, and it pointed the way for those who felt that they had something in common with its hedonistic hero, as Huysmans himself must have done. If a Des Esseintes, with all the resources at his disposal, failed to find a lasting remedy for boredom, it seemed that for anyone

with a similar turn of mind the way led only to suicidal despair. Yet there was another way, as Huysmans realised, for in a conversion with his friend Gustave Guiches in 1887, after expressing his despair in life, work and women, he is reported to have said:
'Perhaps there's still occultism. I don't mean spiritualism, of course—the cheap swindlers with their shady tricks, the mediums with their buffoonery, and the doddering old ladies with their table-turning antics. No, I mean genuine occultism—not above but beneath or beside or beyond reality! Failing the faith of the Primitive or the first communicant, which I should dearly love to possess, there's a mystery there which appeals to me. I might even say that it haunts me ...'[1]

It was the classic Faustian impulse that led Huysmans to the bookshop in the Rue de la Chaussée d'Antin, and he was soon moving freely in occult circles. One of the people who stimulated his interest in the occult was Berthe Courrière, mistress of the writer Rémy de Gourmont, who described her in his *Portraits du prochain siècle* as 'a cabalist and occultist, learned in the history of asiatic religions and philosophies, fascinated by the veil of Isis, initiated by dangerous personal experiences into the most redoubtable mysteries of the Black Art ... a soul to which Mystery has spoken—and has not spoken in vain'.

Huysmans was introduced to her in 1889 by de Gourmont with whom she was then living in a flat in the Rue de Varenne. He spent many evenings there listening to Berthe Courrière discoursing on occultism, and on one occasion he took part in a séance at the flat.

Huysmans also became friendly with the Naundorffists, who used to gather in force at parties given by the writer, Charles Buet, in his flat in the Avenue de Breteuil. He also corresponded with the Marquis de Meckenheim, a close adherent to the Naundorffist cause, and began to collect material from which he hoped to write a novel about the movement. He soon abandoned the scheme, however, and began instead to research on the subject of black magic, and in particular the medieval French satanist Gilles de Rais, who, having been a distinguished soldier and Marshal of France, had turned to the black arts and perpetrated a series of horrifying and bestial crimes. Huysmans examined the records of the Marshal's trial and visited the ruins of his castle. All this was to come out in his novel *Là-Bas*, in which an account of the career of Gilles de Rais is woven into a narrative concerning satanism in nineteenth-century France.

Là-Bas contains a detailed description of a black mass, and there is a great deal of speculation as to whether Huysmans ever attended such an occasion. Rémy de Gourmont and others who knew him said he had not; but his friend Léon Hennique said the opposite. In an interview published in *Nouvelles Littéraires*, of 10th May 1930, he declared that 'Huysmans had been present at a black mass, and afterwards he had told me how frightful and diabolical the spectacle had seemed to him'. But the term 'black mass' is often used rather loosely, and it is possible that what Huysmans described to Hennique was no more than some kind of séance. The best evidence is provided by the account of the black mass in the novel, which I shall outline a little further on. Huysmans's description of the ceremony, although vivid and detailed, does not quite ring true. Like the descriptions of satanist activities in the fanciful works of Montague Summers, it gives the impression of having been concocted from anti-satanist polemics.

Another topic of speculation is the identity of the real-life model for Canon Docre, the satanist priest of *Là-Bas*. The favourite suggestion is that Docre was based on a Belgian priest by the name of the Abbé van Haecke. Some light is thrown on this question by Baron Firmin van den Bosch, who claimed that he had been given by Huysmans a detailed account of the latter's researches into satanism. According to van den Bosch Huysmans had attended a black mass and during the ceremony had noticed a priest standing apart watching. Not long afterwards he had been able to identify the priest from a photograph he had come across in an occult bookshop. Huysmans apparently told van den Bosch that van Haecke had a cross tattooed on the soles of his feet so that he had the pleasure of continually walking on the symbol of Christ. Whether this is true or not, there certainly was a sinister reputation surrounding the Abbé van Haecke which Huysmans believed.

Another character who comes into *Là-Bas* is a white magician referred to as Dr. Johannès. About the real-life identity of Dr. Johannès there is no doubt whatever. He was the Abbé Boullan, an extraordinary person who had a profound influence on Huysmans's life. Boullan was a significant figure in nineteenth-century occultism, and, although Huysmans painted him as practitioner of white magic, there were many who considered him to be a black magician of the darkest hue. The main facts of his life are as follows.

Joseph-Antoine Boullan was born on 18th January 1824, in the village of Saint-Porquier, Tarn-et-Garonne. He studied for the priesthood at the local seminary and later at Rome where he took his doctorate with distinction. He then joined the Missionaries of the Precious Blood and, after taking part in a number of missions to Italy, settled down in one of the Society's houses in Alsace, of which he soon became principal. In 1856 he left the Society and came as an independent priest to Paris where he made a reputation for himself as a theologian and edited a periodical called *Les Annales du sacerdoce*.

Soon after moving to Paris he was given the spiritual direction of a young nun named Adèle Chevalier who had had a series of remarkable visions. In 1859 Boullan and Sister Adèle started a religious community at Bellevue near Paris called the Society for the Reparation of Souls. The purpose was commendable enough, but it was not long before strange complaints began to be made about the community. Fraudulent medicinal remedies were supposed to have been used, and, what was worse, it was rumoured that the two founders had an amorous liaison and were indulging in various hideous practices. It was even said that, during a mass, Boullan had sacrificed on the altar a child born to him by Sister Adèle.[2]

The result of these accusations was that in 1861 Boullan and Adèle Chevalier were put on trial for fraud and indecency. They were found guilty on the first count and sentenced to three years' imprisonment which Boullan served at Rouen from December 1861 to September 1864.

In 1869 Boullan was imprisoned in the cells of the Holy Office in Rome where he wrote a confession of his crimes known as the *Cahier rose*. He was soon rehabilitated by the Holy Office and returned to Paris in the winter of 1869. In January 1870 he brought out a new periodical called *Les Annales de la sainteté au XIXe siècle* which soon attracted unfavourable attention from the ecclesiastical authorities because of certain heretical views expressed in it. Boullan also incurred their displeasure by the unorthodox methods he used in exorcising evil spirits.

Things came to a head in 1875 when the Archbishop of Paris summoned Boullan and questioned him about these procedures. The result of the interview was that the Archbishop placed

Boullan under a solemn interdict. Boullan appealed to Rome to remove the interdict, but the Archbishop's judgement was upheld, and Boullan retaliated by leaving the Church.

Immediately afterwards he entered into correspondence with Eugène Vintras, the prophet of Tilly-sur-Seule. The two met in Brussels on 13th August 1875 and again in Paris on 26th October. On the second occasion Vintras presented Boullan with some of the famous miraculous hosts, which the latter evidently considered as a mark of special favour, for when the prophet died in December of the same year, Boullan immediately declared himself to be the new leader of the sect. Since Vintras had called himself the New Elijah, Boullan announced that he was the reincarnation of John the Baptist. And, in emulation of the dove—symbol of the Paraclete—that Vintras had displayed on his forehead, Boullan had a pentagram tattooed at the corner of his left eye. All this failed, however, to convince most of the followers of Vintras, only a handful of whom accepted Boullan as their new leader.

Undaunted, Boullan established himself at Lyons where he gathered about him a small and loyal coterie, one of the most active members of which was his middle-aged housekeeper, Julie Thibault, otherwise known as Achildaël or the Apostolic Woman. the activities of this group ranged from strange ceremonies such as the Sacrifice of Glory of Melchizedek and the Provictimal Sacrifice of Mary to more secret rites which Boullan called his 'Unions of Life' and which only privileged disciples were allowed to attend. Boullan taught that 'since the fall of our first parents was the result of an act of culpable love, it is through acts of love accomplished in a religious spirit that the Redemption of humanity could and should be achieved. These 'acts of love' took the form of intercourse, either with celestial entities, if the adept wished to redeem himself, or with 'inferior beings' if he wished to help them up the 'ladder of life'.[3]

In 1886 Boullan broke his rule of secrecy by allowing three comparative outsiders to take part in his rites. The first was a priest named Canon Roca who, shortly after being initiated by Julie Thibault into the mysteries of the 'ladder of life', left Lyons horrified by what he had seen and determined to have nothing more to do with Boullan. The second was Stanislas de Guaita, who appears to have approached the group in a spirit of humility, for, according to Boullan, he went down on his knees before Julie Thibault, telling her that he was 'only a little child at school'. It is hard to say whether this humility was sincere, or whether de Guaita was simply carrying on a masquerade in order to gather ammunition for his later attacks on Boullan. But if there is any doubt about de Guaita's motives in his dealings with Boullan there is no doubt whatever about the motives of the third initiate, Oswald Wirth, who deliberately set out to spy on Boullan. For over a year he pretended to be enthusiastic about Boullan's ideas and gradually worked his way into the master's confidence. When he had obtained a written statement setting out Boullan's doctrines he considered that he had enough evidence with which to discredit the sect and wrote Boullan a brutal letter in December 1886 revealing his treachery.

The following year, when Wirth and de Guaita met, they compared notes on their experiences at Lyons and decided to set up an 'initiatory tribunal' to judge Boullan. Having found him guilty they communicated their verdict to him in a letter of 24th May 1887, which was dictated by de Guaita and signed by Wirth. In the letter Wirth informed Boullan that he had made a special trip to Châlons-sur-Marne to interview a certain Mlle M. who had furnished him with a number of Boullan's letters and a forty-page report giving the most minute details about the activities of the sect. The letter continued:

I am now charged with the task of informing you of these facts and of urging you, in your own interests and with charitable motives, to renounce your sacrilegious activities and the repugnant propaganda to which you devote yourself. The true Initiates will tolerate no longer your profanation of the Cabala by calling yourself a Cabalist and your mixing of the dung of your profligate imagination with the exalted doctrines of the Masters of Wisdom.

Renounce your naive pride, for it is this that prevents you from seeing the abomination of your doctrines and your works. Have the courage to acknowledge your error, retract before the dupes of your obscene teaching, ask pardon for your crimes against Nature, the Church and the Holy Spirit!

A last route to salvation is open before you; it is up to you to decide whether you will profit by it.

For you are condemned. But, since it is more enamoured of Christian charity than of strict justice, the tribunal will wait.

The sentence remains suspended over your head until the day when, for lack of any more merciful means, its application will become inevitable.

I have, without doubting the reality of your crimes, done my utmost to appeal to your good faith, which however is more than questionable in view of one fact, among others, recounted by Mlle M., a fact which excited the indignation of your judges to the highest pitch. This concerns an order given to the above-named clairvoyant to make a reply to the Marquise de Saint-Yves, not according to her own conscience and truthfulness, but according to your own interest, calculated beforehand.

May God, taking pity on your obduracy, open your blind eyes and touch your poor heart! I wish this from the bottom of my soul.

Oswald Wirth[4]

This letter was taken by Boullan as a declaration of war. Convinced that de Guaita and his associates would attempt by magical means to execute him, Boullan began elaborate preparations to ward off the attacks, believing that his enemies would use the spells that they had learned from him.

Evidently Boullan's counter-measures were effective, for by 1891 de Guaita considered it necessary to attempt a different line of attack. If Boullan could not be eliminated he could at least be publicly exposed, and in 1891 de Guaita published *Le Temple de Satan*, denouncing the practices of the Lyons sect.

By this time Huysmans had come into contact with Boullan. All that he had heard about the sinister ex-Abbé led him to believe that here was a valuable source of first-hand information on occultism, and in 1889 his friend Gustave Guiches wrote on his behalf to Canon Roca asking how Huysmans might get in touch with Boullan. The Canon wrote back as follows:

'In answer to your letters of 27th instant, I hasten to inform you that I have broken off all relations with M. Boullan of Lyons and that I shall take good care never to renew them ... The man is not known to have any friends, and I very much doubt if there is a single one whom M. Huysmans might ask for an introduction. But I can refer him to a decent young fellow in Paris who knows all Boullan's infamous secrets and can enlighten you completely on both the man and his abominable occultism. Write to the initiate Oswald Wirth, mentioning my name ... and perhaps also to the young Baron Stanislas de

Guaita, who should be in Paris just now and who knew Boullan in the same circumstances as I did, though more briefly. He too is well up in the subject . . .'[5]

Huysmans followed the Canon's advice and wrote to de Guaita and Wirth. The former's reply was unhelpful, but the latter wrote back offering to give Huysmans all the information he possessed, and the two met at Wirth's flat on the evening of 7th February 1890. Huysmans was unimpressed by Wirth as can be seen from the notes he made on the meeting.

'O. Wirth—a shuffler and a stammerer—denies that the Abbé Boullan is a satanist. He's a Naundorffist, hopes for the coming of the great King and wants to be Pope. He dreams of a Religion of "Pure and Free Love". Alleged to be a swindler and a rogue. His occult powers?—Wirth denies these and claims to have exposed Boullan's depravity to Roca and other occultists'[6]

What Wirth did not know at the time of this meeting was that Huysmans had already corresponded with Boullan, having obtained his address from Berthe Courrière, who knew him well and described him as 'a charming man'. In a letter dated 5th February, Huysmans explained to Boullan that he was researching on modern satanism and that he already consulted various Paris occultists, but with disappointing results. These individuals had expounded 'some idiotic theories wrapped up in the most apalling verbiage' and had shown themselves to be 'perfect ignoramuses and incontestable imbeciles'. His letter continued as follows:

'Several times I have heard your name pronounced in tones of horror—and that in itself predisposed me in your favour. Then I heard some rumours that you were the only initiate of the ancient mysteries who had obtained practical as well as theoretical results, and I was told that if anyone could produce undeniable phenomena, it was you and you alone. This I should like to believe, because it would mean that I had found a rare personality in these drab times—and I could give you some excellent publicity if you needed it. I could set you up as the Superman, the Satanist, the only one in existence, far removed from the infantile spiritualism of the occultists. Allow me then, Monsieur, to put these questions to you—quite bluntly, for I prefer a straightforward approach. Are you a satanist? And can you give me any information about succubi—Del Rio, Bodin, Sinistrari and Görres being quite inadequate on this subject? You will note that I ask for no initiation, no secret lore—only for reliable documents, for results you have obtained in your experiments.'[7]

Boullan replied the next day in a letter characteristically headed by the motto *Quis ut Deus?* and signed with the name 'Dr. Johannès' which Huysmans was later to use in *Là-Bas*. Boullan declined Huysmans's offer of publicity and said that he was not a satanist but 'an Adept who has declared war on all demonical cults'. He made it clear that he was not able to give any detailed information until he knew Huysmans's precise intentions in conducting his research.

Huysmans wrote back the following day assuring Boullan that he did not wish to glorify satanism, but merely to establish that it continued to exist and exercise power. He went on:

'It happens that I'm weary of the ideas of my good friend Zola whose absolute positivism fills me with disgust. I'm just as weary of the systems of Charcot, who has tried to convince me that demonianism was an old wives' tale, and that by applying pressure to the ovaries he could check or develop the satanic impulses of the women under his care in La Salpetrière. And I'm wearier still, if that be possible, of the occultists and spiritualists, whose phenomena, though often genuine, are far too often identical.

'What I want to do is to teach a lesson to all these people— to create a work of art of a supernatural realism, a spiritual naturalism. I want to show Zola, Charcot, the spiritualists, and the rest that nothing of the mysteries which surround us has been explained, If I can obtain proof of the existence of succubi, I want to publish that proof, to show that all the materialist theories of Maudsley and his kind are false, and that the Devil exists, that the Devil reigns supreme, that the power he enjoyed in the Middle Ages has not been taken from him, for today he is the absolute master of the world, the Omniarch . . .'[8]

Boullan was impressed by this letter and wrote in reply expressing his approval of Huysmans's aims and promising his co-operation. He confirmed Huysmans's belief that satanism still flourished and stated that it was even more powerful than in the middle ages. 'I can put at your disposal', he wrote, 'documents which will enable you to prove that satanism is active in our time, and in what form and in what circumstances. Your work will thus endure as a monumental history of satanism in the nineteenth century.'[9]

But Boullan was not willing take take Huysmans finally into

his confidence before making sure that he was not going to behave as de Guaita and Wirth had done. He therefore sent Julie Thibault to Paris to see Huysmans and make some discreet inquiries about him. She must at first have seemed to him a slightly unlikely emissary—a little middle-aged woman in a bonnet and a cheap black dress, clutching an umbrella and a prayer book, with a tin crucifix hanging from her neck and a pair of *pince-nez* on the end of her nose. Her austere profile, however, indicated a powerful character, and she soon impressed Huysmans with accounts of her remarkable exploits. She had, it appeared, spent many years visiting shrines to the Virgin Mary all over Europe, walking over 25,000 miles carrying only her umbrella and a bundle of clothes and living on nothing but bread, milk and honey. Huysmans took a liking to this colourful woman; and some years later, after Boullan had died, she was to make her home in the novelist's flat as his housekeeper and companion.

She, on her part, liked Huysmans and reported favourably to her master in Lyons, with the result that the novelist soon found himself deluged with documents from Boullan giving him details about the casting of spells, the Sacrifice of Glory of Melchizedek, the Black Mass and other magical phenomena. Boullan also did Huysmans the favour of performing two magical operations to protect him from any evil spells that might be cast by de Guaita and his friends. The second of these operations lasted two whole days. There is no evidence that de Guaita's fraternity did attempt any magical attacks on Huysmans, but they did try to dissuade him from having any further dealings with Boullan. On 13th February 1890 Wirth wrote to Huysmans drawing his attention to certain passages in Charles Sauvestre's book *Les Congrégations religieuses dévoilées*, dealing with the criminal activities of the Society for the Reparation of Souls. A few days later he called at Huysmans's office at the Ministry of the Interior and delivered a lecture on Boullan's depravities—but to no avail. 'He listened', Wirth reported 'with a smile on his lips, and then remarked that if the old man had found a mystical dodge for obtaining a little carnal satisfaction, that surely wasn't so stupid of him. . . .'[10]

Undeterred by Wirth, Huysmans continued collecting material from Boullan and from other sources, and towards the end of 1890 *Là-Bas* was completed. Somewhat to Huysmans's surprise one of the more respectable newspapers, *Echo de Paris*, asked for the serial rights, and the first instalment appeared on 15th February 1891. In view of the public impact made by the novel and its pre-eminence as a work of occult fiction, a résumé of it might be of interest here.

The story centres on Durtal, a young novelist who has decided to undertake a study of Gilles de Rais. The beginning of the book describes the motives that have led him to seek a supernatural subject. The naturalist school, to which he has hitherto belonged, has, he feels, become sterile; while its methods are valuable, the subjects which it portrays have ceased to be of interest. Durtal therefore is seeking an entirely new kind of subject to which he can apply the objectivity of naturalism. 'It would be necessary, in a word, to follow the main path so deeply carved out by Zola, but it would be necessary also to trace in the air a parallel path, another route . . . to create, in short, a spiritual naturalism . . .'[11]

In his personal life, as well as in his writing, Durtal feels the need for some new source of inspiration. He periodically feels attracted towards religion, but is unable to commit himself because his critical faculties revolt against it. 'He did not believe in it, and yet he acknowledged the supernatural, for, even on this earth, how could one deny the mystery that rose up on all sides . . .?'[12] Durtal's problem clearly reflects that of his creator, as it reflects the problem confronting a large section of French intelligentsia at the time the novel was written.

Huysmans projected himself not only into the character of Durtal, but also into that of Durtal's confidant, des Hermies, a mysterious, withdrawn, fastidious individual, who is profoundly versed in strange subjects and frequents the company of astrologers, cabalists and alchemists. Des Hermies feeds Durtal's interest in occult literature and supplies him with books, including an alchemical manuscript translated and with a commentary by Eliphas Lévi. Durtal is, however, puzzled by the allegorical illustrations and finds Lévi's commentary unhelpful. 'Eliphas Lévi explained as best he could the symbols of these volatile fluids in their glass vessels, but he refrained from giving the famous recipe of the great arcanum and perpetuated the teasing practice of his other books in which, beginning on a solemn note, he affirmed his intention to reveal the ancient arcana and yet kept silent when the moment came, under the ineffable pretext that he would perish were he to betray such powerful secrets.'[13]

A number of other colourful characters appear in the novel. There is Carhaix, an old bell-ringer who lives with his wife in a cavernous dwelling high up in a church tower. In this strange apartment Durtal and des Hermies have many conversations with Carhaix on subjects ranging from the art of bell-ringing to the depravities of black magic. And it is here that they meet the astrologer Gevingey who tells them that the reign of the Paraclete is near.

' "The time awaited by Johannès is close," said Gevingey. "And here is the proof. Raymond Lully attested that the end of the old world would be heralded by the diffusion of the doctrines of the Antichrist, and these doctrines he names as Materialism and the monstrous, re-awakening of Magic. This prediction applies to our time, I believe." '[14]

This statement is made during a long conversation on the subject of the Paraclete, during which Carhaix confesses that the theory answers his most ardent wishes.

' "After all," he went on, sitting down and folding his arms, "if the third Reign is illusory, what consolation can remain to Christians when faced with the general disarray of a world which charity obliges us not to hate? . . .

' "There are three reigns," said the astrologer, compressing the ash in his pipe with his finger. "That of the Old Testament, of the Father, the reign of fear. That of the New Testament, of the Son, the reign of expiation. That of the Gospel of John, of the Holy Spirit, which will be the reign of atonement and love." '[15]

The real-life counterpart of Gevingey was the astrologer Eugène Ledos, while Carhaix was based on a man called Contesse, who was bell-ringer at Saint-Sulpice. Another prominent character in the book is Hyacinthe Chantelouve, Durtal's mistress, who was based partly on Berthe Courrière.

Mme Chantelouve is a member of a satanist circle, and it is she who takes Durtal to a black mass performed by the infamous Canon Docre. The ceremony takes place in the chapel of a former Ursuline convent, now part of a private house belonging to a woman friend of Docre. On the appointed evening Durtal and his mistress travel by carriage to the neighbourhood of the Rue de Vaugirard and alight in a small, quiet street by a wicket gate in a forbidding wall. An old woman opens the gate to them, and Mme Chantelouve leads Durtal across a gloomy garden to the chapel where they are admitted by a little man with a high-pitched, affected voice and a painted face. They enter a sombre chamber reeking of decay where a miserable-looking congregation await the beginning of the mass. The altar is conventional save for the crucifix hanging above it, which bears a grotesque figure of Christ with a strangely elongated neck and a face twisted into an 'ignoble smile'.

At length Docre appears, attended by two choir boys. He is dressed in a scarlet hat, from which two red bison's horns emerge, and a chasuble the colour of dried blood on the back of which is the figure of a goat within a triangle surrounded by a design of the magical herbs of saffron, sorrel and spurge. He bows to the altar and begins the mass, which at first follows the pattern of an ordinary low mass; then, however, the priest, bowing down before the altar, cries out:

'Master of Scandals, Dispenser of the benefits of crime, Prince of sumptuous sins and great vices, Satan, it is thou whom we adore, God of logic, God of justice!' There follows a long panegyric to Satan, after which Docre turns his attention to the figure of Christ on the cross and procedes to hurl the most obscene blasphemies at it.

After Docre's speech is ended the congregation abandon themselves to hysteria, intensified by the fumes given off by pungent herbs burning in chafing dishes. The smell begins to make Durtal feel faint and, being unable to endure the atmosphere any longer, he flees, taking Mme Chantelouve with him, from the reeking chapel.

This description of the black mass strikes the only sensational note in an otherwise subtle and perceptive novel. It was enough, however, to ensure *Là-Bas* a certain *succès de scandale*, which was made all the greater when the Bibliothèque des Chemins de Fer banned the novel from all railway bookstalls when it appeared in book form in April 1891.

After the publication of *Là-Bas*, Huysmans continued to maintain contact with Boullan. He had become convinced that the latter's fears of occult attacks were well founded and was soon making full use of the magical antidotes with which Boullan had supplied him, having instructed him in their use during one of Huysmans's visits to Lyons. One of these antidotes was shown to Jules Huret who interviewed Huysmans for

the *Echo de Paris*. Huret reported that during their conversation the novelist turned to him and asked:
 ' "Would you like to smell some exorcistic paste?"
 ' "Yes," I said. "You have some here?"
 'He got up, opened a box, and took out a square tablet of brownish paste. They he collected a little red-hot ash from the fireplace on a shovel, and laid the tablet on top of it. The paste sizzled, a thick cloud of smoke rose into the air, and a strong smell filled the tiny room—a smell in which there mingled with the perfume of incense the pungent, oppressive smell of camphor.
 ' "It's a mixture of myrrh, incense, camphor and cloves—the plant of St. John the Baptist," he told me. "What's more, it has been blessed in all sorts of ways. It was sent to me from Lyons, by someone who told me: 'As this novel of yours is going to stir up a host of evil spirits about you, I am sending you this to get rid of them.' "[16]
 'There was a long silence. I began to understand des Esseintes and Gilles de Retz, and in the red rays of the setting sun which came slanting in through the fiery window-panes, I almost expected to see twisted forms fleeing from the torments of exorcism....'

The attacks that Huysmans experienced occurred when he was about to retire to bed for the night. According to Edmond de Goncourt, the novelist was 'troubled by the feel of something cold moving across his face, and rather alarmed by the thought that he might be surrounded by some invisible force'.[17] These experiences, which Huysmans rather flippantly termed 'fluidic fisticuffs', continued to plague him for several years. He was not, however, seriously afraid as long as he was able to practise Boullan's counter-measures. One incident must have considerably reinforced his confidence in the Lyons magician: acting on Boullan's advice, he stayed away from his office on a particular day, and when he returned to work the following day discovered that a heavy gilt-framed mirror behind his desk had fallen on the spot where he usually sat.

As soon as Huysmans sensed the onset of an attack he would shut himself away and carry out a ritual. A tablet of exorcistic paste would be burned in the fireplace, a protective circle would be drawn on the floor; then, 'brandishing the miraculous host in his right hand, and with his left hand pressing the blessed scapular of the Elijan Carmel to his body, he would recite conjurations which dissolved the astral fluids and paralysed the power of the sorcerers'.[18]

In the face of these goings-on, Huysmans apparently retained his customary cynical sense of humour. Even on his visits to Lyons he found it impossible to be entirely solemn about the activities of Boullan's coterie. During one visit he wrote to Berthe Courrière:

'In this amazing house I have actually seen Mass said by a woman! Glory be to the regenerated sex and to the celestified organs (to use the style favoured by these people)! I'm having my fortune told by the little somnambulist I told you about, and just now she's reading the future in some glasses of water. After that I'm going to consult another woman who practises the Mozarabic Rite and casts horoscopes with chick-peas and broad beans. And lastly I have an appointment with a former Benedictine Abbess and hope to get some curious documents from her. As you can see, I'm not wasting my time.

'The battles have begun again since I last wrote to you— Wagrams in space. For a time I thought I was in a lunatic asylum. Boullan jumps about like a tiger-cat, clutching one of his hosts. He invokes the aid of St. Michael and the eternal justiciaries of eternal justice; then, standing at his altar, he cries out "Strike down Péladan, strike down Péladan, strike down Péladan!" And Madame Thibault, her hands folded on her belly, announces: "It is done." '[19]

By this time Huysmans was already turning towards Catholicism and was destined to end his days as an oblate attached to a Benedictine monastery. But he undoubtedly owed his conversion to his occult experiences, without which he might never have glimpsed the spiritual world; furthermore he always remembered the Abbé Boullan with a certain affection.

Two years after the publication of *Là-Bas* Huysmans was still corresponding with the ex-Abbé, and at the beginning of 1893 he received the following ominous letter:

Quis ut Deus?
Lyons, Jan. 2nd, 1893

My dear friend Huysmans,
I have received your letter with great joy in which you send me your good wishes for the New Year. This fateful time opens with sombre omens. The figures 8–9–3 form a combina- which foreshadows bad news.

Jan. 3rd

I wrote nothing more yesterday, waiting as I was for a letter from dear Madame Thibault, but during the night a terrible thing happened. At 3 o'clock in the morning I awoke suffocating. I called out twice, 'Madame Thibault. I am suffocating!' She heard me, but when she arrived I was unconscious. From 3 to 3.30 I was between life and death.

At Saint Maximon Madame Thibault dreamt of Guaita and in the morning a black bird of death cried out. It was the herald of the attack. M. Misme also dreamt the same. At 4 o'clock I slept again, the danger was past.[20]

But the reprieve did not last long, and on 4th January Boullan died. Mme Thibault sent to Huysmans the following account of his passing:

'After he had drunk a cup of tea, he breathed more easily. I relit the fire and warmed a shirt for him; he put it on and seemed to return to his normal state. He got up as usual and began to write his article for *La Lumière* which Madame Louise Grange had asked him to do. Then he wrote a letter to a friend. He wanted to take this to the post himself. I would not allow that telling him that it was too cold.

'Dinner time came. He sat down, ate well, and seemed very cheerful. Afterwards he paid his usual visit to his friends, Les Dames G... Whan he returned he asked me if I should be ready for prayer. We offered prayer and a few minutes afterwards he seemed ill at ease. He exclaimed, "What is that?" After saying this he collapsed. M. Misme and I had only time to support him and help him to his chair where he could rest during the prayers which I cut short so as to get him to bed more quickly.

'His chest was congested and his breathing very difficult. In the midst of his struggles his heart and liver were affected. He said, "I am dying. Farewell." I said to him, "But, Father, you are not going to die. What about the book you have written? You must finish it." He was pleased that I said that to him and he asked for "l'eau de salut". Having taken a mouthful he said, "This will save me." I did not feel unduly anxious, because we had seen him so often recover after having been near to the gates of death. I thought this danger would pass.

'I said, "Father, how are you?" Then I realised that he could no longer speak. He gave me a last look of farewell. He seemed in agony. It lasted barely two minutes, and he was dead.'[21]

sans peine les esprits attentifs, raconte cette évolution saturée d'étonnement et de merveilleux. Elle explique avec une incomparable magnificence de langage, la transsubstantiation d'une idée religieuse, quand, au hasard des aventures historiques, deux races devenant contiguës, il se fait un passage de dogme, de l'une à l'autre. En un panorama ennobli de grandes lignes et à personnages rares, il concentre l'immense phénomène du Christianisme s'emparant des rites du Sémitisme pour les purifier et les diviniser en douceur et en mansuétude.

C'est très beau une œuvre de cette envergure,

Caricature par CARAN D'ACHE (*Figaro*).

14a Cartoons by 'Caran d'Ache' in *Le Figaro* showing Péladan and his Rosicrucian orchestra

14b The symbol of Stanislas de Guaita's Cabalistic Order of the Rosy Cross

15 Stanislas de Guaita (1861–1897), leader of the Cabalistic Order of the Rosy Cross: a photograph taken in his last years

Boullan's obituary appeared in *Le Figaro* of 7th January 1893. The author Philippe Auquier, a minor art critic, praised Boullan and described him as the great apostle of 'the most obscure problems of the supernatural'. He also hinted that Stanislas de Guaita and his Rosicrucians might have had something to do with the death of the Lyons adept. Huysmans and his friend the writer Jules Bois were more explicit and through the columns of *Gil Blas* publicly accused de Guaita of murdering Boullan. De Guaita at first kept silent, but was finally provoked into defending himself. In *Gil Blas* of 15th January he wrote:

'For several days now the press has been spreading certain pieces of gossip about me which in fact reflect less on me than on the malicious or naive people who have launched the rumours that dog me so relentlessly.

'There is now no one who has not been informed that I am given to the most odious practices of sorcery; that I am at the head of a Rosicrucian College fervently dedicated to satanism, whose members devote their leisure hours to the evocation of the Black Spirit; that those who oppose us fall, one by one, victims to our malpractices; that I personally have, at a distance, struck down numerous enemies who have died under spells designating me as their assassin . . . That is not all. It is agreed that I mix and manipulate the most subtle poisons with an infernal art; I volatise them with a special felicity so as to make a toxic vapour from them waft to countless faraway places, towards the nostrils of those whose faces displease me; I play the part of Gilles de Rais on the threshold of the twentieth century; I have *friendly and other relations* with the redoubtable Docre, the canon beloved of M. Huysmans; finally, I keep prisoner in a cupboard a familiar spirit who emerges at my command!

'Is this enough? No. All these fine details are nothing but a preamble, the main contention being that the ex-Abbé Boullan—the Lyons thaumaturge whose recent death caused something of a stir—only succumbed because of my efforts combined with those of my black colleagues, the brothers of the Rosy Cross.'

De Guaita went on to deny that Boullan had died from any other cause than a weak heart and a diseased liver; and, castigating Huysmans and Jules Bois for the evil lies that they had spread about him, announced that he had challenged them to a duel and dispatched his seconds, Maurice Barrès and Victor

Emile Michelet. Huysmans chose as his seconds his friends Gustave Guiches and Alexis Orsat. The seconds of both parties were anxious to avoid the scandal which a duel would stir up, and all four did their best to placate de Guaita. As a result of their efforts an agreement was reached, and on 15th January Huysmans published a statement dissociating himself from the views expressed by Bois and declaring that he had never had any intention of disputing de Guaita's honour as a gentleman. In return de Guaita withdrew his challenge to Huysmans. He was also appeased by a similar conciliatory statement from Bois. A few months later, however, Bois published another attack on the Marquis. This time there was no possibility of conciliation, and the two men fought a pistol duel at the Tour de Villebon. The result was indecisive and de Guaita later had the generosity to record that Bois had conducted himself courageously on the duelling-field. Bois also later fought a duel with Papus who was a skilled swordsman and wounded Bois slightly in the forearm. Afterwards they became the best of friends.

Five years later de Guaita was dead, struck down not by magical forces but by an overdose of drugs. Huysmans meanwhile was drifting increasingly further from occultism and was already on the path that was to lead him to Catholicism. He therefore plays no further part in this study.

1. Robert Baldick, *The Life of J.-K. Huysmans*.
2. Boullan, as Huysmans discovered, had many good qualities, and I am disinclined to believe that he could have been guilty of such an appalling crime.
3. Robert Baldick, *The Life of J.-K. Huysmans*.
4. Wirth, *Stanislas de Guaita*.
5. Robert Baldick, *The Life of J.-K. Huysmans*.
6. Ibid.
7. Ibid.
8. Ibid.
9. Ibid.
10. Ibid.
11. J.-K. Huysmans, *Là-Bas* (Livre de Poche edition, Plon, Paris, 1966) p. 8.
12. Ibid., p. 15.
13. Ibid., p. 75.
14. Ibid., p. 260.
15. Ibid., p. 257.
16. Robert Baldick, *The Life of J.-K. Huysmans*.
17. Ibid.
18. Joanny Bricaud, *Huysmans, occultiste et magicien*, p. 27.
19. Robert Baldick, *The Life of J.-K. Huysmans*.
20. H. T. F. Rhodes, *The Satanic Mass*.
21. Ibid.

17 *Writers and the Occult*

Huysmans was not the only French writer to be influenced by occultism. Indeed the influence of the occult in French nineteenth-century literature is so widespread than an exhaustive study of it would be impossible in one volume, let alone a single chapter. The literary aspect of the occult revival can therefore best be shown by picking out a few examples of writers who were interested in the esoteric. These tend to divide into two categories, which sometimes overlap. First, there is the kind of writer for whom occultism is a source of subject matter. Secondly there is the kind for whom it provides a glass through which he sees the world and its phenomena and his role as a writer.

Balzac probably belonged more to the first category than to the second. The most strongly occult of his works is *Séraphita*, which has a Swedenborgian theme. Interest in the Swedish visionary had somewhat dwindled during the early years of the nineteenth century, but in 1820 a revival occurred with the appearance of the first complete French edition of Swedenborg's works, translated by Moët. Another translation, by Le Boys de Guays, appeared in 1840. Balzac's *Séraphita* was published in 1835.

The novel is set in the town of Jarvis on the coast of Norway where there lives a beautiful and mysterious young person known as Séraphitus or Séraphita. It soon becomes clear that Séraphitus/Séraphita is in some strange way bisexual or ambisexual, presenting a male personality to some and a female personality to others. Two people are deeply in love with Séraphita. One is Minna, the daughter of the local pastor, Becker. The other is a dour young man named Wilfrid. Séraphita refuses the advances of both and explains that he/she has a far higher purpose than earthly love. Perplexed by Séraphita's behaviour, Wilfrid calls on Becker and asks if he can explain the mystery surrounding this strange person. Becker explains that in order to do so he must first explain the teaching of Emmanuel Swedenborg. There follows a long résumé of Swedenborg's life and doctrine. Becker then relates how one of Swedenborg's most ardent disciples was a certain Baron Séraphitus. 'The Baron', he explains, 'was the most ardent follower of the Swedish prophet who had opened in him the eyes of the Inner Man and had given him a longing for a life conforming to the higher order.' Swedenborg searched for an 'Angelic Spirit' for him to marry, and found one in a vision. She was the daughter of a London shoemaker. The Baron married her and in due course a child was born, but the child was given no name. By this time Swedenborg was dead, but on the day of birth he manifested himself in Jarvis and filled with light the room where the child was sleeping. 'The work is completed, the heavens rejoice,' he announced. Ten years later the parents died, but the child was unperturbed and insisted that they continued to live in him/her. For convenience the child was given the name of Séraphita.

Séraphita tries to persuade Minna and Wilfrid to marry, but they are still obsessed with the object of their adoration. Gradually, however, they become drawn to the strange world that Séraphita inhabits, and when Séraphita tells them that he/she is about to leave this world, they beg to be taken as well. Their friend refuses, but promises to leave with them 'the keys of the kingdom where His light shines', warning them that the first steps of the way are hard. 'Silence and meditation', they are told, 'are the effective means of travelling along this way. God always reveals himself to the solitary and contemplative person.' After urging them to pray assiduously to achieve union with God, Séraphita bids farewell.

Minna and Wilfrid fall on their knees as the soul departs and have a vision in which they see the spirit of Séraphita ascending into the heavens and being transformed into a Seraph. They also see 'the source from which the terrestrial, spiritual and divine worlds derive their movement. Each world had a centre to which all points of its sphere were drawn. These worlds themselves were points which were drawn to the centre of their group. And each group was drawn towards the great celestial regions that communicated with the shining and inexhaustible *source of all that is*.' When the vision is ended Minna and Wilfrid pledge themselves to each other and resolve to tread the path to heaven together.

There is no hint, in any of these extraordinary descriptions of visions, that the author thought that he was describing hallucinations. Nor is there any hint of insincerity in Séraphita's behaviour. The character who receives the least sympathetic treatment from Balzac is Becker who attributes Séraphita's visions to the intervention of demons. What did Balzac himself believe? It is difficult to see Balzac as a convert, even temporarily, to Swedenborgianism. What seems more likely is that he recognised that there are many ways into the world of the spirit and that Swedenborg's way was a perfectly good one for certain people. Looked at in this way the visions become a subjective reality which have their own kind of truth.

Soon after the publication of *Séraphita* there appeared in 1838, the novel *Le Magicien* by Alphonse Esquiros, who had already been mentioned in connection with Eliphas Lévi. Esquiros is a significant figure in that he was one of the first poets of the period to display occult influences. In his *Chants d'un prisonnier*, published in 1841, he wrote:

> *Dieu seul sait mes tourments et mes inquiétudes,*
> *Le but mysterieux des mes jeunes études.*
> *Tout jeune, j'ai cherché sur les pas de Mesmer*
> *A sonder le sommeil, cette profonde mer.*

(God alone knows my torments and my anxieties, the mysterious aim of my youthful studies. As a young man I sought, following Mesmer, to plumb the deep sea of sleep.)

Esquiros belonged to the class of writer who believes himself to be in some sense endowed with occult powers. Into the same category Victor Hugo can be placed. In Hugo's case occultism—or, to be precise, spiritualism—had for a time a very strong influence on his personal life as well as on his work. Like many of his contemporaries, he came to the occult through reading. To quote Levaillant's interesting study, *La Crise mystique de Victor Hugo*: '. . . an attempt was made to reconstitute the list of reading matter which, after 1830, Victor Hugo had been able to, and must have, read to initiate himself into the great secrets of those called the *"illuminés"*. It was not difficult to find in *Les Contemplations* influences stemming from Pythagoreanism, Saint-Simonism and the seductive theories of Swedenborg; it was possible to discern echoes of his conversations with the Fourierist[1] Pierre Leroux exiled near him, and of the doctrines of the Hebrew Cabala which was expounded to him in 1852 by the Jewish Philosopher Alexandre Weil.' Like certain other nineteenth-century poets, Victor Hugo believed that the poet had a divine mission and was endowed with qualities which made him akin to a priest. As some of his poems show, he saw himself in the role of a prophet, through whom the light from the upper realms shines down to the mass of humanity.

Hugo's interest in the occult might have remained purely intellectual had it not been for the death of his daughter in 1843 which not only caused him great grief but set him wondering whether it might be possible to communicate with the dead. He did not make any practical efforts in this direction until ten years later when he was in exile in Jersey for his political activities and was living with his wife and family in a little house overlooking the sea in Marine Terrace, St. Helier. It was here, in 1853, that he first began to hold séances, aided by his family and a small group of friends, his son Charles often acting as medium. He started by communicating, as he believed, with his dead daughter, but later found himself conversing with illustrious men of letters from the past such as Shakespeare, Dante, Aeschlyus and Molière. It was with Shakespeare that he spoke most often, and a curious kind of astral collaboration soon developed between the spirit of the Bard and his modern admirer. The following sample from this strange dialogue is summarised from the record quoted by Levaillant in his *Crise mystique*.

Shakespeare first manifested himself on Friday, 13th January 1854—Victor Hugo had chosen Friday the 13th as being a suitably portentous day to contact the Bard. After the great man had made his presence known, Hugo, curious to know how he occupied his time on the astral plane, asked him:

'Are you going on with your work? If you are, if this is true of you then it must also be true of all the other geniuses—which would imply that, besides the direct creation by God, there is also what one might call indirect creation, this is to say creation by God through the great minds. Do you wish to reply to my question? Are you continuing with your work? If you are continuing with it are you doing so according to the world of men which you once inhabited or according to the world of souls which you now inhabit?'

Shakespeare objected that the question was invalid. 'Human life has human creators. Celestial life has a divine creator. To create—that is the work; to contemplate—that is the reward . . . Heaven would be incomplete if I were able to create anything, a masterpiece would usurp God . . .'

But Shakespeare's inability to create in the divine plane did not prevent him from continuing to create on the human plane. At another session on 22nd January he informed Hugo that he had some poetry which he would like to recite.

'In English or French?' asked Hugo, to which Shakespeare gave the astonishing reply:

'The English language is inferior to the French language.' Then the great Bard proceeded to recite four quatrains ending with the following:

> O mon Dieu j'agenouille à tes pieds mes victoires;
> Hamlet, Lear, à genoux! à genoux, Roméo!
> Courbez-vous mes drapeaux, devant Dieu des gloires!
> Vous chantez Homini, la tombe dit Deo.

(Oh God, I cause my victories to kneel before you; Hamlet, Lear, on your knees! on your knees, Romeo! My flags bow down before the God of glories. You cry *Homini*, the tomb cries *Deo*.)

From then on Shakespeare communicated almost entirely in verse. On 6th February Hugo was holding a séance with his wife and Charles, with his friend Auguste Vacquerie taking notes. Shakespeare manifested himself and began to dictate a poem expressing the poet's inferiority to God as a creator. In the middle of a verse he hesitated and began to rewrite the verse ending with the line:

> Vous fites le pardon, le soir de la douleur.
> (You gave pardon on the evening of grief.)

Vacquerie questioned the clarity of this line, and Hugo intervened:

'I understand that what you are trying to say is: pardon is the sublime offspring of grief. Is that the sense of it?'

Shakespeare replied, yes: then Hugo said that if the verse were rearranged with a different rhyming scheme the line could then read:

> *Tu fis la douleur enfanter le pardon.*
> (You caused grief to give birth to pardon.)

Following discussion of various alternatives, Hugo decided that the most beautiful rendering of the line would be:

> *Vous écriviez douleur; un ange lut: pardon.*
> (You wrote grief; an angel read pardon.)

Verses were also dictated to Hugo by Aeschylus and Molière. During the sessions Hugo always spoke to his illustrious predecessors as an equal, using the familiar '*tu*'.

Countless posthumous masterpieces might have flowed from the great geniuses of the past, transmitted through Hugo's table. But it was not to be. For some reason he and his little group became frightened, and the experiments were abandoned. Hugo declared that he was afraid of where they might lead. Later he had some regrets about having given up his table-turning activities, but he never returned to them.

Possibly Hugo was right to turn aside before he became too deeply involved, because the world of spirits has its frightening side, as is shown by other writers on the subject. An example is Charles de Sivry, whose story *La Boule de verre* appeared in the journal *La Renaissance* (31st August 1873) which had already published a number of other stories on occult themes. In *La Boule de verre* a young couple are visited by a friend who brings with him a glass ball, declaring that he has 'found the key of hidden doors'. He explains that he wishes to experiment with the hypnotism and is looking for a subject. The young wife, who is the narrator of the story, volunteers, and thus begins a strange adventure. The friend comes three times a week and puts her into a trance. Then one day he tells her to remember what she has experienced during her hypnotic sleep.

'He put his finger on my forehead and said: "Remember". What strange sensations I then experienced! I was here and Down There [*Là-Bas*] at the same time and I remembered...'

The world that she remembered was a strange one. She saw: 'A great light, rather wan, and in this light a scene of enchantment: there were jets of water from which emerged metallic butterflies, marvellous tapestries and splendours of strange architecture; and among these things there whirled, to the sound of a peculiar music, men and women of high stature whose extreme beauty astonished me.'

The young woman sinks further and further into somnambulism and senses the approach of death. 'But', she writes, 'this close death is my hope and my joy! For a long time the familiar voices DOWN THERE have been calling me, and the dear ghost does not leave his willing prey.' At the end of the story it is clear that the narrator will soon vanish completely into the other world.

The hypnotist of the story, referred to throughout as C. C . . ., is based on Charles Cros, a poet whose verse had been published in the same journal and whose work shows a strong preoccupation with occultism.

Writers like Cros and de Sivry drew for their inspiration on the steadily growing volume of occult literature. To learn about the Cabala they could turn to Adolphe Franck's study *La Kabbale*, published in 1843, a serious and detailed work devoted to a close analysis of the *Sepher Jetzirah* and the *Zohar*. On spiritualism they could read the works of Allan Kardec or his journal *La Revue spirite*. On the history of magic and folklore as well as the psychology of occultism they could turn to Alfred Maury whose works included: *Histoire des religions de la Grèce antique* (1857–9), *Des Hallucinations hypnagogiques* (1848), *Le Sommeil et les rêves* (1861) and *La Magie et l'astrologie* (1860). Maury was a sceptic and rationalist, but he approached his subjects with a fair and open mind. There was also Ragon de Bettignies, who wrote a number of books purporting to trace the mystical origins of the masonic movement. These were read in the lodges, but also circulated among the public. The principal one is *La Maçonnerie occulte* (1853) which deals with various initiatory fraternities and their relationship with the occult sciences. Ragon's purpose was to remind the masonic brotherhood of the meaning of its symbols and rites by going back to their supposed origins in Greece and Egypt. He probably found his most willing audience in the small number of occult and religiously minded lodges which stood out in contrast to the

Grand Orient with its Voltairean, free-thinking outlook. But probably the most widely read of all occult writers was Eliphas Lévi, the influence of whose works on literature was enormous. After the appearance of Lévi's books the number of writings on occult themes increased dramatically. Lévi was not alone responsible for the increase, but he did more to contribute to it than any other single author.

There was a belief, expressed by Jules Michelet, that the occult arts were essentially a revolt against established authority. It was this aspect of occultism that first attracted a seventeen-year-old prodigy named Arthur Rimbaud who, at the time when he first came into contact with the occult, was languishing discontentedly in his home town of Charleville writing poetry and desperately trying, through juvenile attempts at dissipation, to make a stand against authority symbolised by a tyrannical mother. It was at this point in his life that he met Charles Bretagne, a customs official with a strong penchant for the occult. The two became close friends, and under the influence of Bretagne Rimbaud read books on mysticism, magic and the Cabala. Once his interest was aroused he ransacked both the municipal library and Bretagne's own collection for books on these subjects. During the course of his reading he must have come across the works of Eliphas Lévi.

From the ideas he extracted from his occult reading, Rimbaud put together a theory of poetry and of the poet's role. The poet, Rimbaud decided, must first become an *illuminé* by achieving oneness with the absolute through self-annihilation, and Rimbaud himself believed that he had achieved this. In *Une Saison en Enfer* he wrote: 'Enfin, ô bonheur, ô raison, j'écartai du ciel l'azur, qui est du noir, et je vécus, étincelle d'or de la lumière nature.' (At last, oh happiness, oh reason, I separated the blue, which is from black, from the sky, and I lived, a golden spark of the light of nature.) Having achieved this state the poet can then through his poetry educate others towards his own clarity of vision. This consciousness of the absolute would, however, be impossible to impart through ordinary language, and therefore a new language must be forged in which words have the quality of the things they express. This idea is derived from occult theories about the power of words and their correspondences on the inner plane.

Perhaps the clearest evidence of the occult influences on Rimbaud is his use of alchemical symbolism, as in his *Sonnet des Voyelles*:

> *A noir, E blanc, I rouge, U vert, O bleu; voyelles,*
> *Je dirai quelque jour vos naissances latentes.*
> *A, noir corset velu des mouches éclatantes*
> *Qui bombinent autour des puanteurs cruelles,*
>
> *Golfes d'ombre; E, candeurs des vapeurs et des tentes,*
> *Lances de glaciers fiers, rois blancs, frissons d'ombelles!*
> *I, pourpres, sang craché, rire des lèvres belles*
> *Dans la colère ou les ivresses penitentes,*
>
> *U, cycles, vibrements divins des mers virides;*
> *Paix des patis sèmes d'animaux, paix des rides*
> *Que l'alchimie imprime aux grands fronts studieux.*
>
> *A, suprême Clairon plein des strideurs étranges,*
> *Silences traverses des Mondes et des Anges . . .*
> *O l'Omega, rayon violet de Ses Yeux!*

As Enid Starkie points out in her study of the poet:

'The colours here used are in the correct alchemical sequence during the process of producing the philosopher's gold, the elixir of life. The first colour to appear in the retort is black. That is the colour of dissolution, of putrefaction—as the alchemists say—when the chemicals are broken down into their several component parts, so as to obtain the elements in an unadulterated state, for without this it is not possible to produce the gold. In this state of putrefaction, dissolution or cadaver—there are many epithets for it—the gold is latent though not visible. During the next stage the colour gradually lightens until it becomes white, the state of purity when all extraneous and impure elements have been removed. Next comes the red when, if fortune favours the alchemist, the gold appears. But according to Philalèthe, the experiment is not always so rapidly successful, the red turns to green, remains there for a few days and then turns to blue. This is the last colour, the omega, before blackness is again reached, and care must be taken that this does not happen, for then the process must be started again from the beginning. If the correct temperature and moisture have been sustained then after the hyacinth blue the gold begins to appear, grains of the purest gold bearing no resemblance to ordinary gold, the philosopher's gold, perfect gold, the universal medicine which prolongs life.

'It will be seen that, in this poem, Rimbaud suggests that the poet is a practiser of alchemy, and "A", the colour of black, evokes the images of dissolution and putrefaction. In alchemy one of the symbols for the white colour is the letter "E", and also the word "vapeur"; and the images which the poet links to the vowel "I" are amongst those which Dom Pernety gives in his *Dictionnaire mytho-hermétique*, to designate the alchemical experiment which has reached the stage of the red colour. Green is the colour of Venus, and she was born of the sea—hence the "*vibrements divins*" of the green seas. Finally, last of all, comes the blue, the suspense before the gold appears, the sound of the trumpet announcing victory. In alchemy the final achievement of the gold is often taken as a symbol of attaining the vision of God. Rimbaud writes, "Ses Yeux" as if to indicate the Divinity.'

At the time that Rimbaud wrote *Sonnet des voyelles* alchemy was enjoying a certain vogue in France—Papus's friend Albert Poisson was a leading practitioner. Another of the writers whom it influenced was Gerard de Nerval whose collection of poems *Les Chimères* (first published in 1877) are full of obscure esoteric imagery. Nerval expresses the belief in the resurgence of ancient occult wisdom when he says in one of these poems, *Delfica*:

> *Ils reviendront, ces Dieux que tu pleures toujours!*
> *Le temps va ramener l'ordre des anciens jours;*
> *La terre a trésailli d'un souffle prophétique.*

(They shall return, these Gods whom you mourn! Time will bring back the order of ancient days; the earth has quivered with a prophetic gust.)

By the time that Nerval was writing, literary occultism had reached its apogee, and writers were drawing for inspiration on all the occult sciences—alchemy, astrology, cabalism, spiritualism—anything that opened the doors to the inner world. But any writer who makes use of occultism soon comes up against a law of diminishing returns, for while the more sensational forms of occultism provide excellent subject matter, those who wish to explore the subtler areas of occult symbolism find that their experiences become increasingly personal and progressively less easy to impart in writing. Certainly occultism began to lose its hold on literature around the turn of the century, and writers began to seek inspiration from less recondite sources. Since then the pendulum has swung back again, and today the influence of occultism can again be seen in literature. Writers will always return periodically to the esoteric, for there is a perennial urge to enter, as Edgar Allan Poe expressed it, that

> ... wild, weird clime that lieth sublime
> Out of Space—out of Time.

---

1. Charles Fourier was a socialist thinker much influenced by certain esoteric ideas.

18 Satanists and anti-Satanists

One of the cruder by-products of the nineteenth-century occult revival was a widespread preoccupation with satanism. Encouraged by an extensive literature on the subject, many people derived titillation from the idea that a great diabolical conspiracy existed. Most of this literature professed to expose the conspiracy, but there were those who came to the defence of Satan. One of these was Jules Michelet, author of *La Sorcière*. In this book Michelet argues that medieval sorcery represented a revolt against the religious dogmas and moral rigour of the Christianity of that time. Far from being supernatural or malevolent, it was merely an effort towards liberation. Its main practitioners, he says, were female because women were mistrusted by the Church and their true nature was kept in suppression. Taken in this light, the black mass could be interpreted as a 'redemption of Eve', a triumph of profound instinct over narrow dogma. This theory was one of the sources of inspiration for the interest in diabolism shown by the writers of the symbolist movement.

Quite a different view of satanism is presented by Jules Bois in his *Le Satanisme et la magie*, published in 1895 with a preface by his friend J.-K. Huysmans and a series of bizarre and horrifying illustrations by Henry de Malvost. Bois declares that there are three Satans: the Satan of the poor dispossessed who turn to him for consolation; the Satan worshipped for perverse pleasure by depraved and rich people; and finally, the Satan of the dilettantes who are drawn away from true religion by an intellectual interest in mysticism. He defines satanism as anything that departs from the worship of the One God. Hence Zoroastrianism, Manicheism, Cabalism, ceremonial magic and spiritualism are all forms of satanism. Cornelius Agrippa's

Fourth Book of Occult Philosophy is added as an appendix to the book, as an example of a 'satanist' manual. Bois' accounts of satanist practices are based mainly on the old accounts of the witch-hunters and on the information given him by Huysmans about the activities of Vintras and Boullan. The account which I quoted of a black mass thwarted by Vintras is fairly representative of the book's style and approach.

An equally sensational view of satanism is presented by *Le Diable au dix-neuvième siècle*, by Dr. Bataille, published in 1892. 'Dr. Bataille' was in reality a man named Charles Hacks, a former ship's doctor who claimed to have first-hand evidence of the fact that Satan was being worshipped all over the world and on a scale larger than ever before. The book, which ran to 800,000 words, was first published in serial form and was avidly read by the public.

Bataille's accounts of satanist activities in various parts of the world make colourful reading. In Calcutta, for example, he witnessed a parody of the marriage ceremony in which a male and female ape were united in wedlock by a priest wearing an Egyptian head-dress adorned with gold horns, who afterwards washed his hands in molten lead while reciting diabolic prayers.

By professing allegiance to satanism, Bataille claimed, he had been able to gain initiation into the innermost circles of the brotherhood and to discover that the satanist conspiracy was run by a network of masonic organisations directed from Charleston in the United States by one Albert Pike. The name by which he commonly refers to Pike's organisation is 'the Palladium'.

Although Hacks was ostensibly the sole author of *Le Diable au dix-neuvième siècle* it is likely that the inspiration for the work and possibly much of the text came from a man named Gabriel Jogand-Pagès, who, under the name of Leo Taxil, was responsible for a large number of ostensibly anti-satanist writings. With Jogand we come to one of the most extraordinary episodes in the whole history of occultism, an episode upon which it is worth dwelling at some length as the story is a complex one.

First, it is necessary to explain that Jogand was a confidence trickster of unique stature, and his polemics against satanism were part of a campaign of deception that must rank as one of the most skilful practical jokes of all time. Jogand's elaborate hoax was the crowning achievement of a life dedicated to rebellion against authority beginning with his boyhood struggles against a tyrannical father. His career is such a bizarre one that it is worth tracing from the beginning.

Gabriel Jogand was born in Provence in about 1854. His mother's maiden name was Pagès, and he later sometimes used the name Jogand-Pagès. He began his education under the Jesuits at the school of the Sacré Cœur in Marseilles. In 1863 he entered the school of Notre Dame de Mongré at Villefranche-sur-Saône, and in 1867 went to the Jesuit College of Saint Louis where he had his first contact with freemasonry. Through a school friend, whose father was a freemason, he obtained a book by Mgr. de Ségur attacking masonry and describing a number of masonic rituals; these he read eagerly until the book was found in his school desk and confiscated. This, however, only reinforced his interest in the forbidden subject which he continued to study. His studies led him to a rejection of religion, and at the age of fourteen he announced to his distressed confessor that he had become a free thinker.

His later activities as a revolutionary journalist were foreshadowed when he started up a schoolboy journal called *Le Type*. The school authorities disapproved of the journal and took the opportunity to suppress it while Jogand was absent with typhoid fever. After his recovery he did not return to the school. He and his brother Maurice began to mix in revolutionary circles in Marseilles and decided to abscond to Italy to escape from their father and his oppressive influence. They set out in a coach for the Italian frontier armed with knives and pistols, but were stopped by a gendarme and taken back. Their father was not disposed to be lenient. As a punishment Gabriel was sent for eight months to a juvenile penal establishment. The experience instilled in him a lasting hatred of his father and, by identification, of the Church.

There followed a short period at the Lycée, during which he continued to be at the forefront of revolutionary activity; then came the outbreak of the Franco-Prussian War when he volunteered for the Army and was sent to serve in Algeria. After the war two violently anti-clerical republican journals, *La Marotte* and *L'Egalité*, were started in Marseilles. Jogand became editor of the former and a regular contributor to the latter. He later took over the editorship of a similar journal, *Le Frondeur*, but, having raised its circulation to 30,000 he left to form an exclusively anti-clerical journal called *A Bas la calotte*.

Then came a curious *volte-face*. Shortly after his initiation as a freemason in 1881, he left masonry and began to fulminate against it. Furthermore he announced his reconciliation with the Catholic Church and in 1887 published a book of memoirs entitled *The Confessions of an Ex-free-thinker*. In the same year he was received in audience by Pope Leo XIII. The Catholic polemicists thought that they had captured an important defector from freemasonry. Only later was it to become apparent how subtly Jogand had deceived them.

Meanwhile Jogand was secretly laying a trap for the Catholics. The bait was a renegade satanist called Diana Vaughan who had apparently held high office in the Palladium. The Catholics saw in her the possibility of bringing over to their side a defector even more valuable than Jogand himself, a person who would be able to provide them with powerful ammunition in the form of inside information on her former colleagues. What they did not realise was that their potential convert did not exist. To all intents and purposes she was a figment of Jogand's fertile imagination. Yet so skilfully did Jogand present her to the world that she quickly became a celebrity. He even invented the most colourful genealogy for her.

She was, the story went, a descendant of the seventeenth-century English alchemist and Rosicrucian, Thomas Vaughan, who had made his life's aim the overthrow of the papacy and who had signed a pact with the devil.[1] In 1646 he had travelled to America and, during a sojourn with an Indian tribe, had received a visitation from Venus-Astarte with whom he had enjoyed a physical union. Eleven days afterwards the goddess had presented him with a daughter and departed. Leaving the daughter, whom he called Diana, in the care of the Indians, he had returned to England. Diana had married the chief of the tribe and conceived a son. It was from this son that Diana Vaughan was supposedly descended, her father being an ardent Palladist who had initiated his daughter into the cult and while she was still a young girl had pledged her in marriage to the demon Asmodeus. On 8th April 1889, when she was twenty-five years old, she was, on the orders of Lucifer, officially presented to her fiancé in the Sanctum Regnum of Charleston. Asmodeus appeared on a diamond-studded throne and announced to Albert Pike that he was consecrating Diana as high priestess and interpreter of his wishes; then he demanded that this be communicated to all branches of the organisation.

This was the person whom Jogand held out as being ripe for conversion to the Catholic cause. But in order to make this possibility credible he had to show that Diana had already taken one step away from Albert Pike and his Palladium. The reasons for her disenchantment with the Palladium centred round another high priestess named Sophia Walder, nominally the daughter of Phileas Walder, a Protestant minister and high-ranking freemason, but in reality the issue of a union between Lucifer and Walder's mistress Ida Jacobsen. According to a prediction, Sophia would go to Jerusalem where, in the summer of 1896, she would, as a result of a union with the demon Bitru, give birth to a daughter. Thirty-three years later this daughter would also have a daughter, by the demon Decarabia, who, after a further thirty-three years (1962) would give birth to the Anti-Christ.

As potential great-grandmother of the Anti-Christ, Sophia Walder was the object of great veneration among the Palladists and received special teaching from Albert Pike himself. She soon quarrelled with her fellow high priestess, Diana Vaughan, and things came to a head during an initiation ceremony in Paris when Diana refused to perform a part of the ritual that involved spitting on a consecrated host and transfixing it with a dagger. This led to Diana's leaving the original Palladium and organising her own 'Luciferains Indépendants et Régénérés' —an association which owed allegiance to Lucifer but not to Satan. A 'convent' was established in London and a propaganda organisation set up under the guidance of Diana.

On 21st March 1895 appeared the first issue of a new periodical entitled *Le Palladium régénéré et libre—Directrice: Miss Diana Vaughan*. In reality, of course, it was Jogand who had launched the journal. It enabled him to lend credence to his story and also, under the guise of Diana Vaughan, to get in a few mischievous pieces of blasphemy. The doctrine of the new sect, as outlined in the journal, was as follows. There are two supreme beings who struggle for supremacy: Lucifer, the principle of intelligence and light; and Adonai, the principle of matter and death. Adonai is the creator of man's physical body, while Lucifer gives him his intelligence and power of reproduction.

Satanists and anti-Satanists

The soul is an emanation of Lucifer which Adonai seeks constantly to seduce. Most of the universe is emancipated from the rule of Adonai, but the earth and a planet called Oolis are still under his sway.

The principal angels of Lucifer, who is the true God, are: Moloch, Beelzebub, Asmodeus, Anti-Christ, Astarte, Leviathan and Behemoth. They are of two sexes. Those of Adonai, who are sexless and are called *maléakhs*, are: Michael, Gabriel, Raphael and Auriel. Another of Adonai's servants who is particularly malevolent and very powerful is the Holy Virgin, called Mirzam by the Palladists. Jesus, the son of Mirzam, had originally had good qualities, but pride had caused him to betray the true God.

In the year 1995, Miss Vaughan's doctrine states, the Anti-Christ will appear and the Pope, a converted Jew, will abandon Catholicism and swear allegiance to Lucifer. This event will be followed by a year of war in which the Catholics will be exterminated. Then will come a celestial struggle between the two powers resulting in a victory for Lucifer and the banishing of the defeated ones to the planet Saturn.

Jogand must have enjoyed concocting this hotch-potch of rather childish blasphemy with its crude reversals of the traditional good and bad attributions. Even more satisfying to him must have been the horrified way in which the faithful reacted to these heresies and the zeal with which they prayed for Diana to abandon the Palladium altogether and enter the Christian fold. After three issues of the journal had appeared Jogand decided that it was time for their prayers to be answered. The *Palladium régénéré* ceased production and, on 1st July 1895, was replaced by another periodical, or rather story in serial form, entitled *Miss Diana Vaughan: Mémoires d'une ex-Paladiste*. Diana, it appeared from this, had quarelled with the London headquarters of her organisation and had been converted to Catholicism. She was now living in retirement in a convent and working on further instalments of her memoirs.

These memoirs, which were later published in book form, provided further startling revelations about the activities of the Palladium. One account of a Palladist mass gives an idea of the tone of the book—and of Jogand's powers of invention. It describes a ceremony presided over by a magus on whose chasuble is embroidered in red the image of a crucifix upside-down. His choir boy is an old Jew who wears a devil's tail attached to his rear. An assistant priest and priestess are also in attendance.

The mass begins when the magus faces the altar dedicated to Baphomet and says: 'Most holy Palladium, pledge of victory, through you comes all our hope.' The liturgy then continues as follows:

JEWISH CHOIR BOY: Brothers and Sisters, the Palladium protects us against the maléakhs.

OFFICIATING MAGUS: Through you comes all our hope; it is our Lord God Satan who has established you among us.

JEWISH CHOIR BOY: All of us, in our hearts, give thanks to our Lord God Satan.

OFFICIATING MAGUS: It is our Lord God Satan who has established you among us; you are the magic symbol of Him whom we call the Great Architect of the Universe and the Father of the Temple who is peace for all men.

JEWISH CHOIR BOY: Glory to the Palladium!

The responses continue in this vein for some time; then the assistant priest brings forward a plate covered with freshly cut herbs.

'As the scythe has cut the herbs,' says the officiating magus, 'so we cut off the heads of the ministers of Adonai, until the day of glory of our Lord God Satan . . .'

The assistant priest places the plate on the ground and lies down with his head close to it. The officiating magus then continues:

'Herbs of the prairie, Satan, the Most High, will give you eternal life. Good demons of our Lord God Satan, enter these herbs. Michael, Gabriel and Raphael, if you are here flee away! I drive you hence. Sarakrom, if you are here flee away! I drive you hence. Lilith, if you are here, flee away! I drive you hence. Good demons, welcome, enter into these herbs . . . Barym! Pella! Golgho! . . . My Brothers and Sisters, take part in the banquet.'

The assistant priest, still lying down, eats a large portion of the herbs; then he rises and passes the plate round the congregation, each of whom takes a pinch.

After this parody of the communion, various other obscenities follow, including the crushing of a spider against a host. The ceremony also included the reading of a letter from Julian the

Apostate which had been dictated by the Emperor when he was evoked in a previous ceremony.

All these revelations were eagerly lapped up by the anti-masonic party. Yet, despite the excitement produced among them by Diana Vaughan's conversion, there were those who were inclined to doubt her credentials. These sceptics seized their opportunity, at a special Anti-masonic Congress held at Trent on 29th September 1896, by calling on Jogand to produce details of Diana's conversion, the names of her godfather and godmother and that of the Bishop who had authorised her first communion. Jogand declared that he had all of these details in his pocket, but was withholding them for fear of giving Diana's enemies a clue to her whereabouts. Ever since the 'conversion' Jogand had maintained that Diana must be kept in rigorous seclusion, for the rage of her former Palladist colleagues knew no bounds, and they might well try to assassinate her.

Jogand's handling of the situation brought immense relief to the supporters of Diana Vaughan, for there were now many people, including a number of high-ranking prelates, who had a vested interest in her. Were she to be proved a myth they would be made to look very foolish indeed—which was, of course, exactly the situation that Jogand had intended to bring about.

By now Jogand was an international celebrity and for a while he basked in the acclaim of his anti-masonic supporters. But meanwhile doubts about the existence of Diana Vaughan continued to be expressed. In November 1896, for example, there appeared in the *Kölnische Volkszeitung* an article declaring that all reports about Diana Vaughan were fairy tales. It was signed by none other than Dr. Bataille, though it is in fact extremely unlikely that Dr. Bataille's *alter ego*, Dr. Hacks, was responsible. What seems more likely is that Jogand himself wrote it as part of a campaign to sow doubt about Diana Vaughan in preparation for the final glorious moment when he would remove his mask.

The demands for the production of Diana became an insistent clamour, and finally Jogand judged the moment ripe to play his final card. In the issue of Diana's memoirs published on 25th February 1897 she announced that she would appear in person on 19th April in the lecture hall of the Geographical Society in the Boulevard Saint-Germain.

On the scheduled day the lecture hall was filled to overflowing with a mixed audience of Catholics and freemasons, with a liberal sprinkling of journalists. At the appointed time, instead of Diana Vaughan there appeared on the platform the imposing figure of Gabriel Jogand, as usual meticulously dressed and with a *pince-nez* clipped to his well-shaped nose. His large, distinguished-looking head turned and scanned the audience. Then, with the greatest self-possession, he began to speak:

'Reverend Fathers, Ladies and Gentlemen:

'I must first of all offer my thanks to my colleagues and to the Catholic Press who have given support to my campaign during the past twelve years.

'But now, in addressing myself to you, I must confess that that campaign is something quite different from what you supposed it to be. When Dr. Bataille published *Le Diable au dix-neuvième siècle* you believed him to be devoted to the Catholic cause, and you believed that he was uncovering the dark secrets of Masonry. You thoroughly approved of that.

'Now, I have to tell you that Dr. Bataille is no Catholic, but on the contrary a free-thinker who, not out of any malice, but for his own personal satisfaction, wrote this to see if he could deceive you. I know this because Bataille is an old schoolfriend of mine, and I inspired him to do it. It was really I who composed and constructed this book.

'And now a word about Diana Vaughan. I could have produced her before you today, but, for reasons which I hope to make clear presently, I have not done so. She is my secretary. That is of no importance, but it is important that she is not a Catholic either, but a Protestant so far as she has any religion at all. We three have co-operated to produce what I like to call this "mystification". They say that in the art of cookery the good roaster of meat is born and not made; and so it is with practical joking. It is in my blood; I was born like that.

'If one were to succeed in a plan of this kind, it was at first absolutely necessary not to confide in anyone. Even my wife was ignorant of what I was really doing. When I repudiated my anti-clerical writings I had to be very careful. The Anti-clerical League, which I founded, expelled me on July 27, 1885, for infamous conduct and treason against the society. I accept it all, but for the word *traitor*. I asked them to strike that out, and I said: "You do not understand what I am saying now, but you will understand later."

'Of course I had to put up with a good deal. They said that, under cover of attending the Anti-clerical Congress at Rome which I had organised, I was secretly received at the Vatican and bribed with a million francs to turn against the anti-clericals.

'This was absolutely untrue. My friend Dr. Baudon is here this evening I believe. He was with me all the time I was in Italy, and knows that I never visited the Vatican, and he also knows that I saw much of General Canzio-Garibaldi, son-in-law of the great Garibaldi, and was loyal to the anti-clericals and the republicans. A good many of my friends think I am mad, but none of them thinks of me as a traitor. They know, in a way, that I am really with them. If Dr. Baudon is in the room now, I am going to ask him if that is how they talk about me.

[A number of voices shout: 'It is true! It is true!']

'And now I come to the mystification itself. I had to be converted like Saul on the road to Damascus. I convinced a very worthy priest, a simple soul, about this, and afterwards a Jesuit who was formerly a military almoner and was a much more difficult proposition. He told me to practise the spiritual exercises of St. Ignatius. I knew nothing about them, but I had to study them so as to make the right impression.

'All this happened after I had written my book on Freemasonry. There was no mystification about that. I think Masonry is indebted to me for the service I did it in publishing the rituals. It seems to me that enlightened Freemasons must find all that hocus-pocus ridiculous and would be glad to see it suppressed.

'This is by the way, and we must return to the facts. After my conversion I found that there was a large number of Catholics who thought that the title "Great Architect of the Universe" was just a polite substitute for Lucifer, Satan or the Devil. They linked it all up with spiritualism and said that Satan used to appear at the lodges and preside at the meetings. It is all very well to say that I imposed upon the credulousness of these people. They forced me into it. Do you know that there was a Canon of Fribourg who came to me at the time of my conversion and said:

'"Monsieur Taxil, you are a saint. God has drawn you out of so deep an abyss that you are overflowing with grace. When I heard of your conversion I immediately took the train to come and see you. When I return I want to be able to say not only that I have seen you but that you have worked a miracle before me."

'I said I did not understand, and I could not do that.

'He ignored that. "Yes," he said, "a miracle. Any kind of miracle you like. For instance change this chair into a walking stick or an umbrella."

'I told him as gently as possible that I could not do things like that, but I could see from his face that he did not believe me. I sent him back to Fribourg firmly believing that it was only on account of my humility that I had not obliged him. Later he sent me a great Gruyère cheese with pious inscriptions and mystic hieroglyphs engraved on the rind with a knife. It was an excellent cheese and I ate it with a feeling of great respect and genuine gratitude to the giver.

'It was not quite like that at Rome, but even there Cardinal Parrochi congratulated me on account of my profound knowledge of the Satanic character of the Masonic rituals although I had been nothing more than an apprentice Freemason. The Holy Father also told me that he had read all my writings on Freemasonry, and that they confirmed all the evidence from other quarters concerning its Satanic character.

'At this stage I realised that I must have assistance because the work was too much for one man. I approached an old school friend, and he agreed to co-operate. You must realise that Dr. Bataille was acting in perfectly good faith. He had been a ship's doctor and was very interested in spiritualism. Also he had seen some very odd things on his travels. It was not difficult to convince him about the Satanism of the Palladium, and it was all the easier because Monsignor Meurin, Bishop of Port Louis, who is a great student of archaeology, was himself thoroughly convinced about the matter. I do not think that Bataille believes in the phenomena himself. But he was quite willing to accept the idea that there were a number of people who did, and who behaved as if they did.

'That is how *Le Diable au dix-neuvième siècle* came to be written. I conceived and inspired the whole thing. It was based upon my earlier works on Freemasonry, but it was written up and expanded so as to appeal to a much wider public. Dr. Bataille fully entered into the spirit of it, but I was the real author of the book.

'Because of what I had said in the earlier work concerning

the feminine cult of Freemasonry, this had to be developed too. That was the reason for the introduction of Diana Vaughan. As I said before, Diana Vaughan actually exists, but from what I have already said it will be evident that no purpose could have been served by my producing her before you.

'Miss Vaughan thoroughly entered into the spirit of this mystification too. It was vastly entertaining to her, and in fact the amusement she got out of it has been her sole reward. The young lady is French, but it is true that her family are of American extraction. She is highly intelligent and very well educated, and her religious traditions are Lutheran or Calvinist. I think that this is what made her so ready to help in the staging of my little comedy. She was not at all averse to taking a rise out of the Catholics.

'Miss Vaughan was my secretary, and I put it to her, when I first suggested that she should co-operate, that her salary should be increased. She was not interested in that. The idea itself appealed to her strongly and stimulated her sense of humour. She thoroughly enjoyed being the high priestess of Lucifer, and the chief inspector of the Palladium. It was amusing to be photographed in semi-masculine costume wearing the sash of the order.

'She did not, of course, write the *Confessions of an ex-Palladist*. I was the author of that, but I could not have done it so successfully without her inspiration. The work had to have the authentic feminine touch which it would have lacked if I had not had the advantage of her help and guidance. And there was also the correspondence with the clergy and her other supporters. She composed the letters herself and wrote them with her own hand. It is a very lively correspondence as I am sure all those who have been favoured with a letter from Miss Vaughan will agree.

'Her instinctive taste for intrigue and mystification was also very useful. I should have found it very difficult to arrange that this correspondence should always come from the right places at the right times. It was a complicated matter, and she arranged it most artistically.

'Although there are some who will not do so, I hope there are a few who will take this little comedy that I have staged in good part. I should be sorry if my mystification were taken too seriously or if anyone had been injured by it; but however that may be, ladies and gentlemen, perhaps I ought to end on a rather more serious note. I am here to announce the decease of something which has been very near to the hearts of some of you. The Palladium exists no more. I was the creator of it, and I have destroyed it. You have nothing more to fear from its sinister influence. The great enemy of Christian men and of the Catholic Church is dead.[2]'

At the end of his speech Jogand bowed politely to his flabbergasted audience, strolled off the platform and calmly retired to a café on the other side of the boulevard where he ordered a coffee and cognac. Immediately after he had left pandemonium broke out. The embarrassment of the Catholics quickly turned to fury, exacerbated by the jeers of the masonic party. Only the prompt action of the police in clearing the hall prevented a riot.

The climax of Jogand's elaborate hoax was followed by the desired results. The anti-masonic party was thrown into complete disarray. After the Diana Vaughan affair it was difficult for anyone to take Satanism seriously as a threat. By the same token it was impossible for Satanism to exercise the sinister fascination that it had done for writers like Huysmans. Jogand's extraordinary prank therefore had, in the end, a salutary effect in that it helped to destroy an unhealthy obsession.

---

1. This story is, of course, far removed from the real facts of Thomas Vaughan's life.
2. H. T. F. Rhodes, *The Satanic Mass*.

19   *The Indian Summer of Occultism*

By the turn of the century the more extravagant forms of magical activity had begun to give way to an armchair occultism which was more of a point of view than a doctrine. It became fashionable to take an 'occult' view of history, such as was propounded by Mme Blavatsky's *Secret Doctrine* and Edouard Schurés' *Les Grands Initiés*. The latter work enjoyed an extraordinary success both in France and abroad. First published in 1889, it ran through eighty-five editions in the next thirty-seven years. Schuré claimed that the founders of the great religions, including Christ, were initiates of the same basic teaching. His references show that he was greatly influenced by Fabre d'Olivet.

Those who were not content to be armchair occultists were, however, still active. Papus's group, with its many ramifications, had become the focal point of esoteric activity, and his two journals, *La Voile d'Isis* and *L'Initiation*, were the main organs of the movement. The other occult journals included: *Le Progrès spirite*, *L'Echo du merveilleux*, *La Vie mystérieuse* and *La Revue spirite*. The number of practising occultists in Paris was enough to support at least one business supplying their needs, for an advertisement appeared regularly in *L'Initiation* proclaiming that Léonis, of 391 Rue des Pyrénées, Paris 20ᵉ, was able to supply 'hypnotic spheres, hypnotic mirrors . . . planchettes with an extra-light touch . . . magic wands, objects for magical altars' and other paraphernalia.

Papus's followers were active in the provinces as well as in Paris. A letter from the president of an affiliated group at Le Havre, which appeared in *L'Initiation* at the beginning of 1895, reported: 'As we are engaging in all branches of occultism the group is necessarily composed of people interested in magnetism, spiritualism, hypnotism etc. and is therefore made up of heterogeneous elements. Some are fervent Cardecists, others are interested only in table turning.' The writer goes on to say that the group had tried magic once without much result and had abandoned it, but that he was continuing with it on his own as he regarded it as 'the only true science'. Another very active provincial group was the Société d'études philosophiques et psychiques at Tours, which published regular reports in *L'Initiation*.

Papus's Martinist Order was also flourishing, and in 1910 a further three grades were added to the existing four. Papus's deputy in the group, and later his successor, was Charles Detré, who called himself Teder. In 1913 the Hermanubis Lodge of the Order issued the following proclamation to the Martinists: 'On Sundays, between two and three o'clock, and on Wednesdays, between ten and eleven o'clock in the evening, the Martinist brothers, having paid homage to the superior plane by an ardent prayer, are invited to concentrate their thought, illumined by the supreme force, Love, in asking our master Christ for the relief and cure of the sick.'

The Martinists appear to have been a highly effective group, for by this time they had succeeded in establishing branches abroad. Articles in *L'Initiation* reported the growth of Martinism in both Italy and Russia. In the issue of July 1910, for example, appeared a notice that a branch of the order had been established at St. Petersburg. Another article, in January 1911, informed readers that in Russia 'Martinist and occult movements are taking on immense proportions . . . Through the teachings expounded in the works of Papus, Eliphas Lévi, Stanislas de Guaita and Saint-Yves d'Alveydre, the ideas of these Masters are manifesting themselves to an extraordinary degree.' In the growth of occult movements in Russia on the eve of the Revolution of 1917 we see an exact parallel to the flourishing of such movements before the French Revolution and again in the periods leading up to the various crises of the nineteenth century.

An interesting offshoot of the Martinist Order was the Gnostic Catholic Church, founded by Jules Doinel, an official in the library of Orleans. It was later headed by Fabre des Essarts, who called himself the Patriarch Synesius and was also a poet of the Symbolist movement. The doctrines of his Church were based on the traditional Gnostic idea that the world was created by an evil god to ensnare spirit in matter and prevent its return to the true source of creation. For the members of the French Gnostic Church the way of escape lay through the two extremes of libertinism or asceticism.

In addition to the Martinists a number of other organisations continued to be active. The Theosophical Society had its small band of faithful adherents, and in 1908 started an offshoot called the Knights of the Round Table. Another group that came into being was the Friends of Saint-Yves d'Alveydre which was formed with the purpose of collating and publishing certain manuscripts of Saint-Yves as well as propagating his ideas. This society published a whole series of works relating to Saint-Yves. It also had a headquarters equipped with a library and a lecture hall.

Meanwhile the Naundorffists continued to hope for the return of the French monarchy in the form of the Naundorff family. They published a journal called *La Revue Naundorffiste historique*, which contained articles on the genealogy of the royal family and its supposed present descendants as well as on the events surrounding the disappearance of the Dauphin. In 1906 the journal carried a report of a commemorative mass held for Marie Antoinette, which was attended by the Naundorffists and certain members of the aristocracy. Cries of '*Vive le roi*' were heard as the faithful band emerged from the church. But it was a forlorn cry, for the world of the twentieth century no longer cared about the fate of the Dauphin, and the review ceased publication in November of the same year.

The followers of the Prophet Vintras fared better; Vintrasian rites were practised in Paris until at least the 1930s and may still be practised today, though I have no information to this effect. Pierre Geyraud, in his *Les Religions nouvelles de Paris*, gives an interesting account of a Vintrasian ceremony which he attended presumably not long before the book was published in 1939. Geyraud relates that, as a result of his investigations into occult sects for his book, he found himself hounded by a group of Satanists who were working spells against him. His occultist friends gave him various pieces of advice. One of them offered to arrange for a Vintrasian priest he knew to perform the Sacrifice of Glory of Melchizedek for Geyraud's protection.

This genealogy of this Vintrasian group was as follows: after the death of the Prophet, the majority of followers, who did not recognise Boullan as the new head, grouped themselves under the leadership of Edouard Souleillon. They celebrated the Sacrifice of Glory in a sanctuary at Champigny-sur-Seine and also in two Vintrasian chapels in Paris, one in the Rue Sainte-Anne, and the other near the church of Montrouge. Persecution instigated by Rome broke up this group, but they continued to practise underground, and it was a priest of this affiliation who came to the aid of Geyraud.

The ritual is described by Geyraud as taking place in a third-floor flat in the Javel district. A chest of drawers, which had been pushed against the wall and covered with a red cloth served as an altar. On it stood a champagne glass, a small plate containing some hosts and a lighted candle in a candlestick. On the wall above the altar was pinned a cloth embroidered with the four letters of the Tetragrammaton, to the left of which hung a framed portrait of Vintras.

The celebrant was barefooted and dressed in a long red chasuble over which he wore a large cross made of white cloth, the cross-piece of which hung below his belly to symbolise 'the crucifixion of the phallus'. He was assisted by his wife, also barefoot, who was dressed in a white tunic and green cape. Only two other worshippers were present.

The priest began by reciting prayers with his wife giving the responses. Having invoked the Archangel Michael, he poured some white wine into the champagne glass while his wife filled another glass with red wine—white wine apparently was a privilege reserved for the male priesthood. The celebrant then turned and pointed his left hand at Geyraud's forehead, extended his right hand upwards and intoned a long formula of exorcism. Then, still muttering formulas which Geyraud was unable to understand, he took a host from the plate, broke it in two, burnt the edge of each fragment in the candle flame and said: 'Here is the communion of bread and fire.' He then ate one of the pieces and offered the other to Geyraud who, much to the priest's consternation, politely refused. After giving Geyraud a disapproving look the priest drank the wine, then his wife drank from her glass. There were more prayers, and finally the proceedings terminated with an invocation to the Holy Spirit.

After the ceremony Geyraud questioned the priest about his doctrines. He was told that the new Vintrasians remained faithful to the old, but laid much greater emphasis on the imminence of the reign of the Paraclete.

Outside the mainstream of French occultism—if the term 'mainstream' can be used of occultism—was a mystical form of Breton nationalism, a parallel to the Celtic romanticism being propagated in Britain and Ireland by such figures as W. B. Yeats, George Russell and William Sharp. In 1899 a Breton called Jean Le Fustec started what he claimed was a French branch of the Welsh Gorsedd. This developed into a society called The Bards, which Geyraud discusses in his *Les Sociétés secrètes de Paris*. The members were divided into three grades: Bards, who were the guardians of words and chants and who dressed in blue; Ovates, the conservers of traditions and symbols, who dressed in green; and Druids, initiators to the divine sciences and wisdom, who wore white.

In the same book Geyraud offers a rather tantalising mention of a highly secret Rosicrucian group. He quotes the following passage from Paul Sédir's *Histoire des Rose Croix* (published in 1910):

'To avoid omitting anything, we should mention here a manifestation of a very elevated Rosicrucian centre, the F.T.L., whose mode of recruitment and the centre itself have never been described. We know that this society began to spread in about 1898 and we suppose that the neophytes are put in touch with the members of the order in a way comparable to that described in the Rosicrucian poster placarded in Paris in 1623.

'The initiation is very pure and essentially Christian.'

Geyraud continues:

'I searched for a long time without result to find out if this F.T.L. still had adepts in Paris. Many who devote their lives to esoteric history and teach it were ignorant even of the existence of this secret society. Very rare were those who were able to assure me that it still exists and that it has in our capital a very small number of followers.

'All the same I did meet one. He was a man who worked in films. He was very surprised to learn that I knew of his affiliation. While acknowledging in a friendly fashion the sincere purpose of my enquiry, he did not feel able to give me the slightest enlightenment about his F.T.L., its aims, its recruitment, its rites—or even its name!

'This F.T.L. is certainly surrounded by mystery! None the less I have been able to find out that its present head is M. C . . ., a friend of Barlet, who was Grand Master of the Cabalistic Order of the Rosy Cross; that it has a branch at Bordeaux called the Saint-Graal; and that is founder was . . . Sédir himself.'

Most of the groups that were active in the early years of the twentieth century were in some sense continuations of the occult movement of the previous century whose antecedents I have traced in this study back to the period preceding the Revolution. The momentum which had carried de Guaita, Papus and Péladan was now slowing down. Though there was a continuation of occult activity which connects with the present day it is possible to discern the setting up of a new momentum after the First World War. If occultism tends to flourish in a period of impending crises, when the crisis actually arrives the opiates of occultism cease to be effective and men must turn their minds to the preservation of their lives or the defence of their country. The era that forms the subject of this book can be said to have ended with the holocaust of the First World War. By the time that the smoke had cleared all the most important figures from the occult movement of the nineteenth century were dead. Papus died in 1916 and Péladan in 1918. Only the visions they had nurtured remained. The Kingdom of the Paraclete had yet to arrive.

APPENDIX A

Eliphas Lévi's Descendants

Eliphas Lévi's son, whom Chacornac refers to as 'M.A.C.' was one of the people who accompanied the body to its last resting place. Chacornac's life of Lévi provides the following information in a footnote (pp. 290–1):

'We were especially acquainted with M.A.C. It was in the spring of 1914 that we had this pleasure. M.A.C. lived in the Rue Chanoinesse, near Notre Dame. He was a fine old man of medium height with white hair; we were immediately struck by his resemblance to Eliphas Lévi. His face radiated goodness and sweetness, and he was very kind.

'We explained the aim of our visit and M.A.C. smiled happily on hearing the name of his father, whom he told us, he held in great veneration. He then showed us numerous manuscripts which he had himself patiently drawn up according to the works of Eliphas Lévi. Then, opening a bookcase, he showed us the entire works of his father, in the sumptuous bindings of the period.

'M.A.C. gave us, in memory of our friendly conversations, a bust of Eliphas Lévi, and one of his manuscripts . . .

'Unfortunately our relationship stopped there, due to the dreadful calamity which shook the entire world at that moment; and in 1916 we learned with sorrow of the death of M.A.C.

'In 1919 we met the son of M.A.C. We are indebted to him for much precious information about the life of his grandfather, and we thank him sincerely for having helped us in our task.'

Levi's only daughter died while still a child.

APPENDIX B

Eliphas Lévi and Aleister Crowley

The English magus Aleister Crowley, who died in 1947 after a remarkably colourful and somewhat notorious life, believed himself to be a reincarnation of Lévi. In his book *Magick in Theory and Practice* he cited a number of points in support of this belief.

'The date of Eliphas Lévi's death was about six months previous to that of Aleister Crowley's birth. The reincarnating ego is supposed to take possession of the foetus at about this stage of development . . .

'Aleister Crowley found a certain district of Paris incomprehensibly familiar and attractive to him. This was not the ordinary phenomenon of the *déjà vu*, it was chiefly a sense of being at home again. He discovered long after that Lévi had lived in the neighbourhood for many years.

'There are many curious similarities between the events of Eliphas Lévi's life and that of Aleister Crowley. The intention of the parents that their son should have a religious career; the inexplicable ostracism which afflicted him and whose authors seemed somehow to be ashamed of themselves; the events related to marriage: all these offer surprisingly close parallels . . .'

More interesting still is the evidence of Crowley's copy of Chacornac's life, still extant, which has a number of pencilled notes made by Crowley in the margins commenting on certain passages which seemed to bear out his reincarnation theory.

On page 108 of Chacornac's book is a quotation from one of Lévi's letters to Baron Spedalieri describing an occasion when his little daughter was terribly ill and at the point of death as a result of having been looked after by an incompetent nurse. Constant bared his chest and placed the child against it, at the same time blowing gently into her mouth and nostrils. Then he took some warm water and sprinkled it on to her forehead calling upon the Father, Son and Holy Ghost. This immediately revived the child, who opened her eyes and began to smile. Crowley's annotation says: 'Cf. saving Lola Zaza', indicating that he believed he had saved his daughter's life by the same means. Lola Zaza was Crowley's child by his first wife Rose.

On page 213 is a passage describing how Lévi often wrote under a kind of involuntary impulse and, on reading over what he had written afterwards, apprehended the words for the first time with 'a sort of delight mingled with terror'. Crowley marked this passage with three vertical strokes and the word 'Yes!' Crowley's *Book of the Law* was written in this way and his reactions to it were the same.

To quote one more example, on page 242 is a description of Lévi's ability to deflate pretentious people: 'One evening he found himself at a dinner party where a lawyer who prided himself as a word-spinner was telling a story as though it were his own. While the raconteur was searching for a telling phrase Eliphas Lévi suddenly broke in and continued the story by reciting an old fifteenth-century narrative poem which the lawyer had plagiarised.' Crowley's note in the margin says: 'As I did with Frank Harris.'

Select Bibliography

The following is a selection of some of the books I have found most useful for this study. Where possible I have given the publisher's name and in some instances have added my comments. In the case of Eliphas Lévi I have attempted to list all his important works published under that name; I have also listed the unpublished manuscripts that I consulted.

Bibliographies
Caillet, Albert L., *Manuel bibliographique des sciences psychiques et occultes* (3 vols., Paris, Dorbon, 1912). This monumental work, covering all aspects of occultism, is an invaluable source of reference.
Châteaurhin, G. de., *Bibliographie du Martinisme* (Lyons, Derain-Raclet, 1939). By definition limited in scope, but extremely useful.
Yves-Plessis, R., *Bibliographie française de la sorcellerie* (Paris, Chacornac, 1900). Very useful classified list of books on all aspects of occultism, though not as wide in scope as Caillet.

Texts
Barruel, the Abbé Augustin, *Mémoires pour servir a l'histoire du Jacobinisme* (French version, London, Le Boussonier, 1797-8; English version, London, the author, 1797-8).
Christian, Paul (pseud. for J.-B. Pitois): (i) *L'Homme rouge des Tuileries.*
(ii) *L'Histoire de la magie* (Paris, Furne, Jouvet, 1870)
Court de Gébelin, Antoine, *Le Monde primitif analysé et comparé avec le monde moderne* (9 vols., Paris, the author, 1773-84).
Esquiros, Alphonse, *Le Magicien*, a novel (Paris, Desessart, 1838).

Etteilla (pseud. for Alliette): (i) *Cours théorique et pratique du livre de Thot* (Paris, 1791).
(ii) *Etteilla, ou manière de se récréer avec un jeu de cartes* (Paris, 1770).
(iii) *Le Zodiaque mystérieux, ou les oracles d'Etteilla* (Amsterdam and Paris, 1820).
Fabre d'Olivet, Antoine: (i) *Les Vers dorés de Pythagore* (Paris, Treuttel et Wurtz, 1813).
(ii) *La Langue hébraïque réstitué* (2 vols., Paris, Barrios, Eberhart, the author, 1815–16).
(iii) *Histoire philosophique du genre humain* (Paris, Brière, 1824).
Franck, Adolphe, *La Kabbale* (Paris, Hachette, 1843).
Grimoires: (i) *Le Grand Grimoire, ou l'art de commander les esprits celestes* (Paris, 1845).
(ii) *Le Grimoire du pape Honorius*, various editions including: (a) dated 1800 'à Rome', but probably published in France; (b) dated 1760 'à Rome', but probably published in France in about 1800—has coloured illustrations and minor textual differences from edition (a); (c) published at Lille in 1840.
(iii) *Grimorium Verum*, various editions including: (a) 1780, translated into French by Plaingière; (b) French edition dated 1517 'à Memphis, chez Alibeck, l'Egyptien'—this is obviously false, and the book is more likely to have been published in France in 1817.
Guaita, Stanislas de, *Essais des sciences maudites*: I, *Au Seuil du mystère* (Paris, Carré, 1886); II, *Le Serpent de la Genèse* (Part i, Chamuel, 1891; Part ii, ibid., 1897).
Huysmans, J.-K., *Là-Bas*, a novel (Paris, Tresse et Stock, 1891; latest edition. Plon, Livre de Poche series, 1966).
Lenain, *La Science cabalistique* (Amiens, the author, 1823).
Kardec, Allan (pseud. for Léon Hippolyte Rivail), *Le Livre des esprits* (Paris, Dentu, 1857).
Lévi, Eliphas (pseud. for Alphonse-Louis Constant): (i) *Dogme et rituel de la haute magie* (first published as one volume, Paris, Germer Baillière, 1856. English translation by A. E. Waite, latest edition, London, Rider, 1968).
(ii) *Histoire de la magie* (Paris, Germer Baillière, 1860. English trans. by A. E. Waite, latest edition, London, Rider, 1969).
(iii) *La Clé des grandes mystères* (Paris, Alcan, 1897 English translation by Aleister Crowley, latest edition, London, Rider, 1969).

(iv) *Paradoxes of the Highest Science* (English translation of a hitherto unpublished manuscript by Lévi, published in *Theosophical Miscellanies*, Calcutta, 1883).

(v) *Le Livre des splendeurs* (Paris, Chamuel, 1894).

(vi) *Clés majeures et clavicules de Salomon* (Paris, Chamuel, (1895).

(vii) *La Science des esprits* (Paris, Germer Baillière, 1865).

(viii) *Le Livre des sages* (Paris, Chacornac, 1912).

(ix) *The Magical Ritual of the Sanctum Regum* (translated by Wynn Westcott, latest edition, London, Crispin Press/ Thorsons, 1970).

(x) *Les Portes de l'avenir* (unpublished manuscript, 1870).

(xi) *Libres pensées sur des idées nouvelles* (unpublished, undated manuscript).

Papus (pseud. for Gérard Encausse): (i) *Traité méthodique de science occulte* (Paris, Carré, 1891).

(ii) *Traité élémentaire de magie pratique* (Paris, Chacornac, 1906).

(iii) *Le Diable et l'occultisme* (Paris, Chamuel, 1895).

(iv) *La Magie et l'hypnose* (Paris, Chamuel, 1897).

(v) *Catholicisme, satanisme et occultisme* (Paris, Chamuel, 1897).

Pasqually, Martines de, *Traité de la réintegration des êtres* (Paris, Chacornac, 1899).

Péladan, Joséphin: (i) *Comment on devient mage* (Paris, 1892).

(ii) *L'Art idéaliste et mystique, doctrine de l'ordre et du salon des Rose Croix* (Paris, Chamuel, 1894).

(iii) *La Décadence esthétique* (Paris, Dalou, 1888).

(iv) *Le Vice suprême* (Paris, Librairie de la Presse, Laurens, 1886).

(v) *Curieuse* (ibid., 1886).

Saint-Yves d'Alveydre (pseud. for Joseph-Alexandre Saint-Yves), *L'Archeomètre* (Paris, 1934).

Star, Ely (pseud. for Eugène Jacob), *Les mystères de l'horoscope* (Paris, Dentu, 1885).

Vaughan, Diana (the name under which Gabriel Jogand-Pagès masqueraded): (i) *Mémoires d'une ex-palladiste* (Paris, Pierret, 1896).

(ii) *La Restauration du Paganisme* (ibid., 1896).

Studies

Alem, Jean-Pierre, *Enfantin, le prophète aux sept visages* (Paris, Pauvert, 1963).

Select Bibliography

Aubrun, R. G., *Péladan* (Paris, Sansot, 1904).
Baldick, Robert, *The Life of J.-K. Huysmans* (Oxford, Clarendon Press, 1955). A masterly work containing a penetrating analysis of the occult influences on Huysmans.
Barlet, François Charles, *Saint-Yves d'Alveydre* (Paris, Durville, 1910).
Barrès, Maurice, *Un Rénovateur de l'occultisme, Stanislas de Guaita* (Paris, Chamuel, 1898).
Berlet, Charles, *Un Ami de Barrès, Stanislas de Guaita* (Paris, 1936).
Bois, Jules: (i) *Le Satanisme et la magie* (Paris, Chailley, 1895).
(ii) *Le Monde invisible* (Paris, Flammarion, 1902).
Bricaud, Joanny: (i) *J.-K. Huysmans et le satanisme* (Paris, Chacornac, 1912).
(ii) *Huysmans, occultiste et magicien* (ibid., 1913).
(iii) *L'Abbé Boullan* (ibid., 1927).
(iv) *Les Illuminés d'Avignon, étude sur Dom Pernety et son groupe* (Paris, Nourry, 1927).
Chacornac, Paul, *Eliphas Lévi, rénovateur de l'occultisme en France* (Paris, Chacornac, 1926).
Cooper-Oakley, Isabel, *The Comte de Saint-Germain* (New York, Steiner Books, 1970)
Encausse, Philippe, *Papus (Dr. Gérard Encausse), sa vie, son œuvre* (Paris, 1932).
Erdan (pseud. for A. A. Jacob), *La France mystique* (Paris, Coulon-Pineau, 1855).
Garçon, Maurice, *Louis XVII ou la fausse énigme* (Paris, Hachette, 1968).
Geyraud, Pierre: (i) *Les Sociétés secrètes de Paris* (Paris, Emile-Paul Frères, 1939).
(ii) *Les Réligions nouvelles de Paris* (ibid., 1939).
Both of these are fascinating works containing much information of a journalistic nature on a wide variety of sects and cults.
Glass, Justine, *The Story of Fulfilled Prophecy* (London, Cassell, 1969).
Lea, H. C., *Léo Taxil, Diana Vaughan et l'Eglise Romaine: histoire d'une mystification* (Paris. 1901). The best account of the Diana Vaughan affair.
Le Forestier, René: (i) *La Franc-maçonnerie occultiste au XVIIIe siècle et l'ordre des Elus Coëns* (Paris, Dorbon, 1928).
(ii) *La Franc-maçonnerie templière et occultiste au XVIIIe et*

XIXe siècles (Paris, Aubier-Montaige/Louvain, Editions Nauwelaerts, 1970). Both of these are monumentally detailed works, invaluable for any study of occult masonry of the period.

Levaillant, M., *La Crise mystique de Victor Hugo* (Paris, Corti, 1954).

Martin, Gaston, *La Franc-maçonnerie française et la préparation de la Révolution* (Paris, Les Presses Universitaires de France, 1926).

Mercier, Alain, *Les Sources ésoteriques de la poésie symboliste* (Paris, A.-G. Nizet, 1969). An extremely interesting and informative analysis.

Michelet, Victor-Emile, *Les Compagnons de la hiérophanie, souvenirs du mouvement hermétiste à la fin du XIXe siècle* (Paris, Dorbon, 1937). Anecdotal and undetailed but quite interesting account of some late-nineteenth-century occultists.

Millet Saint-Pierre, J. B. *Recherches sur le dernier sorcier (Ettiella) et la dernière école de magie* (Le Havre, Le Pelletier, 1859).

Praz, Mario, *The Romantic Agony* (latest edition, London, Oxford University Press, 1970). Contains some interesting references to occult influences in literature.

Rhodes, H. T. F., *The Satanic Mass* (latest edition, London, Jarrolds, 1968). A work of uneven detail, but useful for Vintras, Boullan and Leo Taxil).

Rijnberk, Gerard van, *Le Tarot* (Lyons, 1947). The most thorough and objective history of the Tarot yet written.

Starkie, Enid, *Arthur Rimbaud* (London, Hamish Hamilton, 1947).

Viatte, Auguste, *Les Sources occultes du romantisme* (2 vols., Paris, Champion, 1928).

Webb, James, *The Flight from Reason, Vol. I, The Age of the Irrational* (Macdonald, 1971). An interesting study of occultism in Europe from about 1820 to 1910, well documented and including useful information on most of the leading French occultists of the period.

Wirth, Oswald, *Stanislas de Guaita, souvenirs de son secrétaire* (Paris, Editions du Symbolisme, 1935).

Index

Adam, Paul, 170, 177
Aeschylus, 175, 200
Afre, Mgr., Archbishop of
  Paris, 88
Agrippa, Cornelius, 20, 54,
  147, 206
Alchemy, 26–30, 113–14, 159,
  203–4
Alexander III, Tsar, 161
Alexander VI, Pope, 145
Allenbach, Adèle, 81, 82, 91
Alliette, *see* Etteilla
Alta, Abbé (pseud. for Abbé
  Mélinge), 170
Ambelain, Robert, 163
Anti-Christ, 152, 210–11
Apollonius of Tyana, 18, 101–4,
  151
Apuleius, 143
Arson, pupil of Wronski, 97
Astral Light, 149–50
Astrology, 129–30, 150, 167–8
Auquier, Philippe, 193

Bacon, follower of Pasqually,
  25–6
Bailleul, Aristide, 84, 134–5
Bailly, Edmond, 177
Bailly, Jean, 35, 41
Balzac, Honoré de, 85, 165, 195–7
Balzac, Mme de, 133–4
Barlet, F.-C. (pseud. for A.
  Faucheux), 170

Barrès, Maurice, 164, 193
Barruel, Abbé, 36–9, 42, 62
Bataille, Dr. (pseud. for Charles
  Hacks), 207, 213–14
Bettignies, Ragon de, 201
Blavatsky, Mme H. P., 157,
  168, 219
Bode, 41, 42
Boehme, Jacob, 25, 96
Bois, Jules, 65, 162–3, 193–4, 206
Bornet, Anna, 138
Boullan, Joseph-Antoine, 179–86,
  189–93
Bousselet, Mme Pauline (*née*
  Constant), 139
Braszynsky, Count Alexander,
  116, 118, 121, 125, 127, 139
Bretagne, Charles, 202
Bricaud, Joanny, 29
Buet, Charles, 178
Bulwer-Lytton, Edward, 1st
  Baron Lytton, 101–2, 116,
  120, 127, 164
Byron, Lord, 133

Cabala, 12, 25, 52, 54, 96, 105,
  119, 121, 124, 147–52, 159,
  166, 170, 198, 201, 206
Cabalistic Order of the Rosy
  Cross, 163, 170, 171
Cadiot, Mlle, *see* Noémi
  Constant
Cagliostro, 30, 31, 36, 41, 121

Index

Caithness, Lady, 157
Canzio-Garibaldi, General, 215
Capella, Juliano, 132-3
Catholic Rose Cross, Order of, 171-6
Caubet, 115
Cazotte, Jacques, 34-6, 44
Chacornac, Paul, 11, 88, 225-7
Chamfort, 34-5
Charcot, 185
Charrot, Jacques, 137, 138
Charvoz, Abbé, 63, 105-9
Chaumette, Anaxagoras, 45
Chazal, André, 84, 85
Chemin-Dupontés, J.-B., 46-8
Chenier, Marie Joseph, 44
Chevalier, Adèle, 180
Christian, Paul (pseud. for J.-B. Pitois), 128-30, 167
Clement XII, Pope, 19, 28
Commune, Paris, 137
Comte, Auguste, 69 n
Condorcet, Marquis de, 34-5
Confucius, 47
Constant, Alphonse-Louis, see Eliphas Lévi
Constant, Jean-Joseph, 73
Constant, Mme Jeanne-Agnès, 73, 83-4
Constant, Marie, 92, 225
Constant, Mme Noémi (née Cadiot), 91-4, 100-1
Contesse, 188
Courrière, Berthe, 178, 184, 188
Court de Gébelin, Antoine, 12, 49-51, 73, 148
Cros, Charles, 201
Crowley, Aleister, 11, 109, 141, 226-7

D'Alembert, Jean le Rond, 39, 73
Dansette, Adrien, 45
Danton, Georges Jacques, 41

Dauphin, son of Louis XVI, 61, 221
D'Azyr, Dr. Vicq, 35
Delacroix, Eugène, 111
Desbarrolles, Adolphe, 106, 115
D'Eslon, Charles, 32
Deyrolle, Henri, 139
Diderot, Denis, 39, 73
D'Oberkirch, Baroness, 35
Docre, Canon, 179, 188-9
Doinel, Jules, 220
Doré, Gustave, 105
Dumas, Alexandre, 91, 110
Dupotet, Baron, 56-7

Elect Cohens, Order of, 20-5
Elias, 152
Encyclopaedia, 37
Enfantin, Barthélémi-Prosper, 69 n, 84
Enoch, 152
Erdan (pseud. for A. A. Jacob), 56-9, 86
Esquiros, Alphonse, 85, 87-8, 91, 93-4, 197
Etteilla (pseud. for Alliette), 50-3, 148
Eugénie C . . ., 88, 91-2, 153
Eugénie, Empress, 125

Fabre des Essarts, Léonce, 220
Fabre d'Olivet, Antoine, 53, 69, 79, 96, 162, 219
Faria, Abbé, 55
Fauvety, Charles, 91, 105, 114-15
Favre, Dr. Henri, 115
Fourier, Charles, 205 n
Fournier, Abbé, 21, 26
Franck, Adolphe, 201
Franco-Prussian War, 136-7
Frederick II of Prussia, 28
Freemasonry:
    Growth of movement in France, 19

Index

Occult varieties, 20–31
  Barruel's attacks on, 37–9
  Influence on French
    Revolution, 39–42
  Alleged connection with
    Templars, 62
  Lévi's views on, 115–16
  De Bettignies' writings on,
    201–2
  In the Diana Vaughan hoax,
    208–18
Frère-Colonna, Abbé, 74–6, 94

Ganneau, 62, 85–7, 92
Garibaldi, 215
Gauguin, Paul, 84
Gautier, Judith (Mme Catulle
  Mendès), 138
Gebhard, Mary, 137, 139
Geoffroi, Ferdinand, 62–4
Georgy, Countess von, 17
Germer-Baillière, Mme, 110
Geyraud, Pierre, 221–4
Gilles de Rais, 178, 187, 190
Girardin, Mme de, 85
Gnostic Catholic Church, 220–1
Gnosticism, 96
Gourmont, Rémy de, 178–9
Gozzoli, 64
Gramont, Duchesse de, 34, 35
Grange, Mme Louise, 192
Gregory XVI, Pope, 64
Guaita, Marquis Stanislas de,
  163–77, 181–4, 193–4, 220, 224
Guiches, Gustave, 178, 183, 194

Hacks, Charles, *see* Dr. Bataille
Haven, Marc, 170
Helvetius, Claude Adrien, 39, 41
Hennique, Léon, 179
Hermes Trismegistos, 51
Hermetic Order of the Golden
  Dawn, 141

Home, Daniel Dunglas, 125–7
Hubault, Malmaison, Abbé J.-B.,
  74, 76
Hugand, *see* Jélalel
Hugo, Victor, 138, 197–200
Huret, Jules, 189–90
Hutchinson, Mrs., 131, 138
Huysmans, J.-K., 177–95, 206

Illuminés d'Avignon, 26, 29–30

Jacob, Eugène, *see* Ely Star
Jélalel (pseud. for Hugand), 52
Jobert, Mme, 139
Johannès, Dr., *see* J.-A. Boullan
Julian the Apostate, 212–13
Julius Caesar, 13

Kardec, Allan (pseud. for L. H.
  Rivail), 59, 60, 201
Kaunitz, 32
Knights of the Round Table, 221
Kosciuszko, General, 96

Lacroze, Gary de, 171, 172
Lacuria, Abbé, 164
Lafayette, Marie Joseph, 44
La Harpe, Jean de, 34–5
Lamballe, Princesse de, 31
Langes, Savalette de, 30
Langlet-Dufresnoy, Abbé, 27
Larmandie, Comte Léonce de,
  172
Ledos, Eugène, 188
Lefevre, Father, 88
Le Forestier, René, 21
Le Gallois, Auguste, 87, 89, 91,
  93
Legrand, Mme, 88, 90, 138
Lejeune, Father, 139
Lemmonier, Charles, 105

Lenain, 54
Le Normand, Mlle, 129
Leo XIII, Pope, 209
Levaillant, M., 197
Lévi, Eliphas (pseud. for A.-L. Constant), 11, 12, 33, 36, 164–6, 171, 177, 187, 197, 202, 220, 226–7
 Childhood and education, 73–6
 At Saint-Sulpice, 76–82
 Death of mother, 83
 Friendship with Flora Tristan, 84–5, 90
 Radical activities and imprisonment, 86–8, 92
 At Evreux, 88–9
 Final renunciation of holy orders, 90
 Married life, 91–5
 Friendship with Wronski, 96–100
 Wife's desertion, 100
 Adopts name of Eliphas Lévi, 100
 First visit to England and evocation of Apollonius, 101–4
 Meeting with Charvoz, 105–9
 Experiments in alchemy, 113–14
 Becomes a freemason, 115
 Second visit to London, 116
 Visited by Kenneth Mackenzie, 117–22
 Meeting with Spedalieri, 124
 Views on spiritualism, 125–8
 Friendship with Paul Christian, 128–30
 Old age and death, 136–40
 Assessment of his work, 141–53
 Descendants, 225
Louis XIV, 136
Louis XVI, 34, 36, 42, 44, 61
Louis XVII, 61, 86. *See also* Naundorff
Louis XVIII, 61
Louis-Philippe, King, 92, 133
Lucas, Louis, 114, 159

Mackenzie, Kenneth, 117–22, 141
Magic:
 Ceremonial, 20–4, 101–4, 145, 146, 206
 Lévi's views on, 145–51
Malesherbes, Guillaume de, 34–5
Malvost, Henri de, 206
Mandryka, Captain, 161
Mapah, *see* Ganneau
Marie Antoinette, Queen, 36, 86, 221
Martin, Gaston, 40–3
Martinism, 148, 163, 220–1
Mary Queen of Scots, 157
Mathers, S. L. MacGregor, 141
Mathias-Duval, Professor, 159
Maudsley, 185
Maury, Alfred, 201
Meckenheim, Marquis de, 178
Mélinge, *see* Abbé Alta
Mendès, Catulle, 138, 164
Merci-Argentau, Count, 32
Mesmer, Franz Anton, 31–3, 41, 49, 57, 69, 75
Meurin, Mgr., Bishop of Port Louis, 216
Michelet, Jules, 202, 206
Michelet, Victor-Emile, 193–4
Mniszech, Comte Georges de, 125, 134, 138–9
Molay, Jacques de, 62
Molière, 200
Montferrier, Marquis de, 97, 100

Napoleon Bonaparte, 36, 48, 61, 120
Napoleon III, 99, 125, 133
Naundorff, Charles Edouard, 62
Naundorff, Charles Guillaume, 62

Index

Naundorffist movement, 62–4, 178, 184, 221
Nerval, Gérard de, 204
Niboyet, Mme, 93
Nicholas II, Tsar, 160–1
Nicolai, 35
Nowakowski, 125

Oberlin, Frederick, 58
Olcott, Colonel H. S., 157–8
Olier, Mgr., Bishop of Evreux, 88–90
Orsat, Alexis, 194

Paléologue, 160
Palladium, 207, 209–13, 216–18
Papus (pseud. for Dr. Gérard Encausse), 12, 149, 157–63, 170, 177, 194, 219–20, 224
Paracelsus, 120, 122, 147, 167
Paraclete, 75–6, 139, 151, 188
Pascal, Edouard-Adolphe, 138–9
Pasqually, Martines de, 20–6, 30, 34
Péladan, Dr. Adrien, 164, 167
Péladan, Joséphin, 163–8, 170–6, 224
Pentagram, 150
Pernety, Antoine-Joseph, 26–30
Pestalozzi, Johann Heinrich, 59
Philalèthes, Rite of, 30
Pike, Albert, 207, 210
Pitois, J.-B., *see* Paul Christian
Poe, Edgar Allan, 205
Poisson, Albert, 204
Pradier, 94
Puységur, Marquis de, 55
Pythagoras, 79, 80

Rabelais, 105, 131
Rasputin, 160–1
Rimbaud, Arthur, 202–4

Robespierre, Maximilien, 46
Roca, Canon, 181, 183
Rosencreutz, Christian, 18
Rosicrucianism, 148, 163–4, 223–4. See also Cabalistic Order of the Rosy Cross and Catholic Rose Cross
Rosier, Dr. Fernand, 113
Roucher, 35
Rousseau, Jean-Jacques, 131

Saint-Germain, Comte de, 17–19, 51
Saint-Martin, Louis Claude de, 25, 26, 41, 96, 124, 148
Saint-Simon, Claude Henri, Comte de, 61, 69 *n*
Saint-Sulpice, college of, 76–80, 83
Saint-Yves d'Alveydre, Joseph-Alexandre, 162–3, 220–1
Salons de la Rose Croix, 174
Salverte, Eusèbe, 54
Satanism, 178–89, 193, 206–18
Sauvestre, Charles, 186
Schuré, Edouard, 219
Scott, Sir Walter, 129
Sédir, Paul, 223–4
Shakespeare, William, 198–200
Sibour, Mgr., Archbishop of Paris, 110–11
Sivry, Charles de, 200
Sobrier, 92, 93
Societas Rosicruciana in Anglia, 117, 164
Souleillon, Edouard, 222
Spedalieri, Baron, 124–5, 127, 131, 137–8
Spiritualism, 57–60, 125–8, 201, 215
Star, Ely (pseud. For Eugène Jacob), 167
Starkie, Enid, 203

States General, 42
Summers, Montague, 179
Swedenborg, Emanuel, 30-1, 41, 58, 87, 96, 195-7

Talleyrand, Bishop of Autun, 44
Tarot, 12, 49-52, 120, 148-9, 169-70
Taxil, Leo (pseud. for G. Jogand-Pagès), 207-18
Templars, 62
Théâtre de la Rose Croix, 175
Théophilantropes, 46-8
Theosophical Society, 47-8, 157, 163, 168-9, 221
Thibault, Julie, 181-2, 186, 191-2
Tissot, P. H., 56
Tristan, Flora, 84-5, 88, 90
Trithemius, 147, 151

Vacquerie, Auguste, 199
Van den Bosch, Baron Firmin, 179

Van Haecke, Abbé, 179
Vaughan: the Diana Vaughan hoax, 207-18
Vaughan, Thomas, 209, 218 n
Verger, Louis, 111
Vignon, Claude (pseud.), see Noémi Constant
Vintras, Pierre Michel Eugène, 62-9, 106-9, 116, 181, 221-2
Voltaire, François, 39, 41, 131

Waite, A. E., 11, 24, 141, 144
Walder, Sophia, 210
Walpole, Horace, 18
Washington, George, 58
Wattelet, Dr., 138
Weil, Alexandre, 198
Weishaupt, Adam, 41-2
Willermoz, J.-B., 20, 25-6
Wirth, Oswald, 149, 169-171, 182-4
Wronski, Hoene, 96-100

Zola, Emile, 177, 185